Grammar, Usage & Mechanics
Teacher Edition

STRATEGIES FOR
writers

ZB **Zaner-Bloser**

Grade Level Consultants

Margaret Bateman
Montgomery, Alabama

Cindy Daniel
Bothell, Washington

Suzanne Klein
Hilliard, Ohio

Nancy Morgan
Sharon, Pennsylvania

Joan Pawloski
Grand Rapids, Michigan

Cover photo: Rycus Associates Photography

Illustration: Steve Botts, Tracy Greenwalt

ISBN: 978-0-7367-9265-3

Copyright © Zaner-Bloser, Inc.

Zaner-Bloser, Inc.
1-800-421-3018
www.zaner-bloser.com

SUSTAINABLE FORESTRY INITIATIVE

Certified Chain of Custody
Promoting Sustainable Forestry
www.sfiprogram.org
SFI-00712

Printed in the United States of America

11 12 13 14 15 997 5 4 3 2 1

Teacher Edition Table of Contents

	SE	TE
Program Information		T4
Scope and Sequence		T11
Unit 1: Sentence Structure		T16
Lesson 1 Complete Subjects and Complete Predicates	7	T16
Lesson 2 Simple Subjects and Simple Predicates	9	T17
Lesson 3 Compound Subjects and Compound Predicates	11	T17
Lesson 4 Direct Objects	13	T18
Lesson 5 Indirect Objects	15	T18
Lesson 6 Predicate Nouns and Predicate Adjectives	17	T19
Lesson 7 Prepositional Phrases	19	T19
Lesson 8 Compound Sentences	21	T20
Lesson 9 Dependent and Independent Clauses	23	T20
Lesson 10 Avoiding Fragments, Run-ons, Comma Splices	25	T21
Proofreading	27	T21
Unit 1 Review	29	T22
School Home Connection	31	T22
Unit 1 Assessment	139	T22
Extra Practice Activities	159	
Unit 1 Test	185	T22
Unit 2: Parts of Speech		T24
Lesson 11 Common and Proper Nouns	33	T24
Lesson 12 Plural and Possessive Nouns	35	T25
Lesson 13 Personal and Possessive Pronouns	37	T25
Lesson 14 The Present Tense	39	T26
Lesson 15 The Past and Future Tenses	41	T26
Lesson 16 The Present Perfect Tense	43	T27
Lesson 17 Adjectives	45	T27
Lesson 18 Adverbs	47	T28
Lesson 19 Prepositions	49	T28
Lesson 20 Coordinating and Subordinating Conjunctions	51	T29
Proofreading	53	T29
Unit 2 Review	55	T30
School Home Connection	57	T30
Unit 2 Assessment	143	T30
Extra Practice Activities	164	
Unit 2 Test	187	T30
Unit 3: Usage		T32
Lesson 21 *Their, There, They're*	59	T32
Lesson 22 *Its* and *It's*	61	T33
Lesson 23 *Your* and *You're*	63	T33
Lesson 24 *Like* and *You Know*	65	T34
Lesson 25 Comparing with *Good* or *Bad*	67	T34
Lesson 26 *That, Which, Who*	69	T35
Lesson 27 *Real* and *Very*	71	T35
Lesson 28 *Set* and *Sit*	73	T36
Lesson 29 Irregular Verbs: *Know* and *Grow*	75	T36
Lesson 30 *Learn* and *Teach*	77	T37
Proofreading	79	T37
Unit 3 Review	81	T38
School Home Connection	83	T38
Unit 3 Assessment	147	T38
Extra Practice Activities	169	
Unit 3 Test	189	T38
Unit 4: Grammar		T40
Lesson 31 Subject and Object Pronouns	85	T40
Lesson 32 Pronouns in Pairs	87	T41
Lesson 33 Using *I* or *Me*	89	T41
Lesson 34 Pronoun Antecedents	91	T42
Lesson 35 Making the Subject and Verb Agree	93	T42
Lesson 36 Forms of *Be*	95	T43
Lesson 37 Verb Tense	97	T43
Lesson 38 Negatives	99	T44
Lesson 39 Comparative and Superlative Adjectives	101	T44
Lesson 40 Comparative and Superlative Adverbs	103	T45
Proofreading	105	T45
Unit 4 Review	107	T46
School Home Connection	109	T46
Unit 4 Assessment	151	T46
Extra Practice Activities	174	
Unit 4 Test	191	T46
Unit 5: Mechanics		T48
Lesson 41 Writing Sentences Correctly	111	T48
Lesson 42 Proper Nouns and Proper Adjectives	113	T49
Lesson 43 Initials and Abbreviations	115	T49
Lesson 44 Titles	117	T50
Lesson 45 Apostrophes	119	T50
Lesson 46 Commas in a Series	121	T51
Lesson 47 Commas	123	T51
Lesson 48 Using Semicolons	125	T52
Lesson 49 Direct and Indirect Quotations	127	T52
Lesson 50 Friendly Letters and E-mails	129	T53
Proofreading	131	T53
Unit 5 Review	133	T54
School Home Connection	135	T54
Unit 5 Assessment	155	T54
Extra Practice Activities	179	
Unit 5 Test	193	T54
G.U.M. Handbook	195	
Topic Index	215	
Language Index	216	

STRATEGIES FOR writers

Grammar Usage & Mechanics

- Focuses on grade-level appropriate skills important for writing
- Provides self-directed instruction and practice
- Complements any curriculum with easy-to-follow lessons
- Prepares students for high-stakes tests

Practice Options

Student Edition
- Proofreading practice and checklists
- Activities to involve families and communities
- Comprehensive G.U.M. Handbook
- Flexible testing options and practice with standardized test formats

Teacher Edition
- Quick and easy instruction at a glance
- Strategies to help English Language Learners
- Speaking and Listening activities
- Activities for assessment and remediation
- Annotated student edition

High-Interest Themes

Contemporary high-interest themes hold students' attention, increase their content-area knowledge, and make learning fun all year long.

Looking Back
Connects to history and social studies.

Unforgettable Folks
Focuses on heroes, athletes, inventors, and world leaders—past and present.

Grab Bag
Explores different cultures, fashion, cars, technology, movies—anything goes!

The World Outside
Connects to science—volcanoes, glaciers, weather systems, and more.

Beasts and Critters
Puts the spotlight on remarkable birds, reptiles, insects, mammals, and sea creatures.

Timeless Tales (Grades 7 and 8 only)
Highlights a variety of folktales, myths, and legends.

Great Getaways (Grades 7 and 8 only)
Explores rivers, islands, and near-islands around the world.

Each two-page lesson targets important skills and helps students transfer them to their writing. Our five-step format makes it easy.

STEP 1 Provides an example of the targeted skill in context

STEP 2 States skill information

STEP 3 Offers practice of the skill

STEP 4 Helps students apply their knowledge in writing

STEP 5 Reinforces learning through writing activities, puzzles, and technology connections

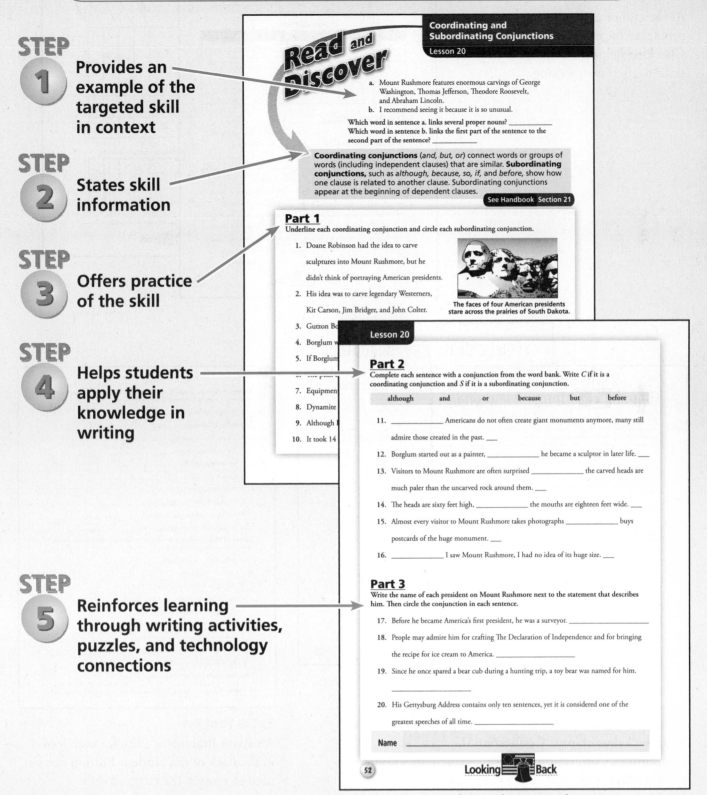

Read and Discover

Coordinating and Subordinating Conjunctions
Lesson 20

a. Mount Rushmore features enormous carvings of George Washington, Thomas Jefferson, Theodore Roosevelt, and Abraham Lincoln.
b. I recommend seeing it because it is so unusual.

Which word in sentence a. links several proper nouns? _____
Which word in sentence b. links the first part of the sentence to the second part of the sentence? _____

Coordinating conjunctions (*and, but, or*) connect words or groups of words (including independent clauses) that are similar. **Subordinating conjunctions,** such as *although, because, so, if,* and *before,* show how one clause is related to another clause. Subordinating conjunctions appear at the beginning of dependent clauses.

See Handbook Section 21

Part 1
Underline each coordinating conjunction and circle each subordinating conjunction.

1. Doane Robinson had the idea to carve sculptures into Mount Rushmore, but he didn't think of portraying American presidents.
2. His idea was to carve legendary Westerners, Kit Carson, Jim Bridger, and John Colter.
3. Gutzon Bo
4. Borglum w
5. If Borglum
7. Equipmen
8. Dynamite
9. Although
10. It took 14

The faces of four American presidents stare across the prairies of South Dakota.

Lesson 20

Part 2
Complete each sentence with a conjunction from the word bank. Write *C* if it is a coordinating conjunction and *S* if it is a subordinating conjunction.

although	and	or	because	but	before

11. _____ Americans do not often create giant monuments anymore, many still admire those created in the past. ___
12. Borglum started out as a painter, _____ he became a sculptor in later life. ___
13. Visitors to Mount Rushmore are often surprised _____ the carved heads are much paler than the uncarved rock around them. ___
14. The heads are sixty feet high, _____ the mouths are eighteen feet wide. ___
15. Almost every visitor to Mount Rushmore takes photographs _____ buys postcards of the huge monument. ___
16. _____ I saw Mount Rushmore, I had no idea of its huge size. ___

Part 3
Write the name of each president on Mount Rushmore next to the statement that describes him. Then circle the conjunction in each sentence.

17. Before he became America's first president, he was a surveyor. _____
18. People may admire him for crafting The Declaration of Independence and for bringing the recipe for ice cream to America. _____
19. Since he once spared a bear cub during a hunting trip, a toy bear was named for him. _____
20. His Gettysburg Address contains only ten sentences, yet it is considered one of the greatest speeches of all time. _____

Name _____

52   Looking Back

Grade 5 student pages shown

T5

Proofreading Practice

At the end of each unit, students proofread for errors. A **Proofreading Checklist** helps students apply targeted skills to their own writing.

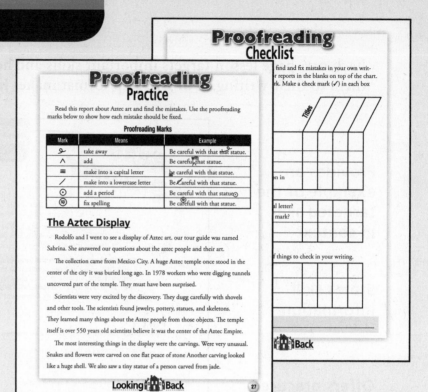

Proofreading Practice

Read this report about Aztec art and find the mistakes. Use the proofreading marks below to show how each mistake should be fixed.

Proofreading Marks

Mark	Means	Example
ℛ	take away	Be careful with that that statue.
∧	add	Be careful that statue.
≡	make into a capital letter	be careful with that statue.
/	make into a lowercase letter	Be Careful with that statue.
⊙	add a period	Be careful with that statue⊙
⊛	fix spelling	Be carefull with that statue.

The Aztec Display

Rodolfo and I went to see a dissplay of Aztec art. our tour guide was named Sabrina. She answered our questions about the aztec people and their art.

The collection came from Mexico City. A huge Aztec temple once stood in the center of the city it was buried long ago. In 1978 workers who were digging tunnels uncovered part of the temple. They must have been surprised.

Scientists were very excited by the discovery. They dugg carefully with shovels and other tools. The scientists found jewelry, pottery, statues, and skeletons. They learned many things about the Aztec people from those objects. The temple itself is over 550 years old scientists believe it was the center of the Aztec Empire.

The most interesting things in the display were the carvings. Were very unusual. Snakes and flowers were carved on one flat peace of stone Another carving looked like a huge shell. We also saw a tiny statue of a person carved from jade.

Looking Back   27

Proofreading Checklist

...find and fix mistakes in your own writ- ...reports in the blanks on top of the chart. ...mark. Make a check mark (✓) in each box

Looking Back

School Home Connection

In Unit 2 of *G.U.M.* students are learning about the jobs different words have in sentences. They are learning that **nouns**, such as *dog* and *planet*, name people, places, and things, and that **verbs** tell about actions. The activities on this page give extra practice with some of the concepts they are learning. You can help your child use the information he or she is learning in school by choosing one or more activities to complete together at home.

Twenty Questions (Nouns)

This guessing game can be played by two to eight people. One person thinks of a person, place, or thing but keeps it a secret. The other players try to guess what noun the person is thinking of by asking questions that can be answered "yes" or "no." Guessers can ask up to twenty questions before the mystery noun is revealed.

Dream Trip (Proper Nouns)

Work with your child to plan a dream trip he or she would like to take. The trip can be to anywhere in the world, and your child's guests can include friends, sports or movie stars, relatives, and others your child might like to invite. Help your child write a plan for the trip on a large sheet of construction paper. Include departure and return dates. Remind your child to capitalize proper nouns such as the names of cities, states, and people.

Unforgettable Folks   57

Community Connection

...different kinds of nouns, pronouns, and adjectives ...own writing. The content of these lessons focuses on ...s. As students completed the exercises, they learned ...kinds of challenges. These pages offer activities that ...unit. They also provide opportunities for the ...materials in the lessons and the community at large.

...enges are available in your community. Look for ...ters, shelters, immigrant resource centers, help ...Contact the organizations to find out what ...create a descriptive list of helpful organizations. ...ization, its phone number and address, and how ...you have finished, decide whether you think your ...on or if other services should also be offered. Add

...that helps people overcome challenges, such as ...nded veterans. Visit or call the organization to find ...the organization as a volunteer. If possible, spend ...Then write an advertisement to convince others to ...de what services the organization offers, what jobs ...portant. You may also want to invite a representative ...out community needs and the value of volunteers.

...or state who have overcome challenges of various ...book of local heroes. In your scrapbook, include a ...nd. Or, choose two or three of the people and write a

...raises money for a good cause. Answer each of these

...in?

...he money go to?

...ds raised?

...tion get people interested in participating?

...s for their participation? If so, what?

...report.

...ttable Folks   97

Extra Practice

Lesson 11 Circle the underlined noun in each sentence. Next to each sentence, write *person, place,* or *thing* to tell what the noun names.

1. The park was crowded. _____
2. The wind blew steadily. _____
3. The day was clear and sunny. _____
4. We flew our kites for hours. _____
5. My kite looks like a fish. _____
6. One kite got caught in a tree. _____
7. The kite's owner climbed the tree. _____
8. He passed the kite to his friend. _____
9. Its string was tangled around a branch. _____
10. We helped him tie new string onto the kite. _____

Lesson 12 Read the sentences. Decide which underlined word or phrase in each sentence is a proper noun. Circle it.

1. Ruth Handler was an inventor.
2. She was born in Denver.
3. That city is the capital of Colorado.
4. She was married to a man named Elliot Handler.
5. Together they moved to California.
6. They helped start a company called Mattel.
7. Ruth Handler invented a doll named Barbie.
8. She named it after her daughter, Barbara.
9. Ruth and Elliot Handler also had a son named Kenneth.
10. They created a doll named Ken, too.

164   Name _____

Connections Beyond the Classroom

Send the **School Home Connection** (Grades 2–6) or **Community Connection** (Grades 7–8) activities home anytime during the unit to reinforce unit skills and to involve families and the community in student learning.

Extra Practice

An **Extra Practice** activity for each lesson in the back of the Student Edition can be used to reteach the targeted skill.

Sentence Diagraming

A sentence diagram is a "picture" of a sentence's structure. Model diagrams and diagraming activities help students understand the relationships between words and phrases within sentences.

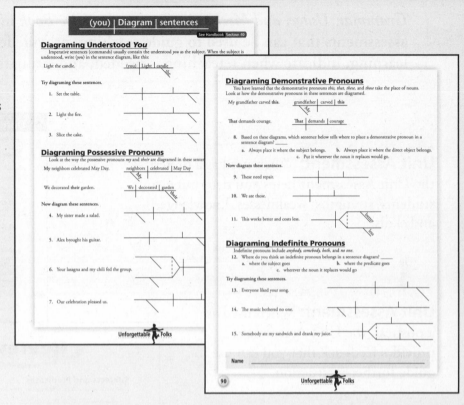

Writing Sentences and Writing a Paragraph

At the end of each unit, students use the skills they have studied to revise poorly constructed sentences, to craft those sentences into a paragraph, and to write an original paragraph. Different types of paragraphs and a variety of sentence constructions provide learners with the tools to become successful writers.

Assessment Options

Diagnostic, Formative, Summative

Grammar, Usage, and Mechanics Student Practice Book includes a variety of assessments that can be used to guide teaching, provide feedback on student learning, indicate when reteaching is needed, and evaluate student achievement.

- **Diagnostic Assessment**
  Unit Assessment: When used as a pretest, the **Unit Assessment** helps you determine your students' strengths, weaknesses, knowledge, and skills.

- **Formative Assessment**
  Unit Assessment: When used as a posttest, the **Unit Assessment** provides feedback that you can use to guide further instruction.

- **Formative Assessment**
  Unit Review: This activity checks students' progress and determines when reteaching is necessary.

- **Summative Assessment**
  Unit Test: This assessment evaluates students' achievement while providing valuable practice for high-stakes tests.

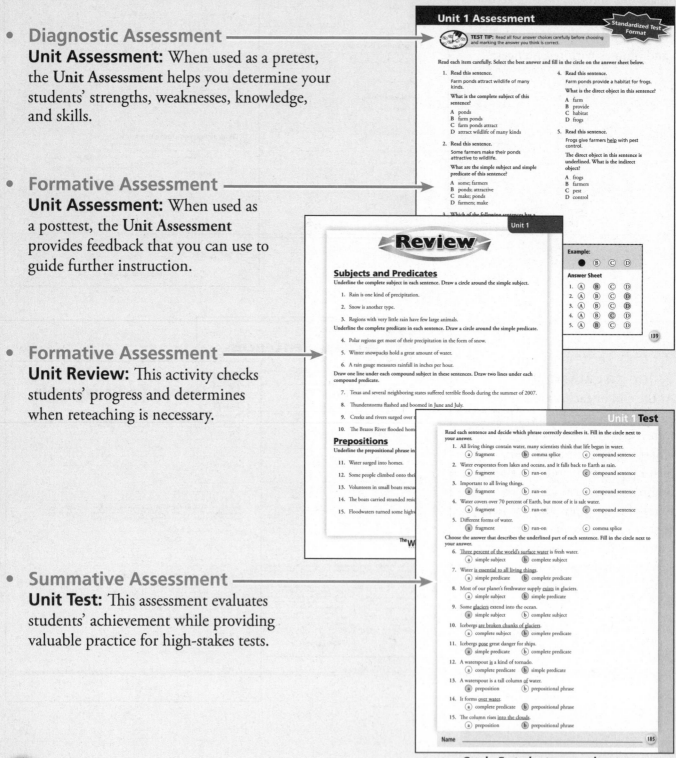

Grade 5 student pages shown

T8

Grammar, Usage, and Mechanics Student Practice Book offers two options for using assessment to differentiate instruction. The lessons are versatile and can be used regularly or as needed to address students' specific skill needs.

Option 1: Whole Class Instruction

Step 1	Instruction and Review	Teach all of the **lessons** in the unit and assign the **Unit Review.**
Step 2	Formative Assessment	Administer the **Unit Assessment** as a posttest to check students' progress. Use the results to determine which lessons require additional instruction.
Step 3	Reteach	Use the corresponding **Extra Practice** activity to reteach the targeted skill.
Step 4	Summative Assessment	Administer the **Unit Test.**

Option 2: Targeted Instruction

Step 1	Diagnostic Assessment	Administer the **Unit Assessment** as a pretest before teaching the unit. Use the results to determine which lessons to teach.
Step 2	Instruction and Review	Teach the appropriate **lessons** in the unit.
Step 3	Formative Assessment	Assign the **Unit Review** to check students' progress and to guide further instruction.
Step 4	Reteach	Use the **Extra Practice** activity for reteaching as necessary.
Step 5	Summative Assessment	Administer the **Unit Test.**

Organizing and Differentiating Instruction

Planning Options

Each book contains a year's worth of study lessons. Additional options for differentiating instruction appear throughout the Teaching Notes for each lesson and are highlighted below the chart.

Three-Day Plan (2 lessons a week)		
Day 1	**Day 2**	**Day 3**
Do **Part 1** in class. Assign **Parts 2** and **3** as homework, or have students complete them cooperatively in class.	Go over **Parts 2** and **3** in class. Complete the **Speaking and Listening** activity in the teacher edition. Assign the **Extra Practice** activity, if necessary.	Do **Part 1** as a group. Have students complete **Parts 2** and **3** cooperatively. Assign the **Extra Practice** activity as homework, if necessary.

Five-Day Plan (2 lessons a week)				
Day 1	**Day 2**	**Day 3**	**Day 4**	**Day 5**
Do **Part 1** in class. Assign **Part 2** as homework, or have students complete it cooperatively in class.	Go over **Part 2** in class. Have students complete **Part 3** cooperatively.	Complete the **Speaking and Listening** activity in the teacher edition.	Do **Part 1** in class. Assign **Parts 2** and **3** as homework, or have students complete them cooperatively.	Go over **Parts 2** and **3** in class. Complete the **Speaking and Listening** activity in the teacher edition. Assign the **Extra Practice** activity, if necessary.

Scaffolding for English Language Learners

Teaching suggestions provide options to meet the needs of students with different language and cultural backgrounds.

Speaking and Listening

Specific **Speaking and Listening** activities in the teaching notes reinforce lesson concepts.

Speaking Alert The megaphone signals specific skills that relate to both oral and written communication. When the megaphone appears, encourage students to discuss how the lesson topic will help their spoken language. Remain sensitive to dialects and regional usage.

Technology

Connections to technology offer students opportunities to apply the grammar, usage, and mechanics skills in today's high-tech world.

Note: Internet use should always be closely monitored. The listed websites have been carefully researched for accuracy, content, and appropriateness. However, websites are subject to change.

Grade	2	3	4	5	6	7	8
Sentence Structure							
subjects							
subject	•	•	•	•	•	•	•
simple and complete subjects	•		•	•	•	•	•
understood *you*					•	•	•
compound subject				•	•	•	•
predicates							
predicate	•	•	•	•	•	•	•
simple and complete predicates	•		•	•	•	•	•
compound predicate			•	•	•	•	•
predicate noun			•	•	•	•	•
predicate adjective			•	•	•	•	•
sentences							
basic (simple) sentences	•	•	•	•	•	•	•
statements and questions	•	•	•	•	•	•	•
commands and exclamations	•	•	•	•	•	•	•
compound sentences		•	•	•	•	•	•
complex sentences			•	•	•	•	•
word order in sentences							•
parallel structure							•
clauses and phrases							
dependent and independent clauses				•	•	•	•
adjective and adverb clauses						•	•
noun clauses							•
prepositional phrases	•	•	•	•	•	•	•
adjectival and adverbial prepositional phrases						•	•
infinitive phrases						•	•
participial phrases						•	•
gerund phrases						•	•
appositives							
appositives					•	•	•
restrictive vs. nonrestrictive						•	•
correcting sentences							
sentence fragments	•	•	•	•	•	•	•
run-on sentences		•	•	•	•	•	•
comma splice			•	•	•	•	•
making sentences say more		•	•			•	•
ramble-on sentences					•	•	•
misplaced subordinate clauses						•	•
objects							
direct object			•	•	•	•	•
indirect object				•	•	•	•
object of the preposition				•	•	•	•
object complement							•

Scope and Sequence (continued)

Grade	2	3	4	5	6	7	8
Parts of Speech							
nouns							
common nouns, proper nouns	•	•	•	•	•	•	•
singular and plural nouns	•	•	•	•	•	•	•
irregular plural nouns			•	•		•	•
possessive nouns		•	•	•	•	•	•
collective nouns						•	•
verbs							
action verbs and linking verbs	•	•	•	•	•	•	•
present tense	•	•	•	•	•	•	•
regular past tense verbs	•	•	•	•	•	•	•
irregular past tense verbs	•	•	•	•	•	•	•
future tense				•	•	•	•
present perfect tense				•	•	•	•
past perfect tense					•	•	•
future perfect tense						•	•
progressive forms (present, past, future)					•	•	•
main verbs and helping (auxiliary) verbs			•	•	•	•	•
transitive and intransitive verbs						•	•
active and passive voice					•	•	•
pronouns							
personal pronouns	•	•	•	•	•	•	•
compound personal pronouns					•	•	•
demonstrative pronouns		•			•	•	•
interrogative pronouns			•		•	•	•
subject pronouns and object pronouns	•	•	•	•	•	•	•
possessive pronouns		•	•	•	•	•	•
indefinite pronouns					•	•	•
pronouns and antecedents				•	•	•	•
relative pronouns						•	•
adjectives							
adjectives	•	•	•	•	•	•	•
demonstrative adjectives			•	•	•	•	•
proper adjectives				•	•	•	•
comparative adjectives and superlative adjectives	•	•	•	•	•	•	•
absolute adjectives						•	•
adverbs							
adverbs			•	•	•	•	•
comparative adverbs				•	•	•	•
superlative adverbs				•	•	•	•
conjunctions							
coordinating conjunctions	•	•	•	•	•	•	•
subordinating conjunctions				•	•	•	•
correlative conjunctions						•	•
prepositions			•	•	•	•	•
interjections					•	•	•
Usage							
homophones							
your and *you're*		•	•	•	•	•	•
their, they're, there	•	•	•	•	•	•	•

Grade	2	3	4	5	6	7	8
Usage (continued)							
its and *it's*	•	•	•	•	•	•	•
whose and *who's*			•		•	•	•
to, two, too			•		•	•	•
than and *then*						•	•
comparatives							
good and *bad* (*better/worse, best/worst*)		•		•		•	•
less and *least*	•					•	•
-er, -est		•	•	•	•	•	•
more and *most*			•	•	•	•	•
irregular verbs							
bring, sing, and *ring*		•					
come and *go*	•	•					
eat and *sleep; give* and *take*	•	•					
forms of *be*	•	•	•	•	•	•	•
know and *grow*				•			
run, fly, and *swim*					•		
throw and *catch*			•				
irregular verbs (general)						•	•
problem words							
very and *real*		•		•			
good and *well*			•		•		
who and *whom*					•	•	•
doesn't and *don't*			•			•	
learn and *teach*				•			
set and *sit*				•		•	•
like, you know, go, and *all*				•		•	•
who, which, and *that*				•	•	•	•
leave, let, rise, and *raise*					•	•	•
lie and *lay*						•	
less and *fewer; over* and *more than*							•
articles							
a and *an*	•	•	•	•	•	•	•
the			•	•	•	•	•
Grammar							
pronouns							
subject and object pronouns	•	•	•	•	•	•	•
pronouns in pairs	•	•	•	•	•	•	•
avoiding extra pronouns		•					
I and *me*	•	•	•	•		•	•
pronoun antecedents				•	•	•	•
verbs							
subject-verb agreement (forms of *be*)	•	•	•	•	•	•	•
subject-verb agreement (regular verbs)	•	•	•	•	•	•	•
subject-verb agreement (special cases)						•	•
choosing verb tense	•	•	•	•	•	•	•
using helping (auxiliary) verbs	•	•	•	•	•	•	•
agreement with compound subjects					•	•	•

Scope and Sequence (continued) Grade	2	3	4	5	6	7	8
Grammar (continued)							
negatives							
avoiding double negatives		•	•	•		•	•
modifiers							
dangling and misplaced modifiers						•	•
Mechanics							
punctuation							
end marks (question mark, period, exclamation point)	•	•	•	•	•	•	•
titles							
books	•	•	•	•	•	•	•
movies, songs, stories, poems, CDs, DVDs			•	•	•	•	•
newspapers and magazines					•	•	
capitalization							
names	•	•	•	•	•	•	•
places	•	•	•	•	•	•	•
titles of respect	•	•	•	•	•	•	•
sentences	•	•	•	•	•	•	•
titles of works	•		•	•	•	•	•
proper adjectives					•	•	•
proper nouns	•	•	•	•	•	•	•
abbreviations of proper nouns	•	•	•	•	•	•	•
direct quotes	•	•	•	•	•	•	•
month, day					•	•	•
abbreviations							
titles of respect, initials	•	•	•	•	•	•	•
streets, cities, states, countries	•	•	•	•	•	•	•
month, day						•	•
kinds of business					•	•	•
acronyms							•
commas							
in a series	•	•	•	•	•	•	•
after introductory words and nouns of direct address		•	•	•	•	•	•
in compound sentences		•	•	•	•	•	•
in direct quotations	•	•	•	•	•	•	•
in greetings and closings (letters and e-mails)					•	•	•
to separate adjectives of the same class						•	•
after introductory adverb clauses						•	•
semicolons							
in compound sentences				•	•	•	•
colons							
to separate independent clauses					•	•	•
before lists					•	•	•
in dialogue						•	•
after an introductory phrase						•	•
in business letters					•	•	•
in expressions of time						•	•
in a bibliography entry						•	•
quotations							
direct	•	•	•	•	•	•	•
indirect		•	•	•	•	•	•

Grade	2	3	4	5	6	7	8
Mechanics (continued)							
apostrophes							
in possessive nouns	•	•	•	•	•	•	•
in contractions		•	•	•	•	•	•
hyphens and dashes							
to separate syllables in a word break						•	•
to link some compound words						•	•
to link word pairs or groups of words that precede nouns						•	•
to link the parts of some numbers						•	•
parentheses							
letters and e-mails							
friendly				•	•	•	•
business						•	•
e-mails				•	•	•	•
Writing Paragraphs							
varying sentence length and type						•	•
writing a topic sentence						•	•
writing supporting details						•	•
writing a concluding sentence						•	•
using time-order words						•	•
using correct verb tense						•	•
writing to support an idea						•	•
writing a description						•	•
writing an informative paragraph						•	•
writing a comparison						•	•
writing a persuasive paragraph						•	•
writing a personal narrative						•	•
writing a friendly letter							•
Research							
Internet searches		•	•	•	•	•	•
library research		•	•	•	•	•	•
bibliography entries						•	•
Diagraming Sentences							
subjects and verbs						•	•
adjectives, articles, and adverbs						•	•
direct objects						•	•
predicate nouns and predicate adjectives						•	•
compound subjects and predicates						•	•
compound sentences						•	•
prepositions and prepositional phrases						•	•
indirect objects						•	•
sentences beginning with *there*						•	•
adjective clauses						•	•
adverb clauses						•	•
inverted sentences							•
complex sentences							•
participial phrases							•
infinitive phrases							•
gerund phrases							•
appositives							•

The World Outside

Unit 1 Sentence Structure

Lesson 1: Complete Subjects and Complete Predicates

Lesson 2: Simple Subjects and Simple Predicates

Lesson 3: Compound Subjects and Compound Predicates

Lesson 4: Direct Objects

Lesson 5: Indirect Objects

Lesson 6: Predicate Nouns and Predicate Adjectives

Lesson 7: Prepositional Phrases

Lesson 8: Compound Sentences

Lesson 9: Dependent and Independent Clauses

Lesson 10: Avoiding Fragments, Run-ons, Comma Splices

Pretest Option

You may use the **Unit Assessment** as a pretest. See pages T8 and T9.

Building Sentence Awareness

Write this phrase on the chalkboard and ask a volunteer to read it aloud: Is in.

Ask students whether this phrase makes sense by itself. (no) Invite students to suggest some words that might be added to this phrase to create a group of words that makes sense. (Examples: The bird is in its cage; A frog is in the pond.) Then tell students that in Unit 1 they will learn about the different parts that make up a sentence. They will also learn how to combine short sentences into longer ones and how to correct sentences that are too long or are incomplete thoughts. Point out that knowing what a sentence is and how it is put together can help them when they speak and write.

Introducing "The World Outside"
Water

Explain to students that the title of Unit 1 is "The World Outside" and that each lesson gives information about water—an important life-giving substance on Earth. Invite students to suggest ways people use water and to name some forms or forces of water. List their ideas in a chart such as this:

Water		
Uses	**Forms or Forces**	
drinking	rain	snow
washing	flood	hail

Lesson 1 (student pages 7–8)
Complete Subjects and Complete Predicates

Objectives

- To learn that every sentence has a subject and a predicate
- To learn what words make up the complete subject and what words make up the complete predicate
- To identify the complete subject and the complete predicate in sentences
- To complete sentences by adding subjects or predicates to phrases
- To compose original sentences

Options for Organizing and Differentiating Instruction

See pages T9 and T10.

Scaffolding for English Language Learners

Explain to students that every living thing is made up of water and that without it there would be no life on Earth. Introduce the words *beverages, industries, agriculture, cultivation,* and *treatment plants.* Use drawings or actual containers to acquaint English Language Learners with the units of measurement mentioned.

Read aloud the sentences in **Part 1,** and then have volunteers reread the sentences orally and identify the complete subject and the complete predicate in each.

Invite volunteers to read each phrase in **Part 2** aloud and to suggest a subject or a predicate to make a complete sentence. (Example: item 13: *A thirsty person* needs water.) Then have students work with English-proficient partners to complete the section.

Students can work with the same partners to complete the writing activity in **Part 3.** Suggest that partners first talk about their favorite water activity and then work together to write their sentences.

Speaking and Listening

Ask students to read aloud the sentences they composed in Part 3. Ask listeners to identify the complete subject and the complete predicate in each. List the water activities students mentioned on the board. Have them orally compose safety tips for each.

Reinforcement and Reteaching

Review **Read and Discover** and the rule statement, refer students to the **G.U.M. Handbook,** or use the **Extra Practice** activity on page 159.

Lesson 2 (student pages 9–10)
Simple Subjects and Simple Predicates

Objectives

- To learn that the simple subject is the most important word or words in the complete subject and the simple predicate is the word or words that tell what the subject did, does, or will do
- To identify simple subjects and simple predicates in sentences
- To write sentences using simple subjects and simple predicates
- To write a descriptive paragraph, and to identify each simple subject and simple predicate in it

Options for Organizing and Differentiating Instruction

See pages T9 and T10.

Scaffolding for English Language Learners

Ask students to study the picture on page 9 as you read the caption aloud. Encourage them to identify the form of each item shown in the picture: ice cube (solid), glass of water (liquid), steam (gas). Note that the steam represents water vapor, which is the invisible gas form of water.

Help students name the forms of the verb *be* and list them on the board. Make sure they understand the difference between *complete subject/predicate* and *simple subject/predicate*. Read all the sentences in **Part 1** aloud. Ask volunteers to reread each sentence orally and to identify the simple subject and the simple predicate.

In **Part 2**, model using a simple subject and a simple predicate from the word bank to compose an oral sentence. (Example: *Hailstones clatter* on the rooftop.) Then have partners work together to complete Part 2.

For **Part 3**, list a word bank of "winter weather words" students might use to write their descriptions.

Speaking and Listening

Have students find weather forecasts in newspapers and read the forecasts, pretending to be weather announcers. Ask listeners to identify the simple subjects and the simple predicates.

Reinforcement and Reteaching

Review **Read and Discover** and the rule statement, refer students to the **G.U.M. Handbook**, or use the **Extra Practice** activity on page 159.

Lesson 3 (student pages 11–12)
Compound Subjects and Compound Predicates

Objectives

- To learn that a compound subject is two or more subjects joined by a conjunction (*and* or *or*) and that a compound predicate is two or more verbs joined by a conjunction
- To identify the simple subjects that make up each compound subject and the verbs that make up each compound predicate in sentences
- To combine phrases to form sentences with compound subjects or compound predicates
- To write a sentence with a compound subject or a compound predicate

Options for Organizing and Differentiating Instruction

See pages T9 and T10.

Scaffolding for English Language Learners

Ask students to study the picture on page 11 and to suggest living things that are affected by the change of tides, such as seashore creatures and beachgoers.

Read the sentences in **Part 1** aloud. In item 1, model how to identify the two simple subjects (ports and harbors). Ask volunteers to reread the other sentences aloud and to identify the compound subject or compound predicate in each one.

Invite volunteers to read the sentences in **Part 2** aloud. Model combining the first sentence pair to form a new sentence with a compound predicate. (Example: Visitors to the beach can swim at high tide or dig clams at low tide.) Then have students work with partners to complete the section.

Have students work independently or in pairs to unscramble the words in **Part 3**.

Speaking and Listening

Ask students to choose two classroom objects and create sentences with compound subjects. (Example: *Pictures* and *posters* decorate the walls.) Have students follow a similar procedure for compound predicates. (Example: We *eat* lunch and then *go* outside.)

Reinforcement and Reteaching

Review **Read and Discover** and the rule statement, refer students to the **G.U.M. Handbook**, or use the **Extra Practice** activity on page 160.

T17

Objectives

- To discover that a direct object receives the action of the verb
- To learn that in a compound direct object, more than one word receives the action of the verb
- To identify direct objects and compound direct objects in sentences
- To choose direct objects to complete sentences
- To compose descriptive sentences with direct objects about a picture

Options for Organizing and Differentiating Instruction

See pages T9 and T10.

Scaffolding for English Language Learners

Read aloud the caption and discuss the picture on page 13. Invite students who have been to the ocean to describe their experiences.

Read each sentence in **Part 1** aloud and explain any unfamiliar terms, such as *reefs, container ships,* and *luxury liners.* Then ask volunteers to reread each sentence orally and to identify the direct object(s) in it. Help students identify the direct object by saying the verb in each sentence and asking "What?" or "Whom?" (Example: item 2: *explore* what? *reefs*).

For **Part 2,** read aloud the words in the word bank, and read each sentence. Work as a group to choose a direct object that makes sense for each sentence. Invite students to draw pictures or to pantomime the action described in the sentence to illustrate the relationship between the verb and the direct object.

Display pictures of underwater scenes before students complete **Part 3.** Explain any unfamiliar terms in the word bank. After students draw, have them work independently to write their descriptive sentences.

Speaking and Listening

Read aloud several sentences from a book or other source that contains action verbs and direct objects. Omit reading the direct objects. Ask students to add new direct objects that make sense.

Reinforcement and Reteaching

Review **Read and Discover** and the rule statement, refer students to the **G.U.M. Handbook,** or use the **Extra Practice** activity on page 160.

Objectives

- To learn that an indirect object is a noun or pronoun that comes before a direct object and that it appears only in sentences that have direct objects
- To identify indirect objects in sentences
- To rewrite words in sentences as indirect objects
- To compose sentences that include indirect objects

Options for Organizing and Differentiating Instruction

See pages T9 and T10.

Scaffolding for English Language Learners

Read the caption on page 15 aloud and, if possible, show students a picture of a bayou. Also display pictures of other bodies of water, such as ponds, lakes, creeks, rivers, and estuaries.

Read aloud the sentences in **Part 1.** Explain that a pothole is a natural depression in the ground that often fills with water. Reread the sentences and have volunteers identify the indirect object in each. Model "testing" whether a word is the indirect object by moving it after the direct object and putting the word *to* in front of it. (Example: item 1: Potholes offer resting places *to migrating ducks.*)

Discuss the directions and example in **Part 2.** Have a volunteer read the first sentence aloud and model rewriting it. (Example: item 15: Eddie sold Rachel his kayak.) Ask student pairs to complete the section.

In **Part 3,** make sure students know what a canoe trip is and what the items in the word bank mean. Pair students with English-proficient partners to compose and write their sentences.

Speaking and Listening

Write this sentence frame on the board:

    __ gave __ (a/some/the) __.

Have students take turns creating oral sentences by filling in the blanks. (Examples: Roger gave his dog a bone; I gave my mom some flowers.) Write the sentences on the board as students say them. Then call on volunteers to identify the direct and indirect objects.

Reinforcement and Reteaching

Review **Read and Discover** and the rule statement, refer students to the **G.U.M. Handbook,** or use the **Extra Practice** activity on page 161.

Lesson 6 (student pages 17–18)
Predicate Nouns and Predicate Adjectives

Objectives
- To discover that predicate nouns follow linking verbs and rename the subject, and predicate adjectives follow linking verbs and describe the subject
- To identify predicate nouns and predicate adjectives in sentences
- To add predicate nouns or predicate adjectives to complete sentences
- To write a question and an answer using a predicate noun or a predicate adjective

Options for Organizing and Differentiating Instruction
See pages T9 and T10.

Scaffolding for English Language Learners
Write glacier on the board. Direct students to the picture on page 17 and read the caption aloud.

Review what a linking verb is and list examples on the board (Examples: is, are, was, were, become, seem, feel). Read each sentence in **Part 1** aloud and have students identify the predicate noun or predicate adjective and the linking verb before they write their answers.

Before beginning **Part 2**, tell students the *Titanic* was a British ship that sank in 1912 when it struck an iceberg. Read the first sentence aloud, and model how to complete it. (Example: A floating chunk of ice from a glacier becomes *an iceberg.*) Have students work in pairs to complete the section.

Read aloud the directions for **Part 3**. Have student pairs role-play survivors and reporters before they write their questions and answers.

Speaking and Listening
Write these sentence starters on the board:

My dog is __.   My friend is __.

Ask students to suggest at least two endings for each one: one with a predicate noun and one with a predicate adjective. (Examples: My dog is a Great Dane; My dog is big.)

Reinforcement and Reteaching
Review **Read and Discover** and the rule statement, refer students to the **G.U.M. Handbook**, or use the **Extra Practice** activity on page 161.

Lesson 7 (student pages 19–20)
Prepositional Phrases

Objectives
- To discover that a prepositional phrase can tell *how, what kind, when, how much,* or *where*
- To learn that a prepositional phrase begins with a preposition and ends with a noun or pronoun that is the object of the preposition
- To identify prepositions and prepositional phrases in sentences
- To add prepositional phrases to sentences
- To use prepositions to complete a puzzle

Options for Organizing and Differentiating Instruction
See pages T9 and T10.

Scaffolding for English Language Learners
Invite students to describe lakes they know of or have visited. Then read aloud the caption on page 19. Discuss how the Great Lakes and their connecting waterways might be vital to the American and Canadian economies (Examples: transporting goods to many ports; providing shipping routes to the sea).

Next, read aloud all the sentences in **Part 1**. Then ask a volunteer to reread each sentence, identifying the prepositional phrase in it and the preposition that begins the phrase.

Read the phrases in **Part 2** aloud. Have students complete this section in small groups. Ask group members to decide which prepositional phrase to use in each sentence. Invite each group to share its rewritten sentences.

Finally, have student pairs complete **Part 3**. To help English Language Learners, write the answers in a word bank on the board and ask students to identify which preposition belongs in each sentence.

Speaking and Listening
Display a picture that shows many objects and events, such as a picture of a fair or a circus. Ask students to orally describe the scene. Remind them to use prepositional phrases in their sentences. Ask listeners to identify the prepositional phrases.

Reinforcement and Reteaching
Review **Read and Discover** and the rule statement, refer students to the **G.U.M. Handbook**, or use the **Extra Practice** activity on page 162.

Lesson 8 (student pages 21–22)
Compound Sentences

Objectives
- To learn that a compound sentence is two simple sentences, or independent clauses, joined either by a comma and a conjunction or by a semicolon
- To identify compound sentences and to rewrite pairs of simple sentences as compound sentences
- To combine independent clauses to form compound sentences

Options for Organizing and Differentiating Instruction
See pages T9 and T10.

Scaffolding for English Language Learners
Explain that many canals have locks that enable ships to move from one water level to another. Read aloud the caption and discuss the diagram on page 21.

Read aloud each sentence in **Part 1**. To help students determine which items are compound sentences, have a volunteer try to restate the two items separated by commas or semicolons as two separate sentences. Ask students to tell how the independent clauses in the compound sentences are joined.

For **Part 2**, read the first pair of sentences aloud and discuss which conjunction to use (and) and why. Have student pairs orally compose possible compound sentences for each item before they write.

Have students work in small groups to complete **Part 3**. Remind them to refer to the page 21 diagram as they reorder the sentences.

Speaking and Listening
Write these sentence frames on the board:

Last summer we went __.

This summer we may go __.

Ask students to complete the frames orally by describing a real or imaginary trip to a river or other body of water. Have them expand each to form a compound sentence. (Example: Last summer we went to Lake Erie, and I had a great time fishing.) Have volunteers tell where to place the comma or semicolon in each.

Reinforcement and Reteaching
Review **Read and Discover** and the rule statement, refer students to the **G.U.M. Handbook**, or use the **Extra Practice** activity on page 162.

Lesson 9 (student pages 23–24)
Dependent and Independent Clauses

Objectives
- To review that an independent clause is a sentence that makes sense by itself
- To learn that a dependent clause has a subject and a verb but cannot stand alone and that it begins with words such as *although, because, if, as,* or *when*
- To identify dependent clauses and independent clauses and the conjunctions that join them
- To match dependent clauses with independent clauses to create new sentences
- To add independent clauses to dependent clauses to make sentences

Options for Organizing and Differentiating Instruction
See pages T9 and T10.

Scaffolding for English Language Learners
Read the caption on page 23 aloud; discuss how waves can carve cliffs or other formations in rock. Ask students how they think ocean waves are created.

Read the sentences in **Part 1** aloud. Clarify the terms *tracking equipment* and *overboard*. Ask volunteers to reread each sentence aloud, to identify the dependent clause and the independent clause, and to explain how they determined the two. Have them also identify the word that begins each dependent clause.

For **Part 2**, have a volunteer model matching the first dependent clause with an independent clause to form a sentence, explaining where to place the comma. Have student pairs complete the remaining sentences.

Have students work in pairs or small groups to complete **Part 3**. Suggest students brainstorm possible independent clauses before they write their sentences.

Speaking and Listening
Write these words on separate index cards: after, although, because, if, as, when, unless, before, since, while. Distribute a card to each student. Ask students to compose a sentence containing a dependent and an independent clause using the word on their card.

Reinforcement and Reteaching
Review **Read and Discover** and the rule statement, refer students to the **G.U.M. Handbook**, or use the **Extra Practice** activity on page 163.

Lesson 10   (student pages 25–26)
Avoiding Fragments, Run-ons, Comma Splices

Objectives
- To learn that a sentence fragment does not express a complete thought, that a run-on sentence is a compound sentence missing a comma and a conjunction, and that a comma splice is a run-on sentence that has a comma but no conjunction
- To identify and correct sentence fragments, run-ons, and comma splices

Options for Organizing and Differentiating Instruction
See pages T9 and T10.

Scaffolding for English Language Learners
Review with students what they learned about waves in Lesson 9. Explain that a *tsunami* is a series of huge, destructive waves.

Read the paragraph in **Part 1** aloud, one sentence at a time. Ask students to examine each sentence to determine whether it expresses one or more complete thoughts. Have them circle any fragments. Ask students to determine whether the clauses are joined and punctuated properly.

Pair students with English-proficient partners to complete **Part 2**. Remind them how the fragment at the beginning of the paragraph in Part 1 should be corrected. (Example: A tsunami is not a single wave but a series of waves sometimes called a wave train.) Then model correcting the comma splice that follows the fragment. Suggest that partners compose their sentences orally before they write them.

Students can work with the same partners to complete **Part 3**, using a dictionary if needed.

Speaking and Listening
Have students form groups of three. Assign each student one of the following topics: comma splice, run-on, fragment. Ask students to prepare a short presentation describing their assigned error, giving an example of it, and explaining how to correct it.

Reinforcement and Reteaching
Review **Read and Discover** and the rule statement, refer students to the **G.U.M. Handbook**, or use the **Extra Practice** activity on page 163.

Proofreading   (student pages 27–28)

Scaffolding for English Language Learners
Have students work with partners who are fluent in English for the proofreading activities.

Proofreading Practice
Ask students to identify the topic of the report on page 27. (wetlands) Explain to students that the report contains several mistakes and that, as they read, they should look for these mistakes.

Review the **Proofreading Marks** chart and the examples. Remind students that these marks are used by professional writers to check their work before publication. Read the first two sentences aloud. Discuss the first error (The *w* in *wetlands* should be a capital letter.) and how it should be marked. Ask students (in pairs or independently) to correct the remaining errors using proofreading marks. You may wish to have students correct the spelling errors, too.

After they have completed the activity, ask volunteers to read each sentence aloud and to identify the errors. Ask students to mark overlooked errors in another color. **Note:** Some errors can be corrected in more than one way.

Proofreading Checklist
Ask students to select a recent piece of their own writing and to write the title of that piece at the top of the chart. Ask students to put a check mark next to each item in the checklist after they have checked it in their work. Students might first work independently and then trade papers with a partner to double-check each other's work. You might model, or ask a student to model, using the **G.U.M. Handbook** (beginning on page 195) to clarify a concept or rule.

Also Remember...
Remind students that capitalization and punctuation are important for clear writing. If necessary, help students use the **Handbook** to clarify when commas should be used and to review the use of capital letters.

Your Own List
Suggest that students look at the errors they did not find in the proofreading activity and add them to the checklist. Also ask students to think about other kinds of errors they make and to add these to the checklist.

Ask students to place this page in their writing portfolios. These pages may be used to assess students' progress over the course of the year.

Assessment Options

See page T9 for ways to use *G.U.M.* assessments to differentiate instruction.

Unit Review

The **Unit Review** (pp. 29–30) allows you to check students' progress and determine when reteaching is necessary. The review pages may be completed in class or as homework. If a student responds incorrectly to two or more items involving the same skill, you may want to work directly with the student to review the relevant lesson. The lesson number to which each review item relates appears in parentheses on the review pages in the Teacher Edition.

Assign the **Extra Practice** activities (pp. 159–163) to reteach targeted skills in a more focused way.

Unit Assessment

The **Unit Assessment** (pp. 139–142) is intended to (1) familiarize students with standardized testing procedures, (2) check students' ability to apply key unit concepts in a different format, and (3) serve as an indicator of student progress.

- When used as a **pretest,** the Unit Assessment helps you determine, prior to instruction, your students' strengths, weaknesses, knowledge, and skills.
- When used as a **posttest,** the Unit Assessment provides feedback that you can use to guide further instruction.

Follow this procedure for administering the Unit Assessment.

1. Read aloud the Test Tip and the test instructions. (**Note:** For additional scaffolding, you may wish to read the test questions and answer choices aloud.)
2. Tell students that they will have 20 minutes to read and answer the questions independently.
3. When time is up, collect and correct the tests. Use the results to measure student progress and guide reteaching.

Assign the **Extra Practice** activities (pp. 159–163) to reteach targeted skills in a more focused way.

Note: The **Unit Review** may be reused after reteaching to check students' understanding of the lesson concepts.

Unit Test

The **Unit Test** (pp. 185–186) helps you judge students' achievement while providing them with valuable practice for high-stakes tests. When you are ready to administer the test, ask students to carefully tear it out of their books. (**Note:** If the test has already been removed, distribute it to students.) Read aloud the directions for each section and make sure students understand how to answer the questions. Ask students to work independently to complete the test.

Students who miss two questions focusing on the same grammar element may need additional help understanding the concept. Reteach the concept, following this procedure:

1. Review **Read and Discover.**
2. Review the rule statement for the concept.
3. Guide students through items a second time. Ask the students to explain why each correct answer belongs in each sentence.
4. Refer students to the **G.U.M. Handbook** for further reinforcement.

School Home Connection (student pages 31–32)

These two pages provide quick, fun activities that review and reinforce the skills and concepts taught in Lessons 1 to 10. These activities also provide opportunities for students to share what they have been learning with their families and for parents to become actively involved in their child's learning. You might utilize the **School Home Connection** pages in one of the following ways:

- Ask students to take the pages home, choose one or two activities to do, and then ask their parents to sign and return the pages.
- Send the pages home without asking that they be returned.
- Ask students to do one activity at school and then send the pages home.

When you are ready to send the pages home, direct students to the activities on pages 31–32. Inform students that these are fun activities they can do at home that will help them practice some of the things they have been learning about in the unit. Then ask students to carefully tear the pages out of the book, and explain how you wish students to use them.

Notes

Looking Back

Unit 2 Parts of Speech

Lesson 11: Common and Proper Nouns
Lesson 12: Plural and Possessive Nouns
Lesson 13: Personal and Possessive Pronouns
Lesson 14: The Present Tense
Lesson 15: The Past and Future Tenses
Lesson 16: The Present Perfect Tense
Lesson 17: Adjectives
Lesson 18: Adverbs
Lesson 19: Prepositions
Lesson 20: Coordinating and
            Subordinating Conjunctions

Pretest Option

You may use the **Unit Assessment** as a pretest. See pages T8 and T9.

Building Grammar Awareness

Write these words on the board and ask a volunteer to read them aloud:

        played Joey well the in game

Have students work in pairs to put the words in an order that makes sense. (Joey played well in the game.) Write this sentence on the board. Explain to students that different words have different jobs in sentences. Ask volunteers to look at the sentence and find a word that names a particular person (Joey), a word that tells of an action (played), and a word that names a thing (game). Inform students that in Unit 2 they will learn about the parts of speech that make up a sentence. Point out that learning about different kinds of words and using them correctly in sentences can help them to be better understood when speaking and writing.

Introducing "Looking Back"
United States History

Inform students that the title of Unit 2 is "Looking Back." Explain that each lesson tells about the history, land, or culture of the United States. Invite students to name some American symbols (apple pie, stars and stripes, bald eagle, the Liberty Bell), celebrations (Thanksgiving, Fourth of July), and tourist attractions (Grand Canyon, Mount Rushmore, Statue of Liberty). You might use a web to record their responses. Encourage students to share what they know about each item they suggest.

Lesson 11   (student pages 33–34)
Common and Proper Nouns

Objectives

- To learn that a common noun names any person, place, thing, or idea
- To discover that a proper noun names a particular person, place, thing, or idea
- To identify common and proper nouns in sentences, and to write sentences using them
- To find hidden nouns in a word search and then identify them as common nouns or proper nouns

Options for Organizing and Differentiating Instruction

See pages T9 and T10.

Scaffolding for English Language Learners

Point out the figure on page 33, and explain that Uncle Sam symbolizes the United States government. Inform students that a meatpacker named Sam Wilson was the inspiration for this national symbol.

Read the sentences in **Part 1** aloud and clarify any unfamiliar concepts or words, such as *packing, friendliness, inspector,* and *curious.* Ask volunteers to read each sentence aloud, to identify which words are common and proper nouns, and to tell how they know.

In **Part 2**, be sure students understand what each symbol refers to. If possible, show pictures of the Great Seal (on which the bald eagle appears), the Liberty Bell, and the White House. Explain that a sea captain gave the name "Old Glory" to the national flag in 1824. Pair students with English-proficient partners to orally compose and then write their sentences.

Partners can work together to complete the word search in **Part 3**. (across: fireworks, flag, Lincoln, America; **down:** independence, Jefferson, parade, Washington)

Speaking and Listening

Have small groups of students work together to brainstorm and list common and proper nouns that refer to people, to places, to things, and to ideas. Have students copy the listed words onto the board under the headings Common Nouns and Proper Nouns.

Reinforcement and Reteaching

Review **Read and Discover** and the rule statement, refer students to the **G.U.M. Handbook,** or use the **Extra Practice** activity on page 164.

Lesson 12 (student pages 35–36)
Plural and Possessive Nouns

Objectives
- To discover that a plural noun names more than one person, place, thing, or idea and that some nouns change spelling in the plural form
- To learn that a possessive noun shows ownership, and to form possessives from plural nouns
- To identify plural and possessive nouns in sentences, and to write the plural and the plural possessive forms of given nouns
- To write a paragraph using plural and possessive nouns

Options for Organizing and Differentiating Instruction
See pages T9 and T10.

Scaffolding for English Language Learners
Read the caption on page 35 aloud. Then, if necessary, introduce and explain the terms *colonists/colony, Pilgrims,* and *harvest.*

In **Part 1,** ask volunteers to read each sentence, to find a word that names more than one person, place, thing, or idea, and to explain how they know the words are plural nouns. Repeat the procedure with possessive nouns. Have students complete Part 1.

Read the sentences in **Part 2** aloud. Discuss the meaning of the word *matches* in item 16. (games, contests) Model completing item 13 and have students work with partners to complete the remaining items.

For **Part 3,** invite students to share ways families might celebrate Thanksgiving today. Pair students with English-proficient partners to compose their paragraphs.

Speaking and Listening
Ask each student to write five nouns that name a person or a thing on separate index cards. Place all the cards in a bag. Have student pairs take turns selecting two cards from the pile. Partners then have one minute to come up with sentences that include both nouns, using their plural or possessive forms. (Examples: *Peter's basketball* is flat. *Peter* has two *basketballs.*)

Reinforcement and Reteaching
Review **Read and Discover** and the rule statement, refer students to the **G.U.M. Handbook,** or use the **Extra Practice** activity on page 164.

Lesson 13 (student pages 37–38)
Personal and Possessive Pronouns

Objectives
- To learn that personal pronouns such as *I* and *me* can be used to refer to oneself, and that personal pronouns such as *she* and *they* can be used to refer to others
- To learn that pronouns such as *his, its,* and *our* show possession
- To identify personal and possessive pronouns in sentences
- To rewrite sentences by replacing nouns with pronouns
- To use personal and possessive pronouns in expository sentences

Options for Organizing and Differentiating Instruction
See pages T9 and T10.

Scaffolding for English Language Learners
Play recordings of "America the Beautiful" and "The Star-Spangled Banner," and introduce the words *melody, anthem, verses,* and *patriotic.*

Read the sentences in **Part 1** aloud. Ask volunteers to identify the pronoun in each and tell whether it is personal or possessive. Call on other volunteers to identify the noun to which each pronoun refers.

In **Part 2,** ask students to rephrase each sentence orally before they write pronouns to replace the underlined words. Point out that the apostrophes in items 11, 12, 14, and 15 show that possessive pronouns are needed. **Note:** Students may choose either the inclusive terms *us* and *We,* or *them* and *They* in their answers for items 12 and 13.

For **Part 3,** students might dictate their sentences to you, an aide, or a peer tutor.

Speaking and Listening
Invite students to briefly tell about their favorite songs or singers. Ask listeners to identify the personal and possessive pronouns each speaker uses.

Reinforcement and Reteaching
Review **Read and Discover** and the rule statement, refer students to the **G.U.M. Handbook,** or use the **Extra Practice** activity on page 165.

Lesson 14 (student pages 39–40)
The Present Tense

Objectives
- To discover that the present tense is used to tell about something that happens regularly or is true now
- To learn to correctly write the present tense form of verbs by adding *s* or *es*, or by dropping *y* and adding *ies* to verbs ending with a consonant and *y*
- To identify present tense verbs in sentences
- To complete sentences using present tense verbs
- To compose a description using present tense verbs

Options for Organizing and Differentiating Instruction
See pages T9 and T10.

Scaffolding for English Language Learners
Point out the map on page 39; explain to students that the Mississippi River is the longest river in the United States.

Read the paragraphs in **Part 1** aloud, and reinforce the meanings of *barges* and *haul*. Have volunteers read aloud each sentence in the paragraph, identify the verb, and tell whether it is in the present tense.

For **Part 2**, read item 14, saying "blank" where there is a blank. Ask a volunteer to reread the sentence with the correct verb in place. (The Mississippi River *begins*...) Have students complete Part 2 in pairs.

Read the instructions for **Part 3** aloud. Help students brainstorm how a captain might use the verbs in the word bank in his description. Have partners brainstorm and compose their descriptions.

Speaking and Listening
Ask students to describe activities in which they have participated. Have listeners restate each sentence, changing the verb to its present tense form. (Examples: I *saw* a movie/I *see* a movie.)

Reinforcement and Reteaching
Review **Read and Discover** and the rule statement, refer students to the **G.U.M. Handbook**, or use the **Extra Practice** activity on page 165.

Lesson 15 (student pages 41–42)
The Past and Future Tenses

Objectives
- To learn that past tense verbs tell about actions that already happened, and to correctly write the past tense form of regular and irregular verbs
- To learn that future tense verbs tell about actions that are going to happen, and to use the helping verb *will* to form the future tense
- To identify past and future tense verbs in sentences, and to complete sentences using past or future tense verbs
- To write a description using future tense verbs

Options for Organizing and Differentiating Instruction
See pages T9 and T10.

Scaffolding for English Language Learners
Write leukemia on the board. Read the word and explain that it is a disease in which white blood cells multiply abnormally. Explain to students that until the late twentieth century, people who were diagnosed with leukemia soon died. Tell them that there are now effective treatments for this disease.

Read each sentence in **Part 1** aloud. Ask students to identify each verb and tell whether it is past or future tense.

In **Part 2**, guide students to determine from sentence clues whether the action in each sentence happened in the past or will happen in the future.

In **Part 3**, encourage student pairs to share their goals orally before they write sentences to express them. Model goal statements using future tense verbs. (Example: I *will take* science courses in high school.)

Speaking and Listening
Write the words Yesterday and Tomorrow as two column headings on the board. Ask students to think of verbs that describe actions they did yesterday or will do tomorrow. Record their responses under the appropriate heading.

Reinforcement and Reteaching
Review **Read and Discover** and the rule statement, refer students to the **G.U.M. Handbook**, or use the **Extra Practice** activity on page 166.

Lesson 16 (student pages 43–44)
The Present Perfect Tense

Objectives
- To learn that verbs in the present perfect tense show action that began in the past and may still be continuing in the present
- To learn how to form the present perfect tense by adding *has* or *have* to the past participle of a verb
- To identify verbs in the present perfect tense in sentences
- To complete sentences using verbs in the present perfect tense
- To compose an ad that has present perfect tense verbs

Options for Organizing and Differentiating Instruction
See pages T9 and T10.

Scaffolding for English Language Learners
Point out the locations of southern California and Vietnam on a map. Explain that the largest Vietnamese community outside Vietnam is in southern California.

In **Part 1**, make sure students understand the words *immigrants, culture, refugees,* and *homeland.* Have volunteers read each sentence aloud while other students identify the verbs in the present perfect tense.

For **Part 2**, ask students to orally compose answers before they write their responses.

In **Part 3**, suggest that students make a list of things they want to emphasize before they write the ad.

Speaking and Listening
Play a game about movies, songs, and books. Have teams of students write questions. Call on teams, one by one, to read the questions aloud. Students should begin with the question Have you seen…?, Have you heard…?, or Have you read…? Then, if the answer is yes, they should ask a question about that movie, song, or book. (If the answer is no, they must start over.) The opposing team has to answer the second question correctly to score a point.

Reinforcement and Reteaching
Review **Read and Discover** and the rule statement, refer students to the **G.U.M. Handbook**, or use the **Extra Practice** activity on page 166.

Lesson 17 (student pages 45–46)
Adjectives

Objectives
- To learn that adjectives describe nouns and pronouns, and that there are different kinds of adjectives
- To identify descriptive adjectives, demonstrative adjectives that tell how many, and articles as adjectives in sentences
- To use adjectives to complete sentences
- To use adjectives to complete a puzzle

Options for Organizing and Differentiating Instruction
See pages T9 and T10.

Scaffolding for English Language Learners
Read the caption on page 45 aloud. Ask a volunteer to find North Carolina on a United States map. Point out Cape Hatteras, a chain of islands that buffers the mainland from the Atlantic Ocean.

Read the sentences in **Part 1** aloud. Then have volunteers read the sentences aloud, one at a time. Ask students to study each boldfaced word in item 1 and identify what type of adjective it is. Be sure students understand the four-part process in the directions as they complete the section.

Read aloud the word bank in **Part 2**. Then have students work in pairs to complete the sentences. Suggest that they complete the sentences orally before they write their answers.

Students can work with the same partners to complete the puzzle in **Part 3**. Suggest that they refer to the rule statement (in the gray box) on page 45 for information about adjectives.

Speaking and Listening
Have students work in pairs to brainstorm three or more sentences that describe themselves, using adjectives that tell how many. (Examples: I have *three* sisters. I like *many* sports. I have a collection of *twenty* comic books.) Give students five minutes. Then ask volunteers to share their sentences and to identify the adjectives in them.

Reinforcement and Reteaching
Review **Read and Discover** and the rule statement, refer students to the **G.U.M. Handbook**, or use the **Extra Practice** activity on page 167.

Objectives

- To learn that adverbs tell more about verbs or adjectives by explaining *how, when, where,* or *to what extent* (*how much*)
- To learn that many adverbs end in *-ly*
- To identify adverbs in sentences, and to tell how they are used
- To find adverbs in a word search and then write sentences using them

Options for Organizing and Differentiating Instruction

See pages T9 and T10.

Scaffolding for English Language Learners

Explain that whaling—the hunting of whales for profit—was a major industry in America in the early 1800s. Then read the caption on page 47 aloud.

Invite volunteers to help you read the sentences in **Part 1** aloud. Make sure students understand the words *abandoned, declined, species,* and *extinct.* Ask students to identify the verb and the adverb in the first sentence. (hunted; first) Have them tell what the adverb explains. (when) Then have students work in pairs to find the remaining adverbs.

Before student pairs begin **Part 2**, make sure they understand the terms *prey, entangled, starves, frantically,* and *shreds.* Read aloud all the sentences. Model identifying the adverb in item 14 and telling what it explains. (yearly; *when* whales migrate)

For **Part 3**, students might complete the word search independently and then work with English-proficient partners to compose their sentences. List on the board the words students should look for. (across: recently, there; **down:** sometimes, very, slowly)

Speaking and Listening

Provide pictures showing various activities. Ask students to compose oral sentences for each picture, using adverbs that help describe the action. List on the board some adverbs students might use. (Examples: quickly, happily, hungrily, extremely, only)

Reinforcement and Reteaching

Review **Read and Discover** and the rule statement, refer students to the **G.U.M. Handbook,** or use the **Extra Practice** activity on page 167.

Objectives

- To learn more about prepositions and prepositional phrases
- To identify prepositions, objects of prepositions, and prepositional phrases in sentences
- To choose appropriate prepositional phrases to complete sentences
- To write descriptive sentences with prepositional phrases

Options for Organizing and Differentiating Instruction

See pages T9 and T10.

Scaffolding for English Language Learners

Display pictures of the Grand Canyon. Then review some of the prepositions students learned in Lesson 7 (Unit 1) and list them on the board. (in, over, of, to, by, for, during, through)

After you read aloud the sentences in **Part 1**, discuss the information and any unfamiliar words with students. Help students identify the prepositional phrase(s) in each sentence, the preposition that begins each, and the object of the preposition.

Before students work on **Part 2**, read the phrases in the word bank aloud and model how to complete item 11. (Most visitors drive or walk to viewing points *above the Grand Canyon.*) Then have students complete the remaining sentences orally before they write their answers.

Read the instructions for **Part 3** aloud and briefly discuss the activities of the squirrels on page 49. Have students work independently to write their sentences or dictate them to you or an aide. Then pair students with partners for the matching part of the activity.

Speaking and Listening

Ask students to describe an outdoor experience, such as a bike ride or a hike. List on the board several common prepositions, such as *from, to, with, near, by, of, over, under, through, around,* and *beside,* and ask students to use them in sentences.

Reinforcement and Reteaching

Review **Read and Discover** and the rule statement, refer students to the **G.U.M. Handbook,** or use the **Extra Practice** activity on page 168.

Objectives

- To discover that coordinating conjunctions connect words or groups of words that are similar
- To learn that subordinating conjunctions, such as *although* and *because,* show how one clause is related to another clause in a sentence
- To identify coordinating and subordinating conjunctions in sentences, and to use them to complete sentences

Options for Organizing and Differentiating Instruction

See pages T9 and T10.

Scaffolding for English Language Learners

Read the caption on page 51 aloud and help students identify the four presidents in the illustration. (George Washington, Thomas Jefferson, Theodore Roosevelt, Abraham Lincoln) To help students fully appreciate the size of the monument, explain that the head of Washington is as high as a five-story building.

Read aloud and discuss the sentences in **Part 1**. If necessary, explain the meanings of *statues, peak,* and *blast away.* Then help students identify the coordinating or subordinating conjunction in each sentence before they mark their answers.

Before students complete **Part 2**, read the conjunctions in the word bank aloud. Then have student pairs work together to complete the section.

In **Part 3**, have pairs work together to read the descriptions, to write the names of the presidents on the lines, and to circle the conjunctions.

Speaking and Listening

Write and, or, and but as well as several subordinating conjunctions on separate index cards. Have students pick a card and compose a sentence. Each sentence should contain the conjunction that was selected. (Examples: We go to the computer room on Tuesdays *and* Thursdays. We can't play outside *because* it is raining.)

Reinforcement and Reteaching

Review **Read and Discover** and the rule statement, refer students to the **G.U.M. Handbook,** or use the **Extra Practice** activity on page 168.

Scaffolding for English Language Learners

Have students work with partners who are fluent in English for the proofreading activities.

Proofreading Practice

Ask students to identify the topic of the report on page 53. (Route 66) Explain to students that the report contains several mistakes and that, as they read, they should look for these mistakes.

Review the **Proofreading Marks** chart and the examples. Remind students that these marks are used by professional writers to correct their work before publication. Read the first sentence aloud. Discuss the error (*is* should be *has*) and how it should be marked. Ask students (in pairs or independently) to correct the remaining errors using proofreading marks. You may wish to have students correct the spelling errors, too.

After students have completed the activity, ask volunteers to read each sentence aloud and identify the errors. Ask students to mark overlooked errors in another color. **Note:** Some errors can be corrected in more than one way.

Proofreading Checklist

Ask students to select a recent piece of their own writing and to write the title of that piece at the top of the chart. Ask students to put a check mark next to each item in the checklist after they have checked it in their work. Students might first work independently and then trade papers with a partner to double-check each other's work. You might model, or ask a student to model, using the **G.U.M. Handbook** (beginning on page 195) to clarify a concept or rule.

Also Remember...

Remind students that capitalization and punctuation are important for clear writing. If necessary, help students use the **G.U.M. Handbook** to clarify when commas should be used and to review the use of capital letters.

Your Own List

Suggest that students look at the errors they did not find in the proofreading activity and add them to the checklist. Ask students to think about other kinds of errors they make and to add these to the checklist.

Ask students to place this page in their writing portfolios. These pages may be used to assess students' progress over the course of the year.

Assessment Options

See page T9 for ways to use *G.U.M.* assessments to differentiate instruction.

Unit Review

The **Unit Review** (pp. 55–56) allows you to check students' progress and determine when reteaching is necessary. The review pages may be completed in class or as homework. If a student responds incorrectly to two or more items involving the same skill, you may want to work directly with the student to review the relevant lesson. The lesson number to which each review item relates appears in parentheses on the review pages in the Teacher Edition.

Assign the **Extra Practice** activities (pp. 164–168) to reteach targeted skills in a more focused way.

Unit Assessment

The **Unit Assessment** (pp. 143–146) is intended to (1) familiarize students with standardized testing procedures, (2) check students' ability to apply key unit concepts in a different format, and (3) serve as an indicator of student progress.

- When used as a **pretest**, the Unit Assessment helps you determine, prior to instruction, your students' strengths, weaknesses, knowledge, and skills.
- When used as a **posttest**, the Unit Assessment provides feedback that you can use to guide further instruction.

Follow this procedure for administering the Unit Assessment.

1. Read aloud the Test Tip and the test instructions. (**Note:** For additional scaffolding, you may wish to read the test questions and answer choices aloud.)
2. Tell students that they will have 20 minutes to read and answer the questions independently.
3. When time is up, collect and correct the tests. Use the results to measure student progress and guide reteaching.

Assign the **Extra Practice** activities (pp. 164–168) to reteach targeted skills in a more focused way.

Note: The **Unit Review** may be reused after reteaching to check students' understanding of the lesson concepts.

Unit Test

The **Unit Test** (pp. 187–188) helps you judge students' achievement while providing them with valuable practice for high-stakes tests. When you are ready to administer the test, ask students to carefully tear it out of their books. (**Note:** If the test has already been removed, distribute it to students.) Read aloud the directions for each section and make sure students understand how to answer the questions. Ask students to work independently to complete the test.

Students who miss two questions focusing on the same grammar element may need additional help understanding the concept. Reteach the concept, following this procedure:

1. Review **Read and Discover**.
2. Review the rule statement for the concept.
3. Guide students through items a second time. Ask the students to explain why each correct answer belongs in each sentence.
4. Refer students to the **G.U.M. Handbook** for further reinforcement.

School Home Connection (student pages 57–58)

These two pages provide quick, fun activities that review and reinforce the skills and concepts taught in Lessons 11 to 20. These activities also provide opportunities for students to share what they have been learning with their families and for parents to become actively involved in their child's learning. You might utilize the **School Home Connection** pages in one of the following ways:

- Ask students to take the pages home, choose one or two activities to do, and then ask their parents to sign and return the pages.
- Send the pages home without asking that they be returned.
- Ask students to do one activity at school and then send the pages home.

When you are ready to send the pages home, direct students to the activities on pages 57–58. Inform students that these are fun activities they can do at home that will help them practice some of the things they have been learning about in the unit. Then ask students to carefully tear the pages out of the book, and explain how you wish students to use them.

Notes

Unforgettable Folks

Unit 3 Usage

Lesson 21: *Their, There, They're*
Lesson 22: *Its* and *It's*
Lesson 23: *Your* and *You're*
Lesson 24: *Like* and *You Know*
Lesson 25: Comparing with *Good* or *Bad*
Lesson 26: *That, Which, Who*
Lesson 27: *Real* and *Very*
Lesson 28: *Set* and *Sit*
Lesson 29: Irregular Verbs: *Know* and *Grow*
Lesson 30: *Learn* and *Teach*

Pretest Option

You may use the **Unit Assessment** as a pretest. See pages T8 and T9.

Building Usage Awareness

Write these sentences on the board:

Sports flash! Get you're tickets now if your going to the championship finals. There selling fast!

Invite a volunteer to read the sentences aloud. Ask students if the words in the sentences **sound** correct. Then ask if all the words in the sentences **look** correct. Invite volunteers to identify those they think are used incorrectly. (you're, your, there) Help students write the correct words above the incorrect words. Explain to students that in Unit 3, they will learn how to correctly use words that sound alike but have different meanings and spellings. They will also learn about other words that are often used incorrectly in writing. Inform students that using the correct words and word forms can help other people understand what they say and write.

Introducing "Unforgettable Folks"
Athletes

Tell students that the title of Unit 3 is "Unforgettable Folks" and that each lesson highlights the achievements of one or more athletes in the United States and around the world. Invite students to name some athletes they admire. You might create a web around the title "Unforgettable Sports Figures." Use questions such as these to guide discussion:

- Do you think sports are an important part of a school, a town, or a country? Why or why not?
- Do you think athletes can be considered heroes or role models? Why or why not?
- What are some traits that most great athletes have?

Lesson 21 (student pages 59–60)
Their, There, They're

Objectives

- To discover that *their, there,* and *they're* sound the same but have different spellings and meanings
- To learn that *their* is a possessive pronoun, *there* is an adverb, and *they're* is a contraction of the words *they* and *are*
- To choose *their, there,* or *they're* to complete sentences, and to write sentences using these words
- To complete clues to a riddle using *their, there,* and *they're* correctly

Options for Organizing and Differentiating Instruction

See pages T9 and T10.

Scaffolding for English Language Learners

Read the caption on page 59 aloud. Explain that Billy Mills (a member of the Lakota, or Sioux, nation in South Dakota) won a gold Olympic medal in the track-and-field competition at the 1964 Olympics.

Read aloud the information in **Part 1** about Mills's race. Then ask volunteers to reread each sentence aloud, to identify the word in parentheses that correctly completes that sentence, and to explain the reason for their choice. Point out that if *they are* makes sense in a sentence, then the contraction *they're* is correct.

For **Part 2**, ask students to work in small groups to discuss races before they write their sentences. Have volunteers read their completed sentences aloud and spell out *their, there,* and *they're* to indicate which word was used in each sentence.

Have groups continue to work together to complete **Part 3**. Remind them to capitalize a word that begins a sentence.

Speaking and Listening

Invite students to work in small groups to compose riddles using *their, there,* and *they're,* as in Part 3. Group members can then take turns saying the sentences in their riddle aloud while classmates identify the use of *their, there,* and *they're* in the sentences.

Reinforcement and Reteaching

Review **Read and Discover** and the rule statement, refer students to the **G.U.M. Handbook,** or use the **Extra Practice** activity on page 169.

Objectives

- To discover that *its* and *it's* sound the same but have different spellings and meanings
- To learn that *its* is a possessive pronoun and *it's* is a contraction of *it* and *is*
- To distinguish between *its* and *it's,* and to use each correctly in sentences
- To complete clues to a riddle using *its* and *it's*

Options for Organizing and Differentiating Instruction

See pages T9 and T10.

Scaffolding for English Language Learners

Ask how many students have played table tennis. Encourage them to talk about the skills a person would need to become a champion table tennis player. Then explain to students that in this lesson they will read about one of the world's greatest table tennis players, Jan-Ove Waldner (YAHN-OH•vuh VAHLD•nehr).

Write *its* and *it's* on the board. Then read aloud the sentences in **Part 1**, one at a time. Have students read each sentence after you. Ask group members to identify which word from the board belongs in each sentence.

Have students work in pairs to read aloud each sentence in **Part 2**, explaining whether *its* or *it's* belongs in the blank before they write their responses.

Have student teams of two or more compete to solve the riddle in **Part 3**. Remind them to capitalize a word that begins a sentence.

Speaking and Listening

Divide the class into two teams. Have one member from each team come to the front of the class, listen as you read aloud a sentence containing *its* or *it's,* and identify which word is used. The first student to raise his or her hand and spell the right answer scores a point. Continue until all students have had a chance to compete.

Reinforcement and Reteaching

Review **Read and Discover** and the rule statement, refer students to the **G.U.M. Handbook**, or use the **Extra Practice** activity on page 169.

Objectives

- To discover that *your* and *you're* sound the same but have different spellings and meanings
- To learn that *your* is a possessive pronoun and *you're* is a contraction of the words *you* and *are*
- To distinguish between *your* and *you're* in sentences, and to answer questions using *your* and *you're* correctly
- To compose a pep talk using *your* and *you're*

Options for Organizing and Differentiating Instruction

See pages T9 and T10.

Scaffolding for English Language Learners

Ask students to identify the skater on page 63. (Michelle Kwan) If possible, obtain a video about figure skating to show to the class.

Read the sentences in **Part 1** aloud. Then have volunteers reread the sentences aloud. After each sentence, ask students to identify the correct word in parentheses and to explain their answer. Point out that if *you are* makes sense in the sentence, then the contraction *you're* is correct.

For **Part 2**, have students work in pairs to compose oral responses to the questions before they write sentences. Model the process with the help of a student volunteer. (Example: Is my coach here yet? No, *your* coach isn't here.)

Have students discuss the meaning of *pep talk* before they work independently to complete **Part 3**. If necessary, students might dictate their sentences to you, an aide, or a peer tutor.

Speaking and Listening

Challenge students to use *your* and *you're* in oral sentences about safety tips for a sport or other activity. Model the process using examples such as these:

Wear *your* helmet when *you're* riding a bike.
When *you're* learning to ski, keep *your* knees bent.

Ask students to identify which word is used at each occurrence.

Reinforcement and Reteaching

Review **Read and Discover** and the rule statement, refer students to the **G.U.M. Handbook**, or use the **Extra Practice** activity on page 170.

Lesson 24 (student pages 65–66)
Like and *You Know*

Objectives
- To learn how to use *like* and *you know* correctly
- To identify the correct and incorrect usage of *like* and *you know* in sentences
- To rewrite sentences using *like* and *you know* correctly
- To correct a paragraph, and to write an advertisement using *like* and *you know* correctly

Options for Organizing and Differentiating Instruction
See pages T9 and T10.

Scaffolding for English Language Learners
Read the caption on page 65 aloud. Ask students to identify similarities and differences between softball and baseball. You might list students' responses in a Venn diagram. Then have volunteers summarize the similarities and differences. If a speaker uses *like* or *you know* as an interruptive word, gently point out that he or she has used the term incorrectly.

Read aloud the sentences in **Part 1**. Then ask volunteers to read each sentence aloud. Have students raise their hands when they hear *like* or *you know* used improperly. Then have students complete Part 1.

Have student pairs complete **Part 2** and **Part 3**, by first reading the sentences in Part 2 and the commercial in Part 3 as written. Tell students to discuss how the sentences in each section should be corrected before they rewrite the sentences and compose their commercials.

Speaking and Listening
Ask pairs of students to compose short dialogues in which *like* and *you know* are used both correctly and incorrectly. Invite volunteers to present their dialogues, and ask listeners to clap once whenever they hear the word or words used incorrectly.

Reinforcement and Reteaching
Review **Read and Discover** and the rule statement, refer students to the **G.U.M. Handbook**, or use the **Extra Practice** activity on page 170.

Lesson 25 (student pages 67–68)
Comparing with *Good* or *Bad*

Objectives
- To learn how to make comparisons using forms of *good* and *bad*
- To understand that *better* and *worse* are used to compare two people or things and *best* and *worst* are used to compare three or more people or things
- To choose the correct form of *good* or *bad* in sentences
- To complete sentences, and to write a comparison using forms of *good* and *bad* correctly

Options for Organizing and Differentiating Instruction
See pages T9 and T10.

Scaffolding for English Language Learners
Read the caption on page 67 aloud. Explain to students that in Lesson 25 they will find out about two baseball players, Ichiro Suzuki and Jackie Robinson.

Work with students to complete **Part 1**. Discuss how many things are being compared in each sentence. Ask students to choose a word to complete each sentence, and have a volunteer read the sentence aloud.

For **Part 2**, review the words in the word bank and ask volunteers to use them in oral sentences. Have students discuss with a partner how many things are being compared in each sentence before they write.

For **Part 3**, draw a Venn diagram on the board and show students how to use it to make comparisons. Have students work in pairs to make diagrams comparing two sports before they write their paragraphs.

Speaking and Listening
Ask volunteers to name their favorite and least favorite foods. Record their responses on the board. Then have students use these responses to make oral comparisons between two or more things, using the correct forms of *good* and *bad*. (Examples: Pizzas are *better* than hot dogs. Celery is the *worst* food of all.)

Reinforcement and Reteaching
Review **Read and Discover** and the rule statement, refer students to the **G.U.M. Handbook**, or use the **Extra Practice** activity on page 171.

Lesson 26 (student pages 69–70)
That, Which, Who

Objectives

- To learn that *that* is used to refer to either people or things, *which* is used to refer to things, and *who* is used to refer to people
- To choose *that, which,* or *who* in sentences
- To complete sentences and clues using *that, which,* or *who* correctly

Options for Organizing and Differentiating Instruction

See pages T9 and T10.

Scaffolding for English Language Learners

Read the caption on page 69 aloud. Explain that Jim Plunkett was one of the first Mexican American players to become a star in the National Football League. Tell students that Plunkett was very good at several sports but had to choose just one to focus on.

In **Part 1,** ask students to pick the word they think belongs in each sentence and to explain their choice. Remind them that they can test whether to use *that* or *which* by reading the sentence without the clause to see if the sentence still makes sense.

For **Part 2,** ask students to read each sentence and discuss their choices with a partner before they fill in the blanks.

Then divide the class into teams of two or more, and have them work cooperatively to solve the riddle poem in **Part 3.**

Speaking and Listening

Help students brainstorm lists of different sports, pieces of sports equipment, and athletes. Ask students to compose oral sentences that contain an item from one or more of the lists and the pronoun *that, which,* or *who.* (Examples: Football, *which* is a popular sport, is very exciting to watch. The position *that* requires the greatest strength is nose tackle. Jim Plunkett, *who* was an exceptional player, helped make the Raiders successful.)

Reinforcement and Reteaching

Review **Read and Discover** and the rule statement, refer students to the **G.U.M. Handbook,** or use the **Extra Practice** activity on page 171.

Lesson 27 (student pages 71–72)
Real and *Very*

Objectives

- To learn that *real* is an adjective that means "actual" and that *very* is an adverb that means "extremely"
- To identify correct and incorrect usage of *real* and *very*
- To write sentences, and to complete a poem using *real* and *very* correctly

Options for Organizing and Differentiating Instruction

See pages T9 and T10.

Scaffolding for English Language Learners

Invite students to share what they know about hockey. Discuss the picture of Canadian Mario Lemieux on page 71 and help students pronounce his name (MAH•ree•oh lu•MYOO). Tell students that Lemieux enjoyed a long and highly successful career despite disabling injuries and a serious illness.

Read each sentence in **Part 1.** After each one, ask students to tell whether *real* or *very* is used correctly. Ask volunteers to correct the sentences that have the wrong words and then to reread them aloud.

For **Part 2,** invite students to complete each item orally. (Example: item 11: Basketball is *very* exciting to watch.) Have student pairs compose oral sentences using *real* and *very* before they write.

Have students work with the same partners to solve the riddle poem in **Part 3.** Invite students to read the poem chorally after it has been completed.

Speaking and Listening

Guide students in telling a round-robin story using *real* or *very* in each sentence. You might write the sentences below on the board as story starters and have small groups of storytellers choose which one they would like to use.

One day Joshua found a real gold coin.

Anna was very happy to see the brown envelope on the desk.

Reinforcement and Reteaching

Review **Read and Discover** and the rule statement, refer students to the **G.U.M. Handbook,** or use the **Extra Practice** activity on page 172.

Lesson 28 (student pages 73–74)
Set and Sit

Lesson 29 (student pages 75–76)
Irregular Verbs: Know and Grow

Objectives

- To learn how to use the verbs *set* and *sit* correctly
- To choose a correct form of *set* or *sit* in sentences
- To rewrite sentences with correct forms of *set* or *sit*
- To write lists that reflect correct use of *set* and *sit*

Objectives

- To learn that the irregular verbs *know* and *grow* change spelling in the past tense
- To choose a form of *know* or *grow* in sentences, and to write answers to questions using correct forms of these words
- To complete a crossword puzzle using correct forms of *know* and *grow*

Options for Organizing and Differentiating Instruction

See pages T9 and T10.

Options for Organizing and Differentiating Instruction

See pages T9 and T10.

Scaffolding for English Language Learners

Read the illustration caption on page 73 aloud. Inform students that Carly Patterson, of Baton Rouge, Louisiana, won two silver medals in the 2004 Olympics. Then invite students who may be involved in gymnastics or who may have seen gymnastic competitions to describe the equipment and events related to the sport.

Read each sentence in **Part 1** aloud twice, using a different answer choice each time. Have students circle the answer choice that correctly completes the sentence. If students have difficulty, remind them to ask themselves, "Set what?" If they cannot answer that question, then the correct word is *sit*.

For **Part 2,** suggest that students ask themselves the same question ("Set what?") before they write their answers. Then ask a volunteer to model rewriting item 12. (Example: The members of the audience...*sat down*.) Have students complete the remaining items with partners.

Have students work independently to complete **Part 3.** Invite volunteers to compose oral sentences using the items they listed and the word *set* or *sit*.

Scaffolding for English Language Learners

Ask students to state some rules for staying safe in and around water. Then ask students to brainstorm ways that swimming regularly could help a person.

In **Part 1,** review the verb forms on page 75. Read each sentence from Part 1 aloud twice, saying a different answer choice each time. Have students pick the correct word and reread the complete sentence aloud.

Read aloud the questions in **Part 2** and invite volunteers to respond orally to each one. Model this process with the help of a student volunteer. Students might then work independently or in pairs to discuss and write their answers.

Have students work cooperatively to complete the puzzle in **Part 3.** Suggest that they refer to the rule statement (in the gray box) on page 75 if they need help remembering the forms of *know* and *grow*.

Speaking and Listening

Invite students to take turns pantomiming actions that involve *sitting* or *setting* things down. Ask other students to compose oral sentences describing each action that uses forms of *set* or *sit* correctly.

Speaking and Listening

Invite students to tell about themselves. Ask them to use as many different forms of *know* and *grow* as possible. Write the verb forms on the board and review them before students begin. You might prompt their responses with questions such as *What is something you know a lot about?* and *In what year did you grow the most in height?* After each speaker is finished, have listeners identify the forms of *know* and *grow* that were used.

Reinforcement and Reteaching

Review **Read and Discover** and the rule statement, refer students to the **G.U.M. Handbook,** or use the **Extra Practice** activity on page 172.

Reinforcement and Reteaching

Review **Read and Discover** and the rule statement, refer students to the **G.U.M. Handbook,** or use the **Extra Practice** activity on page 173.

Objectives

- To understand that the verbs *learn* and *teach* are both related to knowledge, and to learn how to use the two words correctly
- To choose a form of *learn* and *teach* in sentences, and to write answers to questions using the correct forms of these words
- To write a paragraph using correct forms of *learn* or *teach*

Options for Organizing and Differentiating Instruction

See pages T9 and T10.

Scaffolding for English Language Learners

Ask students what they have *learned* about how to play soccer, and who *taught* them. Then read the caption on page 77 aloud and discuss the picture.

Read each sentence in **Part 1** aloud twice, inserting a different answer choice each time. Allow students to answer orally before they underline their answers. Write *goalie, goalkeeper,* and *goaltender* on the board. Explain that these are synonyms.

For **Part 2**, invite students to respond orally before they write their answers.

Then have students work independently or in pairs to write their paragraphs in **Part 3**. Invite volunteers to read their paragraphs aloud.

Speaking and Listening

Ask students to compose oral sentences about subjects they are studying or activities they are involved in, using present and past tense forms of *learn* and *teach*. (Examples: I *learn* about athletic champions in class. I *taught* my mother how to use the computer.)

Reinforcement and Reteaching

Review **Read and Discover** and the rule statement, refer students to the **G.U.M. Handbook**, or use the **Extra Practice** activity on page 173.

Scaffolding for English Language Learners

Have students work with partners who are fluent in English for the proofreading activities.

Proofreading Practice

Ask students to identify the topic of the report on page 79. (cycling) Explain to students that the report contains several mistakes and that, as they read, they should look for these mistakes.

Review the **Proofreading Marks** chart and the examples. Remind students that these marks are used by professional writers to check their work before publication. Read the second sentence in the second paragraph aloud. Discuss the error (*which* should be *who*) and how it should be marked. Ask students (in pairs or independently) to correct the remaining errors using proofreading marks. You may wish to have students correct the spelling errors, too.

After students have completed the activity, ask volunteers to read each sentence aloud and to identify the errors. Ask students to mark overlooked errors in another color. **Note:** Some errors can be corrected in more than one way.

Proofreading Checklist

Ask students to select a recent piece of their own writing and to write the title of that piece at the top of the chart. Ask students to put a check mark next to each item in the checklist after they have checked it in their work. Students might first work independently and then trade papers with a partner to double-check each other's work. You might model, or ask a student to model, using the **G.U.M. Handbook** (beginning on page 195) to clarify a concept or rule.

Also Remember...

Remind students that capitalization and punctuation are important for clear writing. If necessary, help students use the **Handbook** to clarify when commas should be used and to review the use of capital letters.

Your Own List

Suggest that students look at the errors they did not find in the proofreading activity and add them to the checklist. Ask students to think about other kinds of errors they make and to add these to the checklist.

Ask students to place this page in their writing portfolios. These pages may be used to assess students' progress over the course of the year.

Assessment Options

See page T9 for ways to use *G.U.M.* assessments to differentiate instruction.

Unit Review

The **Unit Review** (pp. 81–82) allows you to check students' progress and determine when reteaching is necessary. The review pages may be completed in class or as homework. If a student responds incorrectly to two or more items involving the same skill, you may want to work directly with the student to review the relevant lesson. The lesson number to which each review item relates appears in parentheses on the review pages in the Teacher Edition.

Assign the **Extra Practice** activities (pp. 169–173) to reteach targeted skills in a more focused way.

Unit Assessment

The **Unit Assessment** (pp. 147–150) is intended to (1) familiarize students with standardized testing procedures, (2) check students' ability to apply key unit concepts in a different format, and (3) serve as an indicator of student progress.

- When used as a **pretest,** the Unit Assessment helps you determine, prior to instruction, your students' strengths, weaknesses, knowledge, and skills.
- When used as a **posttest,** the Unit Assessment provides feedback that you can use to guide further instruction.

Follow this procedure for administering the Unit Assessment.

1. Read aloud the Test Tip and the test instructions. (**Note:** For additional scaffolding, you may wish to read the test questions and answer choices aloud.)
2. Tell students that they will have 20 minutes to read and answer the questions independently.
3. When time is up, collect and correct the tests. Use the results to measure student progress and guide reteaching.

Assign the **Extra Practice** activities (pp. 169–173) to reteach targeted skills in a more focused way.

Note: The **Unit Review** may be reused after reteaching to check students' understanding of the lesson concepts.

Unit Test

The **Unit Test** (pp. 189–190) helps you judge students' achievement while providing them with valuable practice for high-stakes tests. When you are ready to administer the test, ask students to carefully tear it out of their books. (**Note:** If the test has already been removed, distribute it to students.) Read aloud the directions for each section and make sure students understand how to answer the questions. Ask students to work independently to complete the test.

Students who miss two questions focusing on the same grammar element may need additional help understanding the concept. Reteach the concept, following this procedure:

1. Review **Read and Discover**.
2. Review the rule statement for the concept.
3. Guide students through items a second time. Ask the students to explain why each correct answer belongs in each sentence.
4. Refer students to the **G.U.M. Handbook** for further reinforcement.

School Home Connection (student pages 83–84)

These two pages provide quick, fun activities that review and reinforce the skills and concepts taught in Lessons 21 to 30. These activities also provide opportunities for students to share what they have been learning with their families and for parents to become actively involved in their child's learning. You might utilize the **School Home Connection** pages in one of the following ways:

- Ask students to take the pages home, choose one or two activities to do, and then ask their parents to sign and return the pages.
- Send the pages home without asking that they be returned.
- Ask students to do one activity at school and then send the pages home.

When you are ready to send the pages home, direct students to the activities on pages 83–84. Inform students that these are fun activities they can do at home that will help them practice some of the things they have been learning about in the unit. Then ask students to carefully tear the pages out of the book, and explain how you wish students to use them.

Notes

Grab Bag

Unit 4 Grammar

Lesson 31: Subject and Object Pronouns
Lesson 32: Pronouns in Pairs
Lesson 33: Using *I* or *Me*
Lesson 34: Pronoun Antecedents
Lesson 35: Making the Subject and Verb Agree
Lesson 36: Forms of *Be*
Lesson 37: Verb Tense
Lesson 38: Negatives
Lesson 39: Comparative and Superlative Adjectives
Lesson 40: Comparative and Superlative Adverbs

Pretest Option

You may use the **Unit Assessment** as a pretest. See pages T8 and T9.

Building Grammar Awareness

Write this sentence on the board and ask a volunteer to read it aloud:

My mom, dad, aunt, and uncle took my brother, sister, and me to the car races.

Ask students whether there is a shorter, easier way to say this sentence. (*They* took *us* to the car races.) Tell students that in Unit 4 they will learn how to use words such as *they* and *us* in sentences. Explain that they will also learn how to use different types of verbs, comparing words, and words that mean "no." Tell students that using words correctly in sentences can help other people understand what is meant when writing and speaking.

Introducing "Grab Bag"
Cars

Explain that each lesson in Unit 4 gives information about auto racing and cars. Invite students to name some racecars or car races they know of. List their responses in a web labeled "Cars." Use questions such as those below to guide discussion.

- How is driving a racecar different from driving a normal car on a city street?
- What safety precautions do racecar drivers need to take?

Objectives

- To discover that a subject pronoun takes the place of a noun in a sentence
- To learn that object pronouns can be used after action verbs or prepositions
- To identify subject and object pronouns in sentences, and to rewrite sentences using subject and object pronouns
- To write descriptive sentences using subject and object pronouns

Options for Organizing and Differentiating Instruction

See pages T9 and T10.

Scaffolding for English Language Learners

Write Indy 500 on the board. Explain that it is short for the Indianapolis 500-mile car race that is held every Memorial Day weekend in Indiana.

In **Part 1,** ask students to read each sentence and to tell whether the boldfaced word is a subject or an object pronoun. **Note:** For item 4, because *you* can be either a subject or an object pronoun, model changing the question into a statement to find the subject.

For **Part 2,** have student pairs read each sentence aloud, decide which pronoun should replace each boldfaced phrase, and then rewrite the sentence.

Before students begin **Part 3,** list on the board the subject and object pronouns from the rule statement on page 85. Have students work in groups of three or four to compose sentences using subject and object pronouns. Suggest that they begin by brainstorming things they might see, hear, and feel at the Indy 500.

Speaking and Listening

Encourage students to find pictures of racecars and car races in magazines. Have them use subject and object pronouns to describe the pictures.

Reinforcement and Reteaching

Review **Read and Discover** and the rule statement, refer students to the **G.U.M. Handbook,** or use the **Extra Practice** activity on page 174.

Lesson 32 (student pages 87–88)
Pronouns in Pairs

Objectives
- To learn how to use subject and object pronouns correctly in sentences
- To choose appropriate subject or object pronouns to complete sentences
- To rewrite sentences, substituting nouns with appropriate subject or object pronouns
- To complete a crossword puzzle, using pronouns as clues

Options for Organizing and Differentiating Instruction
See pages T9 and T10.

Scaffolding for English Language Learners
Explain that *drag* can be a slang term for a street or road (for example, the main *drag*). Then ask students what a *drag race* is (a high-speed car race on pavement). Explain that usually two cars race at a time to determine which can accelerate faster.

Before students mark their answers in **Part 1,** ask them to identify whether the answer choices are part of the subject or part of an object. To help students determine the correct pronoun, suggest that they say each sentence without *and* and the name of the other person. (Example: item 1: Take away *Betty and* and read the sentence as (*He/Him*) takes turns driving their dragster.) Have students identify the pronoun that fits.

For **Part 2,** help students determine which subject or object pronoun each boldfaced noun should be replaced with. Explain that a "funny car" (in item 13) is one of three types of professional drag-racing cars.

For **Part 3,** tell students that the answers to the crossword puzzle are the names of the people in Part 2.

Speaking and Listening
Ask students to describe races they have watched. Encourage speakers to use as many personal pronouns as they can, and have listeners identify each as a subject or an object pronoun.

Reinforcement and Reteaching
Review **Read and Discover** and the rule statement, refer students to the **G.U.M. Handbook,** or use the **Extra Practice** activity on page 174.

Lesson 33 (student pages 89–90)
Using *I* or *Me*

Objectives
- To review that *I* is a subject pronoun and *me* is an object pronoun
- To understand that when talking about oneself and another person, the other person should always be named first
- To choose whether to use *I* or *me* in sentences
- To complete and write sentences using *I* or *me* with the name of another person

Options for Organizing and Differentiating Instruction
See pages T9 and T10.

Scaffolding for English Language Learners
Ask students whether they have ever watched a demolition derby. Ask those who have seen such a race to describe the event.

Read aloud each sentence in **Part 1** twice, saying a different answer choice each time. To test for the correct subject pronoun, have students read the answer choices without the other name. Remind them to always name the other person first in sentences such as these.

Pair students with English-proficient partners to complete **Part 2.** Have them read each sentence aloud, decide whether a subject or an object pronoun is needed, and complete the sentence orally before they write.

Have students draw their own pictures and then work in pairs to write sentences in **Part 3.** Ask them to compose their sentences orally before writing them.

Speaking and Listening
Ask pairs of students to perform simple actions and then to describe the actions using subject or object pronouns. For example, ask a student to give an object to someone and then describe what he or she did. (Example: *I* gave the book to Amy.) Ask the receiver to also describe the action using the pronoun *me.* (Reza gave a book to *me.*)

Reinforcement and Reteaching
Review **Read and Discover** and the rule statement, refer students to the **G.U.M. Handbook,** or use the **Extra Practice** activity on page 175.

Lesson 34 (student pages 91–92)
Pronoun Antecedents

Objectives
- To discover that an antecedent is the word or words that a pronoun refers to and that pronouns and antecedents must agree in number and gender
- To identify antecedents of pronouns in sentences
- To replace nouns with appropriate pronouns to complete sentences
- To identify pronouns and then find their antecedents in a word search

Options for Organizing and Differentiating Instruction
See pages T9 and T10.

Scaffolding for English Language Learners
Read the caption aloud on page 91, and ask students what three continents the contestants crossed. (North America, Asia, Europe)

In **Part 1,** ask volunteers to read the sentences and to identify the word each boldfaced pronoun refers to. Have them verify their answer by rereading the sentence with the antecedent they identified. (Example: item 1: Six teams left New York City on February 12. Not all of the *teams* would finish the race.)

For **Part 2,** help students decide whether a subject or an object pronoun should replace the boldfaced word or phrase in the first item. Then have student pairs complete the remaining items.

Partners can complete the word search and answer the riddles in **Part 3.** Tell students that the answers are in the sentences in Part 1 and Part 2. (across: train, Germans; **down:** Americans, Italians, tires)

Speaking and Listening
Invite students to compose oral sentences using these phrases as the subject or the object of a sentence: the racecar, a car race, the driver, the mechanic, the racers, the fans. Write the sentences on the board. Have students replace the phrase(s) and other nouns in each sentence with the appropriate pronouns. (Example: Betty won the car race. *She* won *it* by two laps.)

Reinforcement and Reteaching
Review **Read and Discover** and the rule statement, refer students to the **G.U.M. Handbook,** or use the **Extra Practice** activity on page 175.

Lesson 35 (student pages 93–94)
Making the Subject and Verb Agree

Objectives
- To learn that the subject and the verb of a sentence must agree
- To learn how to make present tense regular verbs agree with singular and plural subjects
- To choose verb forms that agree with the subjects to complete sentences and puzzle clues

Options for Organizing and Differentiating Instruction
See pages T9 and T10.

Scaffolding for English Language Learners
Point out the picture and caption on page 93. Explain that Formula One races feature cars with one seat, a rear engine, and front and back wings.

In **Part 1,** ask students to identify each simple subject and to identify the correct verb.

Have students complete **Part 2** with partners. You may need to introduce *series* and *Grand Prix*. Explain that the Grand Prix series is made up of about 15 races held in Canada, France, the United States, and other countries.

Have pairs of students work cooperatively to complete the puzzle in **Part 3.**

Speaking and Listening
Write subject/verb pairs on separate index cards. Each subject should be singular and each verb should have the *s* or *es* ending (Examples: The Formula One car/zooms, The fan/cheers). Give one card to each pair of students. Ask each pair to compose a sentence using the subject/verb pair on the card. (Example: *The Formula One car zooms* around the curve.) Write it on the board, and read it aloud. Ask a volunteer to restate the sentence with a plural subject and write it under the original. Discuss how the subject and verb must agree as you review each pair of sentences.

Reinforcement and Reteaching
Review **Read and Discover** and the rule statement, refer students to the **G.U.M. Handbook,** or use the **Extra Practice** activity on page 176.

Lesson 36 (student pages 95–96)
Forms of *Be*

Objectives
- To learn which forms of *be* to use with singular subjects and plural subjects
- To choose the correct form of *be* to complete sentences
- To write sentences using forms of *be*

Options for Organizing and Differentiating Instruction
See pages T9 and T10.

Scaffolding for English Language Learners
Have students look at the picture on page 95 as you read the caption aloud. Tell students that "banked corners" refers to the angle of incline of the track. The incline helps a stock car get around a curve.

Read the sentences in **Part 1** aloud, saying both answer choices. Help students identify whether the subject of each sentence is singular or plural before having them underline their answers. Ask volunteers to reread the sentences aloud with the correct answer choices in place.

Before students complete **Part 2**, have them identify the singular and plural subjects in the sentences in the paragraph. **Note:** To help students decide which verb fits the first sentence, you might have them rephrase the question as a statement: You _____ at the NASCAR races last Saturday.

Have pairs of students compose the sentences in **Part 3**. Suggest that partners describe what auto racers are like before they write their sentences. (Example: Auto racers are brave. I am a brave auto racer.)

Speaking and Listening
Write each form of *be* on a separate index card and place the cards facedown in a pile. Have students take turns picking a card and using the verb form in an oral sentence about themselves or their classmates.

Reinforcement and Reteaching
Review **Read and Discover** and the rule statement, refer students to the **G.U.M. Handbook**, or use the **Extra Practice** activity on page 176.

Lesson 37 (student pages 97–98)
Verb Tense

Objectives
- To learn that all the verbs in a sentence must be used in the correct tense, to give an accurate sense of time
- To choose verb forms that give correct sense of time
- To rewrite sentences by changing the present tense to the past tense
- To compose sentences using verbs in the correct tense

Options for Organizing and Differentiating Instruction
See pages T9 and T10.

Scaffolding for English Language Learners
Write Ferrari and Porsche on the board and ask volunteers to pronounce the names and describe these sports cars. Point out that these two sports cars are among the fastest racecars in the world.

Say both answer choices as you read the sentences in **Part 1** aloud. To help students select the correct verb form, suggest that they look for time clues such as dates.

Read the caption on page 98 aloud. Explain that the 24 Hours of Daytona held in Daytona Beach, Florida, is a famous endurance race. Then read the sentences in **Part 2** aloud. Have student pairs reread each sentence aloud, first with the present tense verb in place and then with the past tense verb, before they write their answers.

Have partners complete the activity in **Part 3**.

Speaking and Listening
Write the words past and future on several slips of paper and put them in a bag. Have students, in turn, pick a slip from the bag. If the word on the slip says *past,* ask them to describe an exciting or amusing incident that took place in the recent past. Encourage students to use time clues to indicate past action. If the slip says *future,* ask them to make a prediction about some future event.

Reinforcement and Reteaching
Review **Read and Discover** and the rule statement, refer students to the **G.U.M. Handbook**, or use the **Extra Practice** activity on page 177.

Lesson 38 (student pages 99–100)
Negatives

Objectives
- To learn that a negative is a word that means "no" or "not" and that the words *no, not, nothing, none, never, nowhere,* and *nobody* are negatives
- To learn that using two negatives in a sentence should be avoided
- To identify double negatives in context, and to rewrite sentences to eliminate double negatives
- To find negatives in a word search and write them

Options for Organizing and Differentiating Instruction
See pages T9 and T10.

Scaffolding for English Language Learners
Explain that the Mille Miglia was a grueling 1,000-mile cross-country auto race that started and ended in Brescia, Italy. Have students look at the map of the race route on page 99. Explain that Taruffi, nicknamed the "Silver Fox" for his gray hair, was the victor (after many previous failures) in the final race held in 1957.

Read aloud the sentences in **Part 1** and ask students to identify the negative(s) in each. Then have them mark the incorrect sentences. Ask volunteers to correct the sentences containing double negatives.

Have students identify the negatives in each sentence in **Part 2**. Ask volunteers to model correcting item 13 in two different ways. (Examples: After 1957, the Mille Miglia wasn't held anymore. The Mille Miglia was not held after 1957.)

Student pairs can complete the word search in **Part 3**. Ask students to identify contractions with the word *not* (Examples: don't, doesn't, weren't, and isn't).

Speaking and Listening
Invite students to play a "Negatives" game by using negative expressions to make silly observations about people or things. (Examples: *Nobody* can hang upside down from the classroom ceiling. The chairs have legs, but *none* of them can walk.)

Reinforcement and Reteaching
Review **Read and Discover** and the rule statement, refer students to the **G.U.M. Handbook,** or use the **Extra Practice** activity on page 177.

Lesson 39 (student pages 101–102)
Comparative and Superlative Adjectives

Objectives
- To learn that comparative forms of adjectives compare two or more people, places, or things and are often followed by the word *than*
- To learn that superlative forms of adjectives compare three or more people, places, or things and often follow the word *the*
- To learn how to create the comparative and superlative forms of adjectives
- To choose the correct forms of adjectives in sentences, and to complete sentences using these forms
- To find adjectives in a word search, and to identify the comparative or superlative form of each

Options for Organizing and Differentiating Instruction
See pages T9 and T10.

Scaffolding for English Language Learners
Explain that a soap box race is for 9- to 16-year-olds who build their own motorless racecars that they coast downhill.

In **Part 1**, have volunteers correct the first two items. Then have student pairs complete the activity.

Help students identify what is being compared in each sentence in **Part 2** before pairs complete the activity. Help students determine whether to use *more* or *most* or the endings *-er* or *-est*.

Students can work independently to complete the word search in **Part 3**. (across: wildest, earliest, faster; down: lowest, softer, highest)

Speaking and Listening
Ask students to orally compose comparisons about racecars and races. Each sentence should use a comparative or a superlative adjective. (Example: The *most difficult* race was the New York-to-Paris race in 1908. That Porsche may be the *fastest* of all the cars at this race.)

Reinforcement and Reteaching
Review **Read and Discover** and the rule statement, refer students to the **G.U.M. Handbook,** or use the **Extra Practice** activity on page 178.

Lesson 40 (student pages 103–104)
Comparative and Superlative Adverbs

Objectives
- To learn that adverbs that end in *-ly* are preceded by *more* in the comparative form and are followed by the word *than*
- To learn that adverbs that end in *-ly* are preceded by *most* in the superlative form
- To choose the correct forms of adverbs in sentences, and to complete sentences using these forms
- To write a comparison using a comparative or a superlative adverb

Options for Organizing and Differentiating Instruction
See pages T9 and T10.

Scaffolding for English Language Learners
Read the caption on page 103. If any students have driven a midget car, have them describe the experience.

Review the meaning of *comparative* and *superlative*. Then read the sentences in **Part 1** aloud, and help students clarify how many people or things are being compared in each (Example: item 2: two: the last lap and the first lap). Have student pairs reread each sentence aloud, decide which adverb form correctly completes the sentence, and underline their answer.

In **Part 2**, suggest that partners read each sentence aloud and determine what is being compared before they complete the activity.

Read the directions in **Part 3** aloud. Ask students to name different competitions. Then list them on the board (Examples: car races, track-and-field events, swimming, gymnastics, figure skating). Have partners compose their sentences orally before they write them.

Speaking and Listening
Write several comparative and superlative forms of adverbs on the board (Examples: **comparative:** faster, more carefully; **superlative:** fastest, most carefully). Invite students to suggest words and phrases of their own. Then ask students to use these forms in oral sentences.

Reinforcement and Reteaching
Review **Read and Discover** and the rule statement, refer students to the **G.U.M. Handbook**, or use the **Extra Practice** activity on page 178.

Proofreading (student pages 105–106)
Scaffolding for English Language Learners
Have students work with partners who are fluent in English for the proofreading activities.

Proofreading Practice
Ask students to identify the subject of the report on page 105. (Racecar driver Kelly Sutton) Explain that the report contains several mistakes and that, as they read, they should look for these mistakes.

Review the **Proofreading Marks** chart and the examples. Remind students that these marks are used by professional writers to check their work before publication. Read the first few sentences aloud. Discuss the errors and how they should be marked. Ask students (in pairs or independently) to correct the remaining errors using proofreading marks. You may wish to have students correct the spelling errors, too.

After students have completed the activity, ask volunteers to read each sentence aloud and to identify the errors. Ask students to mark overlooked errors in another color. **Note:** Some errors can be corrected in more than one way.

Proofreading Checklist
Ask students to select a recent piece of their own writing and to write the title of that piece at the top of the chart. Ask students to put a check mark next to each item in the checklist after they have checked it in their work. Students might first work independently and then trade papers with a partner to double-check each other's work. You might model, or ask a student to model, using the **G.U.M. Handbook** (beginning on page 195) to clarify a concept or rule.

Also Remember...
Remind students that capitalization and punctuation are important for clear writing. If necessary, help students use the **Handbook** to clarify when commas should be used and to review the use of capital letters.

Your Own List
Suggest that students look at the errors they did not find in the proofreading activity and add them to the checklist. Also ask students to think about other kinds of errors they make and to add these to the checklist.

Ask students to place this page in their writing portfolios. These pages may be used to assess students' progress over the course of the year.

T45

Assessment Options

See page T9 for ways to use *G.U.M.* assessments to differentiate instruction.

Unit Review

The **Unit Review** (pp. 107–108) allows you to check students' progress and determine when reteaching is necessary. The review pages may be completed in class or as homework. If a student responds incorrectly to two or more items involving the same skill, you may want to work directly with the student to review the relevant lesson. The lesson number to which each review item relates appears in parentheses on the review pages in the Teacher Edition.

Assign the **Extra Practice** activities (pp. 174–178) to reteach targeted skills in a more focused way.

Unit Assessment

The **Unit Assessment** (pp. 151–154) is intended to (1) familiarize students with standardized testing procedures, (2) check students' ability to apply key unit concepts in a different format, and (3) serve as an indicator of student progress.

- When used as a **pretest,** the Unit Assessment helps you determine, prior to instruction, your students' strengths, weaknesses, knowledge, and skills.
- When used as a **posttest,** the Unit Assessment provides feedback that you can use to guide further instruction.

Follow this procedure for administering the Unit Assessment.

1. Read aloud the Test Tip and the test instructions. (**Note:** For additional scaffolding, you may wish to read the test questions and answer choices aloud.)
2. Tell students that they will have 20 minutes to read and answer the questions independently.
3. When time is up, collect and correct the tests. Use the results to measure student progress and guide reteaching.

Assign the **Extra Practice** activities (pp. 174–178) to reteach targeted skills in a more focused way.

Note: The **Unit Review** may be reused after reteaching to check students' understanding of lesson concepts.

Unit Test

The **Unit Test** (pp. 191–192) helps you judge students' achievement while providing them with valuable practice for high-stakes tests. When you are ready to administer the test, ask students to carefully tear it out of their books. (**Note:** If the test has already been removed, distribute it to students.) Read aloud the directions for each section and make sure students understand how to answer the questions. Ask students to work independently to complete the test.

Students who miss two questions focusing on the same grammar element may need additional help understanding the concept. Reteach the concept, following this procedure:

1. Review **Read and Discover**.
2. Review the rule statement for the concept.
3. Guide students through items a second time. Ask the students to explain why each correct answer belongs in each sentence.
4. Refer students to the **G.U.M. Handbook** for further reinforcement.

School Home Connection (student pages 109–110)

These two pages provide quick, fun activities that review and reinforce the skills and concepts taught in Lessons 31 to 40. These activities also provide opportunities for students to share what they have been learning with their families and for parents to become actively involved in their child's learning. You might utilize the **School Home Connection** pages in one of the following ways:

- Ask students to take the pages home, choose one or two activities to do, and then ask their parents to sign and return the pages.
- Send the pages home without asking that they be returned.
- Ask students to do one activity at school and then send the pages home.

When you are ready to send the pages home, direct students to the activities on pages 109–110. Inform students that these are fun activities they can do at home that will help them practice some of the things they have been learning about in the unit. Then ask students to carefully tear the pages out of the book, and explain how you wish students to use them.

Notes

Beasts & Critters

Unit 5 Mechanics

Lesson 41: Writing Sentences Correctly
Lesson 42: Proper Nouns and Proper Adjectives
Lesson 43: Initials and Abbreviations
Lesson 44: Titles
Lesson 45: Apostrophes
Lesson 46: Commas in a Series
Lesson 47: Commas
Lesson 48: Using Semicolons
Lesson 49: Direct and Indirect Quotations
Lesson 50: Friendly Letters and E-mails

Pretest Option

You may use the **Unit Assessment** as a pretest. See pages T8 and T9.

Building Mechanics Awareness

Write this sentence on the board and ask a volunteer to read it aloud:

> James asked, "Do you have the book called <u>Snake</u> by Caroline Arnold?"

Ask students to point out the different punctuation marks they see in the sentence. Inform students that in Unit 5 they will learn how to use these and other punctuation marks that make writing easier to read. Explain that they will also learn some rules for capitalizing words, and for writing initials, abbreviations, titles, quotations, friendly letters, and e-mails. Point out to students that using correct punctuation and capitalization can make their sentences and paragraphs easier to understand.

Introducing "Beasts and Critters"
Amphibians and Reptiles

Explain to students that each lesson in Unit 5 gives information about a different amphibian or reptile. Invite students to name some amphibians and reptiles they have seen or read about, and to describe features of each. Write their responses in a chart with the headings Amphibians and Reptiles. Use questions such as these to guide discussion:

• How are reptiles different from amphibians?
• What kind of climate is good for an alligator? a snake? a frog?
• What special features have some amphibians and reptiles developed that help them survive?

Lesson 41 (student pages 111–112)
Writing Sentences Correctly

Objectives
• To learn the names of the different sentence types, and to correctly punctuate and capitalize each
• To identify types of sentences, and to correct capitalization and punctuation errors in sentences
• To compose imperative, interrogative, declarative, and exclamatory sentences
• To add correct end punctuation

Options for Organizing and Differentiating Instruction
See pages T9 and T10.

Scaffolding for English Language Learners

Point out the picture of the turtle on page 112. Explain that the leatherback, the largest living turtle, is one of seven species of sea turtles.

Read aloud the sentences in **Part 1**, one at a time. Use voice inflection to emphasize the end mark in each sentence. Ask students to listen to your voice to help them decide whether the end punctuation in the sentence is correct. Have students discuss the correct end mark and any changes in capitalization that should be made. Point out that commands usually begin with a verb, and have students identify the verbs that begin items 1 and 10.

Have students review the four sentence types before they begin **Part 2**. Read aloud the caption on page 112 and encourage students to comment on the features of the leatherback turtle. Then brainstorm sentence ideas with students before they begin writing.

Ask student pairs to read aloud the sentences and to complete the activity in **Part 3**.

Speaking and Listening

Encourage students to think about the most unusual animal that they have ever seen. Ask them to describe the animal. Speakers should try to use all four kinds of sentences, and listeners should identify each type the speakers use.

Reinforcement and Reteaching

Review **Read and Discover** and the rule statement, refer students to the **G.U.M. Handbook,** or use the **Extra Practice** activity on page 179.

Lesson 42 (student pages 113–114)
Proper Nouns and Proper Adjectives

Objectives
- To learn that a proper noun names a specific person, place, or thing and a proper adjective is an adjective formed from a proper noun
- To learn that a title of respect is used before a person's name and that titles of respect, proper nouns, and proper adjectives are capitalized
- To correct capitalization errors in sentences
- To rewrite sentences to correct capitalization errors
- To find proper nouns, proper adjectives, and titles of respect in a word search, and to write a sentence using them

Options for Organizing and Differentiating Instruction
See pages T9 and T10.

Scaffolding for English Language Learners
In **Part 1**, ask volunteers to read the sentences aloud, one at a time; identify the words that contain capitalization errors; and explain each of their choices. Encourage students to identify the proper nouns, proper adjectives, and titles of respect in the sentences.

For **Part 2**, invite students to identify the capitalization errors aloud before they rewrite the sentences. Ask them to identify each corrected word as a proper noun, a proper adjective, or a title of respect.

Students can work independently to complete the word search in **Part 3** and then work with partners to write sentences.

Speaking and Listening
Distribute pages from a newspaper or a nature magazine to pairs of students. Ask them to look for proper nouns and proper adjectives as well as titles of respect and to share them with the group. Have them tell whether each proper noun names a person, a place, or a thing and what each proper adjective describes.

Reinforcement and Reteaching
Review **Read and Discover** and the rule statement, refer students to the **G.U.M. Handbook**, or use the **Extra Practice** activity on page 179.

Lesson 43 (student pages 115–116)
Initials and Abbreviations

Objectives
- To learn that an abbreviation is a shortened form of a word and usually begins with a capital letter and ends with a period
- To learn that an initial takes the place of a name and is written as a capital letter followed by a period
- To correct capitalization and punctuation errors in abbreviations and initials in sentences
- To rewrite words using abbreviations and initials
- To address an envelope

Options for Organizing and Differentiating Instruction
See pages T9 and T10.

Scaffolding for English Language Learners
Invite students to describe snakes they have seen or kept as pets. Have students name different kinds of snakes and share what is known about snakes' habits.

For **Part 1**, write the first sentence on the board. Invite a volunteer to model marking errors according to the directions. Have student pairs complete the remaining items. You may need to explain what *inc* (item 4) and *corp* (item 6) stand for.

Read the items in **Part 2** aloud. Before student pairs rewrite the items, discuss which items can be abbreviated and where initials can be used. Suggest that pairs refer to the corrections in Part 1 to help them recall how certain words are abbreviated.

Have students work independently to write the names and addresses on the envelope in **Part 3**. Display an addressed envelope, and discuss what goes on each line before students begin.

Speaking and Listening
Distribute an advertisement to student pairs. Ask partners to look for abbreviations and titles of respect and then to share with the group what each abbreviation or title of respect stands for. Then have pairs speculate about what names are represented by the initials they found.

Reinforcement and Reteaching
Review **Read and Discover** and the rule statement, refer students to the **G.U.M. Handbook**, or use the **Extra Practice** activity on page 180.

Objectives

- To discover that book and movie titles are under-lined and that quotation marks are used around titles of songs, stories, and poems
- To learn which words in a title should be capitalized
- To identify and correct the capitalization and punctuation in titles
- To complete a matching activity containing titles

Options for Organizing and Differentiating Instruction

See pages T9 and T10.

Scaffolding for English Language Learners

Invite students to describe books, movies, poems, or short stories they have seen or read about snakes, lizards, frogs, or other amphibians and reptiles. Then display pictures of a cobra, a rattlesnake, and a newt and help students identify each.

In **Part 1,** ask volunteers to read each sentence aloud, to identify the title, and to tell whether it is the title of a book, movie, story, poem, or song. Have a volunteer model completing the first item before student pairs complete the remaining items.

In **Part 2,** invite a volunteer to read aloud the titles on the bookshelf. Then have students work with partners to respond to each item. Make sure students understand the meaning of *treat, horror film,* and *painted turtles.*

Student pairs can continue working together to complete **Part 3.**

Speaking and Listening

Invite students to take a poll of favorite books, poems, movies, and songs among students in other classes. Have students record the information in a chart. Remind them to use proper capitalization and punctuation when writing titles. Encourage students to share their results.

Reinforcement and Reteaching

Review **Read and Discover** and the rule state-ment, refer students to the **G.U.M. Handbook,** or use the **Extra Practice** activity on page 180.

Objectives

- To learn how to form possessive nouns and contractions using apostrophes
- To identify possessive nouns and contractions, and to choose the correct possessive noun or contraction to complete sentences
- To rewrite sentences using apostrophes correctly in possessive nouns and contractions
- To find words in a word search and then use them to form possessive nouns and contractions

Options for Organizing and Differentiating Instruction

See pages T9 and T10.

Scaffolding for English Language Learners

Point out the picture and the caption on page 119. Explain that frogs are among some 3,000 species that make up the animal group called *amphibians.*

In **Part 1,** ask volunteers to read each sentence aloud and to tell whether the words in parentheses are possessives or contractions. Then have them identify each correct choice and explain why it is correct.

For **Part 2,** have students identify the sentences that should be rewritten using a possessive noun and those that require a contraction. Introduce the word *caecilians* (suh•SIHL•yunz) in item 17 and help stu-dents pronounce it. Explain that few biologists have seen a live caecilian.

Students can work independently to complete the activity in **Part 3** and then work with partners to check each other's word search and list.

Speaking and Listening

Write these nouns and phrases on the board: girls, boys, chair; is not, will not, they are. Ask students to pick a word or phrase and compose oral sentences in-cluding a contraction or possessive form of the word(s) they chose. (Examples: The *girls'* team is practicing now. We *won't* have time to finish our project today.) After students write their sentences on the board, have volunteers verify the correct use of the apostrophes.

Reinforcement and Reteaching

Review Read and Discover and the rule state-ment, refer students to the G.U.M. Handbook, or use the **Extra Practice** activity on page 181.

Objectives
- To discover that a series is a list of three or more words or phrases and that commas separate items in a series
- To add missing commas in a series, and to delete unnecessary commas
- To compose and complete sentences using commas correctly

Options for Organizing and Differentiating Instruction
See pages T9 and T10.

Scaffolding for English Language Learners
Discuss the picture and caption on page 121. Explain to students that the spotted salamander is one of about 360 species of salamander. Invite students who have seen salamanders to describe them.

Read aloud the sentences in **Part 1**, pausing where commas are needed. Have students circle the items in the series in each sentence. Ask them to tell whether any commas are missing or misplaced and how the errors should be corrected. You may want to clarify the words *grubs, mold, acid rain, larvae,* and *gills.*

For **Part 2**, have students work with partners to read the sentences aloud and to brainstorm answers before they write their responses. Ask a volunteer to model completing item 13. (Example: Spotted salamander larvae eat fleas, shrimps, and grubs.)

Read the adjectives in the word bank in **Part 3** aloud, and then have students work independently to complete the activity. Have them draw on other paper.

Speaking and Listening
Ask students to find three or more similar objects in the classroom (Examples: three round things; four things on a table; three blue things). Ask students to compose sentences that begin with *I spy* followed by the list of objects. Have them say the sentence aloud and then write it on the board. Other students should check it for proper use of commas. Listeners should guess what characteristic the objects have in common.

Reinforcement and Reteaching
Review **Read and Discover** and the rule statement, refer students to the **G.U.M. Handbook,** or use the **Extra Practice** activity on page 181.

Objectives
- To learn that commas are used to indicate a pause and to separate introductory words, independent clauses, and nouns of direct address
- To correct and explain comma usage in sentences
- To rewrite sentences and to write a paragraph using commas correctly

Options for Organizing and Differentiating Instruction
See pages T9 and T10.

Scaffolding for English Language Learners
Read the caption on page 123 aloud. Explain that some frogs live mostly in or near water, others live mostly on land, and some live in underground burrows.

Read the sentences in **Part 1** aloud, pausing briefly where commas belong. After each sentence is read, ask students where and why the pause occurred before having them add the comma. Then have them write *I, C,* or *D* to indicate why a comma is needed in the sentence.

For **Part 2**, ask student pairs to read each sentence aloud, including the words in parentheses. Have them discuss how the sentence should be rewritten, including the placement of the comma, before they write their answers.

Read the directions in **Part 3** aloud. Review with students what they have learned about amphibians in Unit 5 (Lessons 45, 46, 47). Then have students work with English-proficient partners to write their paragraphs. Suggest that students discuss the information they want to include in their paragraphs before they write. If possible, have students do Internet research to learn more about amphibians.

Speaking and Listening
Ask student pairs to look in fiction and nonfiction books to find an example of each of the rules for commas they learned about in Lesson 47. Have them read each example aloud to the group, write it on the board, and explain what rule it follows.

Reinforcement and Reteaching
Review **Read and Discover** and the rule statement, refer students to the **G.U.M. Handbook,** or use the **Extra Practice** activity on page 182.

Lesson 48 (student pages 125–126)
Using Semicolons

Objectives
- To learn that a semicolon can be used instead of a comma and a conjunction to separate independent clauses in compound sentences
- To add semicolons to separate clauses in sentences, and to combine sentences using semicolons
- To write sentences using a semicolon to separate independent clauses

Options for Organizing and Differentiating Instruction
See pages T9 and T10.

Scaffolding for English Language Learners
Write chameleon on the board and help students pronounce it. Ask students what they know about this reptile. (a lizard that can change its color) Then have students look at the chameleon pictured on page 125 and describe its features.

Be sure students understand what an independent clause is. Then read each sentence in **Part 1** aloud, pausing where a semicolon is needed. Ask volunteers to identify the two independent clauses in each sentence and to tell where the semicolon belongs.

For **Part 2**, read the sentences aloud. Ask students to work with partners to match the sentences and to discuss how they will combine them. Invite a volunteer to model the process with one sentence pair. Remind students to check capitalization in their sentences.

Discuss possible answers to the questions in **Part 3**, and then have students work in pairs to complete the activity.

Speaking and Listening
Hold up a book and say something about it, such as This is a nature book. Ask a volunteer to say something more about the book. (Example: It tells about plants and animals.) Write both sentences on the board. Invite a volunteer to form a compound sentence using a semicolon to separate the clauses. Follow a similar procedure with other objects that you or the students choose.

Reinforcement and Reteaching
Review **Read and Discover** and the rule statement, refer students to the **G.U.M. Handbook**, or use the **Extra Practice** activity on page 182.

Lesson 49 (student pages 127–128)
Direct and Indirect Quotations

Objectives
- To discover that a direct quotation is a speaker's exact words and an indirect quotation is a retelling of a speaker's words
- To identify indirect quotations, to add missing punctuation to direct quotations, and to correct capitalization in sentences
- To rewrite indirect quotations as direct quotations and vice versa
- To write dialogue to go with pictures

Options for Organizing and Differentiating Instruction
See pages T9 and T10.

Scaffolding for English Language Learners
Point out the picture on page 127 and read the caption aloud. Inform students that there are about 30 species of rattlesnake; some are large, and some are small. If necessary, explain the meaning of *hibernate*.

Read the sentences in **Part 1** aloud, one at a time. Ask volunteers to identify each sentence as a direct or an indirect quotation. If the sentence is a direct quotation, ask the volunteer to read aloud only the part that is spoken by the character. Then have students decide where to add the missing punctuation.

Have volunteers read aloud and model completing items 13 and 14 in **Part 2**. (Example: item 13: Nico asked Joe how a rattlesnake makes its rattling sound. item 14: Joe said, "A rattlesnake sheds its skin a few times every year.") Ask partners to complete the section.

Before they draw their pictures and write their dialogue to complete **Part 3**, have partners brainstorm what might happen next to Joe, Nico, and Tony.

Speaking and Listening
Have students take turns restating the indirect quotations in Part 1 as direct quotations and vice versa. They should tell where the quotation marks belong in each direct quotation. (Items 1, 3, 6, and 10 should become direct quotations; the other items should become indirect quotations.)

Reinforcement and Reteaching
Review **Read and Discover** and the rule statement, refer students to the **G.U.M. Handbook**, or use the **Extra Practice** activity on page 183.

Lesson 50 (student pages 129–130)
Friendly Letters and E-mails

Objectives
- To learn that a friendly letter has a heading, a greeting, a body, a closing, and a signature
- To learn that an e-mail has the same parts as a letter, but its header contains the sender's and recipient's e-mail address, the date, and a subject line
- To label the five parts of a letter
- To rewrite a friendly letter correctly
- To write a formal e-mail

Options for Organizing and Differentiating Instruction
See pages T9 and T10.

Scaffolding for English Language Learners
Ask students to discuss whether they prefer to write and receive letters or e-mails. Point out that before the invention of the telephone, the telegraph, and the Internet, people communicated over long distances by letter.

Ask a volunteer to read aloud the letter in **Part 1** and to identify the heading. Have students identify the remaining letter parts before they label each.

Ask students to work in pairs to complete **Part 2**. Partners should read the letter aloud and discuss how to correct it before they rewrite it on the lines.

Before students begin **Part 3**, review formal e-mail format and discuss proper netiquette for communicating with a professional person. Have pairs of students decide on questions to ask and compose their e-mails aloud before word processing them. Have students print out their work and check to see that they have used correct form, capitalization, and punctuation.

Speaking and Listening
Invite pairs of students to write friendly letters to each other. Then have them switch letters and check the form of each other's letter. Invite partners to read their correspondence aloud.

Reinforcement and Reteaching
Review **Read and Discover** and the rule statement, refer students to the **G.U.M. Handbook**, or use the **Extra Practice** activity on page 183.

Proofreading (student pages 131–132)

Scaffolding for English Language Learners
Have students work with partners who are fluent in English for the proofreading activities.

Proofreading Practice
Ask students to identify the topic of the letter on page 131. (chuckwallas, iguanas) Explain to students that the letter contains several mistakes and that, as they read, they should look for these mistakes.

Review the **Proofreading Marks** chart and the examples. Remind students that these marks are used by professional writers to check their work before publication. Read the first line aloud. Discuss the error (*st* should be *St.*) and how it should be marked. Ask students (in pairs or independently) to correct the remaining errors using proofreading marks. You may wish to have students correct the spelling errors, too.

After students have completed the activity, ask volunteers to read each sentence aloud and to identify the errors. Ask students to mark overlooked errors in another color. **Note:** Some errors can be corrected in more than one way.

Proofreading Checklist
Ask students to select a recent piece of their own writing and to write the title of that piece at the top of the chart. Ask students to put a check mark next to each item in the checklist after they have checked it in their work. Students might first work independently and then trade papers with a partner to double-check each other's work. You might model, or ask a student to model, using the **G.U.M. Handbook** (beginning on page 195) to clarify a concept or rule.

Also Remember...
Remind students that capitalization and punctuation are important for clear writing. If necessary, help students use the **G.U.M. Handbook** to clarify when apostrophes should be used and to review the use of capital letters.

Your Own List
Suggest that students look at the errors they did not find in the proofreading activity and add them to the checklist. Ask students to think about other kinds of errors they make and to add these to the checklist.

Ask students to place this page in their writing portfolios. These pages may be used to assess students' progress over the course of the year.

Assessment Options

See page T9 for ways to use *G.U.M.* assessments to differentiate instruction.

Unit Review

The **Unit Review** (pp. 133–134) allows you to check students' progress and determine when reteaching is necessary. The review pages may be completed in class or as homework. If a student responds incorrectly to two or more items involving the same skill, you may want to work directly with the student to review the relevant lesson. The lesson number to which each review item relates appears in parentheses on the review pages in the Teacher Edition.

Assign the **Extra Practice** activities (pp. 179–183) to reteach targeted skills in a more focused way.

Unit Assessment

The **Unit Assessment** (pp. 155–158) is intended to (1) familiarize students with standardized testing procedures, (2) check students' ability to apply key unit concepts in a different format, and (3) serve as an indicator of student progress.

- When used as a **pretest,** the Unit Assessment helps you determine, prior to instruction, your students' strengths, weaknesses, knowledge, and skills.
- When used as a **posttest,** the Unit Assessment provides feedback that you can use to guide further instruction.

Follow this procedure for administering the Unit Assessment.

1. Read aloud the Test Tip and the test instructions. (**Note:** For additional scaffolding, you may wish to read the test questions and answer choices aloud.)
2. Tell students that they will have 20 minutes to read and answer the questions independently.
3. When time is up, collect and correct the tests. Use the results to measure student progress and guide reteaching.

Assign the **Extra Practice** activities (pp. 179–183) to reteach targeted skills in a more focused way.

Note: The **Unit Review** may be reused after reteaching to check students' understanding of the lesson concepts.

Unit Test

The **Unit Test** (pp. 193–194) helps you judge students' achievement while providing them with valuable practice for high-stakes tests. When you are ready to administer the test, ask students to carefully tear it out of their books. (**Note:** If the test has already been removed, distribute it to students.) Read aloud the directions for each section and make sure students understand how to answer the questions. Ask students to work independently to complete the test.

Students who miss two questions focusing on the same grammar element may need additional help understanding the concept. Reteach the concept, following this procedure:

1. Review **Read and Discover**.
2. Review the rule statement for the concept.
3. Guide students through items a second time. Ask the students to explain why each correct answer belongs in each sentence.
4. Refer students to the **G.U.M. Handbook** for further reinforcement.

School Home Connection (student pages 135–136)

These two pages provide quick, fun activities that review and reinforce the skills and concepts taught in Lessons 41 to 50. These activities also provide opportunities for students to share what they have been learning with their families and for parents to become actively involved in their child's learning. You might utilize the **School Home Connection** pages in one of the following ways:

- Ask students to take the pages home, choose one or two activities to do, and then ask their parents to sign and return the pages.
- Send the pages home without asking that they be returned.
- Ask students to do one activity at school and then send the pages home.

When you are ready to send the pages home, direct students to the activities on pages 135–136. Inform students that these are fun activities they can do at home that will help them practice some of the things they have been learning about in the unit. Then ask students to carefully tear the pages out of the book, and explain how you wish students to use them.

Notes

Notes

Grammar, Usage & Mechanics
Student Practice Book

STRATEGIES FOR

writers

ZB Zaner-Bloser

Grade Level Consultants
Margaret Bateman
Montgomery, Alabama

Cindy Daniel
Bothell, Washington

Suzanne Klein
Hilliard, Ohio

Nancy Morgan
Sharon, Pennsylvania

Joan Pawloski
Grand Rapids, Michigan

Cover photo: Rycus Associates Photography

Illustration: Steve Botts, Tracy Greenwalt

ISBN: 978-0-7367-9272-1

Zaner-Bloser, Inc.
1-800-421-3018
www.zaner-bloser.com

SUSTAINABLE FORESTRY INITIATIVE

Certified Chain of Custody
Promoting Sustainable Forestry
www.sfiprogram.org
SFI-00712

Printed in the United States of America

11 12 13 14 15   997   5 4 3 2 1

Table of Contents

Unit 1 Sentence Structure

The World Outside Water

Lesson 1 Complete Subjects and Complete Predicates 7
Lesson 2 Simple Subjects and Simple Predicates 9
Lesson 3 Compound Subjects and Compound Predicates 11
Lesson 4 Direct Objects 13
Lesson 5 Indirect Objects 15
Lesson 6 Predicate Nouns and Predicate Adjectives 17
Lesson 7 Prepositional Phrases 19
Lesson 8 Compound Sentences 21
Lesson 9 Dependent and Independent Clauses 23
Lesson 10 Avoiding Fragments, Run-ons, Comma Splices 25
Proofreading Practice 27
Proofreading Checklist 28
Unit 1 Review 29
Unit 1 School Home Connection 31

Unit 2 Parts of Speech

Looking Back United States History

Lesson 11 Common and Proper Nouns 33
Lesson 12 Plural and Possessive Nouns 35
Lesson 13 Personal and Possessive Pronouns 37
Lesson 14 The Present Tense 39
Lesson 15 The Past and Future Tenses 41
Lesson 16 The Present Perfect Tense 43
Lesson 17 Adjectives 45
Lesson 18 Adverbs 47
Lesson 19 Prepositions 49
Lesson 20 Coordinating and Subordinating Conjunctions 51
Proofreading Practice 53
Proofreading Checklist 54
Unit 2 Review 55
Unit 2 School Home Connection 57

Unit 3 Usage

Unforgettable Folks Athletes

Lesson 21 *Their, There, They're* 59
Lesson 22 *Its* and *It's* 61
Lesson 23 *Your* and *You're* 63
Lesson 24 *Like* and *You Know* 65
Lesson 25 Comparing with *Good* or *Bad* 67
Lesson 26 *That, Which, Who* 69
Lesson 27 *Real* and *Very* 71
Lesson 28 *Set* and *Sit* 73
Lesson 29 Irregular Verbs: *Know* and *Grow* 75
Lesson 30 *Learn* and *Teach* 77
Proofreading Practice 79
Proofreading Checklist 80
Unit 3 Review 81
Unit 3 School Home Connection 83

Unit 4 Grammar

Grab Bag Cars

Lesson 31 Subject and Object Pronouns 85
Lesson 32 Pronouns in Pairs 87
Lesson 33 Using *I* or *Me* 89
Lesson 34 Pronoun Antecedents 91
Lesson 35 Making the Subject and Verb Agree 93
Lesson 36 Forms of *Be* 95
Lesson 37 Verb Tense 97
Lesson 38 Negatives 99
Lesson 39 Comparative and Superlative Adjectives 101
Lesson 40 Comparative and Superlative Adverbs 103
Proofreading Practice 105
Proofreading Checklist 106
Unit 4 Review 107
Unit 4 School Home Connection 109

Unit 5 Mechanics

Beasts & Critters Amphibians and Reptiles

Lesson 41 Writing Sentences Correctly 111
Lesson 42 Proper Nouns and Proper Adjectives 113
Lesson 43 Initials and Abbreviations 115
Lesson 44 Titles 117
Lesson 45 Apostrophes 119
Lesson 46 Commas in a Series 121
Lesson 47 Commas 123
Lesson 48 Using Semicolons 125
Lesson 49 Direct and Indirect Quotations 127
Lesson 50 Friendly Letters and E-mails 129
Proofreading Practice 131
Proofreading Checklist 132
Unit 5 Review 133
Unit 5 School Home Connection 135

Unit Assessments

Unit 1 Test 139
Unit 2 Test 143
Unit 3 Test 147
Unit 4 Test 151
Unit 5 Test 155

Extra Practice

Lessons 1–2 159
Lessons 3–4 160
Lessons 5–6 161
Lessons 7–8 162
Lessons 9–10 163
Lessons 11–12 164
Lessons 13–14 165
Lessons 15–16 166
Lessons 17–18 167
Lessons 19–20 168
Lessons 21–22 169

Lessons 23–24 170
Lessons 25–26 171
Lessons 27–28 172
Lessons 29–30 173
Lessons 31–32 174
Lessons 33–34 175
Lessons 35–36 176
Lessons 37–38 177
Lessons 39–40 178
Lessons 41–42 179
Lessons 43–44 180
Lessons 45–46 181
Lessons 47–48 182
Lessons 49–50 183

Unit Tests

Unit 1 Test 185
Unit 2 Test 187
Unit 3 Test 189
Unit 4 Test 191
Unit 5 Test 193

G.U.M. Handbook

. . . . 195

G.U.M. Indexes

Topic Index 215
Language Index 216

Water / covers most of Earth's surface.
a.   b.

Which part (a. or b.) of this sentence tells whom or what the sentence is about? _a._ **Which part (a. or b.) tells what happens?** _b._

Every sentence has a subject and a predicate. The **complete subject** is made up of a noun or pronoun and words that tell about it. The subject tells whom or what the sentence is about. The **complete predicate** is made up of a verb and words that tell what the subject is, has, or does.

See Handbook Sections 10 and 11

Part 1

Underline the complete subject once. Underline the complete predicate twice.

1. The human body is about two-thirds water.

2. A typical American uses almost 100 gallons of water every day.

3. An adult needs about 2¹/₂ quarts of water each day.

4. This water comes from food and beverages.

5. A 15-minute shower uses about 75 gallons of water.

6. Many different industries use water.

7. Gasoline production requires water.

8. Agriculture needs large quantities of water, too.

9. The cultivation of wheat for one loaf of bread requires 150 gallons of water.

10. Some farmers use water-saving techniques.

11. The world's oceans contain salt water.

12. Special treatment plants can remove the salt from the water.

Drinking water is tested regularly throughout the United States.

The World Outside

Part 2   Answers will vary. Accept all reasonable responses.

Create a sentence from each phrase. Add either a subject or a predicate. Underline the complete subject in your sentence.

13. a thirsty person _____

_____

14. a cold, clear stream _____

_____

15. must be watered often _____

_____

16. uses large quantities of water _____

_____

17. rain and snow _____

_____

Part 3

Write three sentences about your favorite water activity, such as swimming, fishing, boating, or wakeboarding. Circle each complete subject and underline each complete predicate.

18. **Answers will vary.** _____

_____

19. _____

_____

20. _____

_____

Name _____

The World Outside

(Heat) changes the water in the kettle from a liquid into a gas.
The (steam) from the kettle rises toward the ceiling.

The complete subject in each sentence is in boldfaced type. Circle the most important word in each complete subject. Underline the verb in each sentence that tells what the subject did.

The **simple subject** is the most important word or words in the complete subject. It is a noun or pronoun and tells whom or what the sentence is about. The **simple predicate** is the most important word or words in the complete predicate. It is a verb. The simple predicate may tell what the subject did or what was done to the subject. It may also be a form of the verb *be*.

See Handbook Sections 10 and 11

Part 1

Circle the simple subject in each sentence. Draw a line under the simple predicate.

1. (Water) occurs as a liquid, a solid, and a gas.

2. (Steam) is a gaseous form of water.

3. Solid (forms) of water include ice and snow.

4. No other (substance) on Earth exists in all three forms.

5. (Rain) replenishes Earth's water supply.

6. (Moisture) evaporates from Earth's surface.

7. (Vapor) collects in the clouds.

8. One (cloud) contains billions of water molecules.

9. The (molecules) inside the cloud grow heavy.

10. (Water) returns to Earth in the form of rain or snow.

11. All (animals and plants) need water.

12. Some desert (creatures) get water from plants.

Water is the only substance on Earth that is present in three forms: solid, liquid, and gas.

Part 2

Write five sentences about water in its solid state. You may use nouns and verbs from the word bank as simple subjects and simple predicates.

hailstones	glisten	snowball	glacier	crashes
icicles	iceberg	melts	whizzes	clatter

13. __Answers will vary.__

14. _____

15. _____

16. _____

17. _____

Part 3

See Handbook | Section 32

Ask an adult to help you search the Internet for infomation about winter weather in your area. Then write a brief paragraph describing winter weather where you live. Underline each simple subject in red. Underline each simple predicate in blue.

__Answers will vary.__

Name _____

The World Outside

<u>P</u>   Tides in the ocean rise and fall regularly each day.

<u>S</u>   The sun and the moon cause the tides.

Write *S* next to the sentence with two or more subjects. Write *P* next to the sentence with two or more verbs.

A **compound subject** is two or more subjects joined by the conjunction *and* or *or*. A **compound predicate** is two or more verbs joined by a conjunction.

See Handbook   **Sections 10 and 11**

Part 1

Circle the two simple subjects that make up each compound subject. Underline the two verbs that make up each compound predicate.

1. (Ports) and (harbors) are helped by tides in many ways.

2. Tides <u>clean</u> the channels and <u>keep</u> them deep enough for ships.

3. Ocean (liners) and cargo (ships) sail through channels at high tide.

4. A high tide <u>can lift</u> a large ship and <u>guide</u> it into port.

5. Tides <u>pick</u> up waste from the shore and <u>carry</u> it far out to the bottom of the sea.

6. Fishing (crews) and (sailors) pay close attention to the tides in their area.

7. The new (moon) and the full (moon) bring spring tides, the highest and lowest tides of each month.

8. Long ago sailors <u>observed</u> the moon and <u>used</u> a compass.

High tide

9. Today fishing boat (crews) and ship (captains) rely on the Internet for information on tides.

10. Tide (charts) and weather (reports) help navigators.

Low tide

Part 2   Suggested answers appear below. Accept all reasonable responses.

Combine each pair of sentences to form one sentence that has either a compound subject or a compound predicate.

11. Visitors to the beach can swim at high tide. They can dig clams at low tide.

    Visitors to the beach can swim at high tide or dig clams at low tide.

    _____

12. Sea stars are often left high and dry at low tide. So are sea anemones.

    Sea stars and sea anemones are often left high and dry at low tide.

    _____

13. Tides contain energy. Waves contain energy, too.   Tides and waves contain energy.

    _____

14. Underwater machines harness tidal power. They convert it into valuable energy.

    Underwater machines harness tidal power and convert it into valuable energy.

    _____

Part 3

Unscramble these words. Each word names something found in harbors. All of the words appear on page 11.

15. scanelnh _____ channels _____   17. rostp _____ ports _____

16. sited _____ tides _____   18. iorslas _____ sailors _____

Now use two of the words to write a sentence with a compound subject or a compound predicate.

Answers will vary.
_____

_____

Name _____

Read and Discover

The **oceans** of the **earth** contain many (plants) and (fish).

Circle the boldfaced nouns that tell what the oceans contain.

The **direct object** is the noun or pronoun that receives the action of the verb. Only action verbs can take a direct object. A **compound direct object** occurs when more than one noun or pronoun receives the action of the verb. To find the direct object, say the verb, and then ask "What?" or "Whom?" For example, to find the direct object of *The oceans of the earth contain many plants and fish,* ask "Contain what?" The answer is "Plants and fish."

See Handbook Section 20

Part 1

Circle the direct object or compound direct object in each sentence.

1. We use the (ocean) for many purposes.

2. Divers explore its colorful (reefs).

3. Diners eat its (fish).

4. Surfers ride its wild (waves).

5. Workers take (minerals), (pearls), (sponges), and (salt) from it.

6. Boats harvest (seaweed) from the ocean.

7. Manufacturers make (medicines), (ice cream), and (cosmetics) from seaweed.

8. Container ships use the (oceans) as superhighways.

9. Luxury liners use the (oceans) as a vast playground.

10. Water purification plants turn (seawater) into drinking water for our thirsty planet.

Coral reefs are home to many colorful species of fish.

Part 2 Possible answers appear below. Accept all reasonable responses.

Write a direct object or a compound direct object after each action verb. Use words from the word bank and your own words.

treasures	clouds	ocean	pictures	creatures	plants	rain	coral

11. People mine the rich _____ ocean _____ for valuable minerals.

12. Divers gather precious _____ treasures _____ from the ocean bottom.

13. Photographers take beautiful _____ pictures _____ of colorful fish.

14. Scientists study strange _____ creatures and plants _____ in the ocean's depths.

15. Moisture from the ocean forms _____ clouds _____.

16. These clouds eventually bring _____ rain _____ to our mountains and valleys.

Part 3

Draw an underwater scene below, or use a computer graphics program to create such a scene. You can use the action words and direct objects in the word bank for ideas. Then write two sentences describing your scene.

sank	gave	reef	octopus	found	made	fins	cave

17. __Answers will vary.__ _____

_____

18. _____

_____

Name _____

The World Outside

14

Read and Discover

Bodies of water give Earth's (creatures) many **gifts**.

Circle the boldfaced word that tells to whom gifts are given.

An **indirect object** is a noun or pronoun that comes before a direct object. The indirect object tells to whom something has been given, told, or taught. Indirect objects appear only in sentences with direct objects. To test whether a noun or pronoun is an indirect object, try moving it after the direct object and putting the word *to* or *for* in front of it: *Bodies of water give many gifts to Earth's creatures.*

See Handbook Section 20

Part 1

The direct object in each sentence is in boldfaced type. Circle each indirect object.

1. Potholes offer migrating (ducks) resting **places**.

2. Estuaries give (shellfish) a peaceful **habitat**.

3. Bayous offer (alligators) many hiding **places**.

4. Ponds give (frogs) a wet, wonderful **home**.

5. Flooding rivers bring (farmers) rich **silt** for their fields.

6. Rivers also give spawning (salmon) a **nursery** for their young.

7. Hot springs offer (people) with sore muscles **relief** from pain.

8. Creeks offer (hikers) a pleasant, warbling **song**.

9. Waterfalls give (photographers) a magnificent **subject** for a picture.

10. Oceans send the (skies) **water vapor** that eventually returns to Earth as precipitation.

11. Bays provide (boats) a safe **haven** in stormy weather.

12. Sweetwater springs give (hikers) lifesaving drinking **water**.

13. Underground aquifers give (farmers) **water** for irrigation.

14. Lakes offer (boaters) a **place** to have fun.

Alligators move slowly through the shallow, stagnant waters of the bayous.

The World Outside

Part 2

Rewrite each sentence so the boldfaced word becomes an indirect object.

> **Example**   Rachel drew a map of the river for her **brother**.
> *Rachel drew her brother a map of the river.*

15. Eddie sold his kayak to **Rachel**. <u>Eddie sold Rachel his kayak.</u>

_____

16. Eddie gave two life jackets to **Benvi**. <u>Eddie gave Benvi two life jackets.</u>

_____

17. Hobie sang a sea song to the **crew**. <u>Hobie sang the crew a sea song.</u>

_____

18. Ernesto wrote a letter about his canoe trip to **Maia**. <u>Ernesto wrote Maia a letter about</u>

<u>his canoe trip.</u>

19. Chul told a story about his days as a sailor to **Dexter**. <u>Chul told Dexter a story about</u>

<u>his days as a sailor.</u>

Part 3

Imagine you and three friends are planning a canoe trip. Write three sentences with indirect objects. Each sentence should tell to whom you will give each item in the word bank.

first-aid kit	camera	portable stove

20. <u>Answers will vary.</u>

_____

_____

21. _____

_____

22. _____

_____

Name _____

The World Outside

If a snowpack remains frozen for many years, a glacier may form. The many snow crystals become thick (layers.) These layers are very **heavy**.

Circle the boldfaced noun that tells what the subject is or becomes. Underline the boldfaced adjective that describes the subject.

A **predicate noun** follows a linking verb and renames the subject. A **predicate adjective** follows a linking verb and describes the subject.

See Handbook Section 11

Part 1

Draw one line under each boldfaced word that is a predicate noun. Draw two lines under each boldfaced word that is a predicate adjective. Circle the linking verb in each sentence.

1. The layers (become) a **mass** of solid ice.

2. A mass of solid ice (is) a **glacier**.

3. Continental glaciers and valley glaciers (are) two **types** of glaciers.

4. Continental glaciers (are) **sheets** of thick ice.

5. Valley glaciers (are) **long** and **thin**.

6. Alaska's Glacier Bay National Park (is) **home** to bears, wolves, and mountain goats.

7. A glacier's movement (is) quite **slow**.

8. A glacier's surface (is) its hardest **part**.

9. Mountain climbers (become) extremely **cautious** on glaciers.

10. The crevasses in a glacier's surface (are) **dangerous**.

11. Crevasses (are) deep **cracks** in the ice.

Mountain climbers use special equipment to scale glaciers.

Part 2 Suggested answers appear below. Accept all reasonable responses.

Write a predicate noun or a predicate adjective to complete each sentence. You may use words from the word bank if you wish. Use an article (*a, an,* or *the*) if it is needed.

obstacle	iceberg	essential	cause
visible	disastrous	shock	ocean liner

12. A floating chunk of ice from a glacier becomes __an iceberg__.

13. Only the very tip of an iceberg is __visible__.

14. A collision between a passenger ship and an iceberg can be __disastrous__.

15. A life vest for every passenger on board a ship is __essential__.

16. The *Titanic* was a large __ocean liner__ that sank in 1912.

17. An iceberg was the __cause__ of its destruction.

18. The sinking of the "unsinkable" *Titanic* was __a shock__ to the world.

Part 3

Out of 2,200 passengers aboard the *Titanic,* only 705 were rescued. Ask an adult to help you find an article in an online encyclopedia about the sinking of the *Titanic.* Then imagine that you are interviewing a survivor. Write a question and an answer for a "news flash" of April 15, 1912. Use at least one predicate noun or predicate adjective to complete each item.

19. Question: __Answers will vary.__

_____

_____

20. Answer: __Answers will vary.__

_____

_____

_____

Name _____

The World Outside

Read and Discover

A large lake can affect the weather in nearby areas.

Which words tell where the weather is affected?

in nearby areas

A **prepositional phrase** can tell *how, what kind, when, how much,* or *where*. A prepositional phrase begins with a **preposition,** such as *in, over, of, to,* or *by*. It ends with a noun or pronoun that is the **object of the preposition**. Words between the preposition and the object of the preposition are also part of the prepositional phrase. A prepositional phrase can appear at the beginning, middle, or end of a sentence.

See Handbook **Section 19**

Part 1

Underline each prepositional phrase. Circle the preposition that begins the phrase.

1. A lake absorbs heat (during) the summer.

2. It releases this heat slowly (over) the following months.

3. A lake warms cold winds (in) cooler months.

4. The winds (off) the lake are relatively warm.

5. These temperate winds can extend the growing season (of) an area.

6. The Great Lakes are important (to) Michigan's fruit crops.

7. The lakes help keep the air (around) the orchards warm.

8. Michigan cherries are shipped (to) many American cities.

9. The cherries are harvested (before) the winter frost.

10. Much produce is shipped (by) train.

The Great Lakes and the waterways that connect them are vital to the economies of the United States and Canada.

Part 2 Suggested answers appear below. Accept all reasonable responses.

Add a prepositional phrase or two to each sentence. Then rewrite each sentence. You may use phrases from the word bank or think of your own.

without their water	to cities and towns	for recreation
during summer months	for irrigation	for manufacturing

11. Lakes are important. Lakes are important during summer months.

_____

12. People use them. People use them for recreation.

_____

13. Industries use their water. Industries use their water for manufacturing.

_____

14. Farmers use their water. Farmers use their water for irrigation.

_____

Part 3

Use the clues to complete the puzzle.
Each answer is a preposition.

Across
3. My family visits Lake Michigan __ the summer months.
4. We drive __ the state of Michigan.
6. I enjoy going __ the lake.
8. It takes several days to drive __ the entire lake.
9. The lake reflects the color of the sky __ it.

Down
1. We swim in the lake __ July and August.
2. I wear goggles when I swim __ the water.
4. I don't like it when fish swim __ me.
5. We pass factories and orchards __ our journey.
7. I like diving __ the cool water.
10. Once I saw a fish swim __ me.

Crossword solution:
- 1 Down: DURING
- 2 Down: UNDER
- 3 Across: IN
- 4 Across: THROUGH
- 4 Down: TOWARD
- 5 Down: ON
- 6 Across: TO
- 7 Down: INTO
- 8 Across: AROUND
- 9 Across: ABOVE
- 10 Down: BY

Name _____

The World Outside

Read and Discover

a. For a hundred years people dreamed of a waterway between the Great Lakes ~~and~~ the Atlantic Ocean.

b. De Witt Clinton planned a canal, ~~but~~ people sneered at his idea.

Cross out the boldfaced conjunction in each sentence.
Which sentence could become two separate sentences? ___b.___

A **compound sentence** is two or more closely related simple sentences. A simple sentence is also called an *independent clause*. The two clauses can be joined by a comma and a conjunction (*and, but, or*) or by a semicolon (;).

See Handbook Sections 8, 12, and 21

Part 1

Write *S* next to each simple sentence and *C* next to each compound sentence. Circle the conjunction or semicolon in each compound sentence.

1. The federal government would not give Clinton any money for his canal, (but) he did not give up. __C__

2. Clinton asked the New York legislature for money, (and) the State of New York agreed to his request. __C__

3. The governor of New York named Clinton the head of the canal commission in 1816(;) Clinton became governor of New York the next year. __C__

A lock allows a ship to pass from one body of water to another.

4. His crew began construction on July 4, 1817. __S__

5. The Erie Canal grew, (and) the towns along its course became busier. __C__

6. The first section opened in 1820, (but) the canal was not completed until 1825. __C__

7. Now raw materials from the Great Lakes region could be shipped to the East, (and) manufactured goods from Eastern cities could be shipped to the upper Midwest. __C__

8. The canal cost over seven million dollars, (but) tolls earned 17 times that by 1882. __C__

9. Early opponents feared the canal would never pay for itself(;) they were proven wrong. __C__

The World Outside

Part 2 Suggested answers appear below. Accept all reasonable responses.
Rewrite each pair of simple sentences as one compound sentence.

10. The <u>Seneca Chief</u> made the first journey through the Erie Canal in ten days. De Witt Clinton was one of the happy passengers.

    The <u>Seneca Chief</u> made the first journey through the Erie Canal in ten days, and

    De Witt Clinton was one of the happy passengers.

11. The Erie Canal cost more than seven million dollars. It proved to be a good investment.

    The Erie Canal cost more than seven million dollars, but it proved to be a good

    investment.

12. Barges moved slowly along the canal. They carried heavy loads cheaply and dependably.

    Barges moved slowly along the canal; they carried heavy loads cheaply and

    dependably.

Part 3 Suggested answers appear below. Accept all reasonable responses.
Many canals have locks to raise and lower boats. The diagram on page 21 shows what happens when a boat passes through a lock. Put the independent clauses below in order to tell what is happening in the diagram. Then combine the clauses to form three compound sentences.

5 The lock is opened a second time.   2 The lock is opened for the first time.
4 The water in the lock rises.   3 The ship enters the lock.
6 The ship sails out of the lock.   1 The ship sails up to the lock.

13. The ship sails up to the lock, and the lock is opened for the first time.

14. The ship enters the lock; the water in the lock rises.

15. The lock is opened a second time, and the ship sails out of the lock.

Name

The World Outside

As the wind pushes against the water, <u>the wind creates waves</u>.

Look at the two parts of this sentence. Which part makes sense by itself?

    a. the boldfaced part   **b.** the underlined part

An **independent clause** is a sentence that makes sense by itself. A **dependent clause** has a subject and a verb, but it does not make complete sense by itself. It needs—or is dependent on—an independent clause. A dependent clause often begins with a word such as *although, because, if, as,* or *when*.

See Handbook Sections 12 and 21

Part 1

Draw one line under each independent clause. Draw two lines under each dependent clause. Circle the word that begins each dependent clause.

1. (Although) some people think waves are caused by tides, the wind causes most waves.

2. (When) the wind blows for a long time at great speed, the waves grow larger.

3. (Because) waves keep moving even after the winds stop, some waves travel far from where they began.

4. (Although) storms often produce gigantic waves, few huge waves have ever been measured precisely.

5. (When) a ship is in the middle of a storm, its crew members must focus on survival.

The power and repetition of waves can carve steep cliffs.

6. Navigating a ship through a storm is still extremely difficult, (though) modern tracking equipment does provide some help.

7. (If) the crew members are careless, they may be washed overboard by a large wave.

8. A sailor aboard *USS Ramapo* measured a 112-foot wave (when) the ship was caught in a hurricane in 1933.

9. (As) *Weather Reporter* sailed the Atlantic in 1972, its instruments recorded an 86-foot wave.

10. (By) the time they reach the shore, most waves have traveled for many miles.

The World Outside

Part 2

Draw a line to match each dependent clause on the left with an independent clause on the right. Then write the new sentences you created. Be sure to add a comma in between clauses.

Because waves often hurl 100-pound rocks at it

Although most waves are harmless

When an earthquake struck in Alaska in 1946

Because people had no warning

A giant tsunami hit Waipi'o Valley on the big island of Hawaii.

Many lives were lost.

Tillamook Lighthouse in Oregon has steel bars built around it.

Some huge waves cause damage.

11. **Because waves often hurl 100-pound rocks at it, Tillamook Lighthouse in Oregon has steel bars built around it.**

12. **Although most waves are harmless, some huge waves cause damage.**

13. **When an earthquake struck in Alaska in 1946, a giant tsunami hit Waipi'o Valley on the big island of Hawaii.**

14. **Because people had no warning, many lives were lost.**

Part 3

Wave warnings often appear near beaches where rough surf is common. Add an independent clause to each dependent clause below to create sentences that warn people of the danger.

when you walk on the beach	if you use caution

15. **Answers will vary.**

16. _____

Name _____

The World Outside

Read and Discover

Avoiding Fragments, Run-ons, Comma Splices

Lesson 10

a. *Tsunami* is a Japanese word meaning "port wave."
b. A huge wave with enormous power.
c. If people are not warned beforehand.
d. Tsunamis should not be called tidal waves, they are not caused by tides.

Which item is a correct sentence? **a.**
Which item has no verb? **b.**
Which item is a dependent clause? **c.**
Which item is made up of two independent clauses without a conjunction? **d.**

A **fragment** does not tell a complete thought. A **run-on sentence** is a compound sentence that is missing a comma and a conjunction. A **comma splice** is a run-on sentence that has a comma but is missing a conjunction. Avoid fragments, run-ons, and comma splices in the final versions of your written work.

See Handbook Sections 13 and 21

Part 1

Circle each fragment. Draw a box around each run-on. Underline each comma splice. (1–6)

(A tsunami, not a single wave but a series of waves sometimes called a wave train.) Tsunamis are dangerous, they are incredibly powerful and travel very fast. Some are caused by earthquakes others are caused by volcanic eruptions. A mighty earthquake occurred under the Indian Ocean on December 26, 2004. (Created a massive tsunami.) Without warning, the tsunami struck Indonesia, Thailand, and other nearby countries. (Caused many deaths and left millions homeless.) Its powerful waves also traveled westward 3,000 miles to the coast of Africa. (Death and destruction there, too.)

One tsunami that struck the Shetland Isles around 4950 B.C. was almost as tall as the Empire State Building.

The World Outside

25

Part 2 Possible answers appear below. Accept all reasonable responses.

Rewrite the incorrect sentences from Part 1. Correct all fragments, run-ons, and comma splices. There may be more than one way to correct the errors.

7. A tsunami is not a single wave but a series of waves sometimes called a wave train.

8. Tsunamis are dangerous because they are incredibly powerful and travel very fast.

9. Some are caused by earthquakes, and others are caused by volcanic eruptions.

10. The earthquake created a massive tsunami.

11. It caused many deaths and left millions homeless.

12. The tsunami caused death and destruction there, too.

Part 3

Read each description of a weather event. Then unscramble the word that names the event.

13. This is a tropical windstorm with heavy rains that starts in the Atlantic Ocean, in the Caribbean Sea, or on the Pacific coast of Mexico. It comes from the Spanish word *huracán*.

    C H R A U N I R E _____ HURRICANE _____

14. This is a wind system that produces the dry and wet seasons in India and southern Asia. It comes from the Arabic word *mausim*, which means "season."

    S O N O M O N _____ MONSOON _____

15. This is a tropical storm in the western Pacific Ocean or China Sea. It comes from the Cantonese *tai fung*.

    O P O N Y T H _____ TYPHOON _____

Name _____

The World Outside

Proofreading
Practice

Read this report about wetlands and find the mistakes. Use the proofreading marks below to show how each mistake should be fixed.

Suggested answers appear below. Accept all reasonable responses.

Proofreading Marks

Mark	Means	Example
ℰ	take away	Bogs and swamps are ~~are~~ two types of wetlands.
∧	add	Bogs and swamps are two types ∧of wetlands.
≡	make into a capital letter	b̲ogs and swamps are two types of wetlands.
/	make into a lowercase letter	Bogs and S̸wamps are two types of wetlands.
⊙	add a period	Bogs and swamps are two types of wetlands⊙
ⓢⓟ	fix spelling	Bo(sp)ggs and swamps are two types of wetlands.

Wetlands

Wetlands are low-lying areas that are saturated with water for long periods. wetlands are classified according to the tipes (sp) of vegetation that grow in them. Swamps are wetlands that have many trees, (and) marshes are wetlands where mostly grasses grow. Bogs are filled with different types of mosses. All three types, (are) havens for many kinds of wildlife.

Birds throughout the world they depend on wetlands as a place to live and raise (their) young. Many migrating birds rely on wetlands as a resting place on they're (sp) long migrations. The prairie fringed orchid and other rare plants thrive in wet, mossy bogs. Wetlands provide a natural clasroom (sp) where scientist (s) can study a wide variety of Plant and animal life⊙

Wetlands also teaches us about the past the chemical composition of most bogs is ideal for preserving remains. Scientists have discovered well-preserved animals and other preserved life forms in bogs all over the world. One group of scientists in florida found artifacts of a Native American people who lived 7,000 to 8,000 years ago. The items revealed that this group had advanced weaving and tool-making skills.

Although milliones (sp) of acers (sp) of wetlands in the United States, (have) been destroyed by pollution or drained for farming or industry, Many groups are working to preserve the Wetlands that remain.

Proofreading
Checklist

You can use the list below to help you find and fix mistakes in your own writing. Write the titles of your own stories or reports in the blanks on top of the chart. Then use the questions to check your work. Make a check mark (✓) in each box after you have checked that item.
Answers will vary.

Titles

Proofreading Checklist for Unit 1

Have I joined compound sentences correctly?				
Does each sentence have both a subject and a predicate?				
Have I avoided run-on sentences, comma splices, and fragments?				
Does each sentence end with the appropriate end mark?				

Also Remember . . .

Does each sentence begin with a capital letter?				
Have I spelled each word correctly?				
Have I used commas correctly?				

Your Own List

Use this space to write your own list of things to check in your writing.

Name _____

The World Outside

Review

Subjects and Predicates

Underline the complete subject in each sentence. Draw a circle around the simple subject.

1. (Rain) is one kind of precipitation.   **(1, 2)**

2. (Snow) is another type.   **(1, 2)**

3. (Regions) with very little rain have few large animals.   **(1, 2)**

Underline the complete predicate in each sentence. Draw a circle around the simple predicate.

4. Polar regions (get) most of their precipitation in the form of snow.   **(1, 2)**

5. Winter snowpacks (hold) a great amount of water.   **(1, 2)**

6. A rain gauge (measures) rainfall in inches per hour.   **(1, 2)**

Draw one line under each compound subject in these sentences. Draw two lines under each compound predicate.

7. Texas and several neighboring states suffered terrible floods during the summer of 2007.   **(3)**

8. Thunderstorms flashed and boomed in June and July.   **(3)**

9. Creeks and rivers surged over their banks.   **(3)**

10. The Brazos River flooded homes and carried away cars.   **(3)**

Prepositions

Underline the prepositional phrase in each sentence. Draw a circle around the preposition.

11. Water surged (into) homes.   **(7)**

12. Some people climbed (onto) their roofs.   **(7)**

13. Volunteers (in) small boats rescued many people.   **(7)**

14. The boats carried stranded residents (to) higher ground.   **(7)**

15. Floodwaters turned some highways (into) lakes.   **(7)**

Complements

Decide whether the boldfaced word in each sentence is a direct object (DO), an indirect object (IO), a predicate noun (PN), or a predicate adjective (PA). Write *DO, IO, PN,* or *PA* after each sentence to identify each boldfaced word.

16. Usually rivers give **people** many benefits. __IO__ (5)

17. They provide **people** with a place to swim and fish. __IO__ (5)

18. In 2007, however, the Brazos River became **dangerous**. __PA__ (6)

19. The raging river was an **enemy**. __PN__ (6)

20. Its surging waters flooded **neighborhoods**. __DO__ (4)

Dependent and Independent Clauses

Circle each sentence that has two independent clauses. Draw a box around each sentence that has one independent clause and one dependent clause.

21. When rain warms the ocean, some of the surface water changes into water vapor. (9)

22. Because the moist air is warm, it rises. (9)

23. (The upper air is colder, and it cannot hold all the moisture.) (8, 9)

24. When the air cools to a certain point, the water vapor forms clouds of water droplets. (9)

25. (Most water vapor is invisible, but we can see water vapor in the form of clouds.) (8, 9)

Fragments, Run-ons, and Comma Splices

Identify each item below as a comma splice, a fragment, or a run-on by writing *CS, F,* or *RO* next to each.

26. Deserts in Australia, northern Africa, and the southwestern part of North America. __F__ (10)

27. The driest desert in the world is in South America it is called the Atacama Desert. __RO__ (10)

28. No rain for fourteen years. __F__ (10)

29. Very little precipitation falls in Antarctica, it is considered a desert. __CS__ (10)

30. On Earth's South Pole. __F__ (10)

Name _____

The World Outside

School 🏠 Home Connection

In Unit 1 of *G.U.M.* we are learning about different types of sentences and about the important parts of a sentence. The activities on this page give extra practice with some of the concepts we're learning. You can help your child use the information he or she is learning in school by choosing one or more activities to complete with your child at home.

Sentence Scramble (Complete Subjects and Complete Predicates)

With your child, read the weather forecasts in your local newspaper. Ask your child to copy four sentences from the forecasts onto strips of paper. Have your child underline the complete subject and circle the complete predicate. (The subject is the part of the sentence that tells whom or what the sentence is about. The predicate is the part of the sentence that tells what happens.)

Example	<u>Wednesday</u> (will be sunny.)
	<u>Rain</u> (is expected by Friday.)

Then snip the strips in half between the subject and predicate, and scramble the parts to make silly new sentences.

Example	<u>Rain</u> (will be sunny.)
	<u>Wednesday</u> (is expected by Friday.)

Back Then (Simple Subjects and Simple Predicates)

Have your child interview an older relative or friend and ask that person what life was like when he or she was in the fifth grade. Have your child record the conversation or take notes. Afterward, help your child write three sentences about the interview. Ask your child to underline the simple subject and circle the simple predicate in each sentence. (The simple subject is the most important word or phrase in the subject. The simple predicate is the verb that tells what the subject did, or links the subject to descriptive information.)

Example	<u>Grandma</u> (rode) a trolley car to school.
	<u>She</u> (worked) in her parents' restaurant after school.
	Her <u>friend</u> (had) a pet donkey.

Able to Leap Tall Buildings (Compound Sentences)

Ask your child to think of some superhuman power he or she would like to have. Then have your child write three compound sentences about how things are now and how they would be different if he or she had that power. (A compound sentence is two separate sentences joined by a comma and *and, or,* or *but.*)

Example   If your child chooses the power to fly, he or she might write, "Now it takes me forty minutes to get to school by bus, **but** with the power to fly, I could get there in five minutes!"

Work with your child to underline the conjunction *and, or,* or *but* in each sentence.

Find the Shoe (Prepositional Phrases)

You can play this game with the whole family. First, have the other players close their eyes. Then take a shoe and hide it somewhere in the room. Have the other players guess where the shoe is, using prepositional phrases. (A prepositional phrase can tell where something is. Prepositional phrases begin with words such as *in, under, through,* or *beyond.*)

Example   Is it **in the refrigerator?** Is it **under the sink?**

When a player asks a question, have him or her identify the prepositional phrase in the question and then go look for the shoe. When the shoe has been found, the finder can then hide the shoe.

What Is Wrong? (Prepositional Phrases)

Ask your child to write three sentences about what is wrong with this picture. Then work with your child to identify any prepositional phrases he or she used. (Prepositional phrases begin with words such as *around, at, by, for, from, in, near, of, off, on, to,* or *with.*)

Example   The cow is floating **in the air.**

Name _____

The World Outside

Thanks to the bravery of (Samuel Wilson) the town of (Metonymy) was saved from the British. When the (Revolutionary War) began, Sam was eight years old. He was given the job of drummer boy in his **town**. When he saw the **redcoats** coming, Sam banged his **drum**. He alerted the **townspeople** in time for them to stop the **soldiers**.

Circle the boldfaced words that name particular persons, places, things, or ideas.

A **common noun** names any person, place, thing, or idea. A **proper noun** names a particular person, place, thing, or idea. Proper nouns must be capitalized.

See Handbook Section 14

Part 1
Underline each common noun. Circle each proper noun.

1. (Sam Wilson) later started a plant for packing meat in (Troy, New York)

2. Because of his friendliness, (Sam) was called ("Uncle Sam") by his workers.

3. During the (War of 1812,) (Sam) printed (U.S.) on the meat being sent to the army.

4. A curious inspector asked a worker what the letters stood for.

5. The worker didn't know, so he said they might stand for (Uncle Sam.)

6. Soon people all over (America) were saying that things

   that came from the government were from (Uncle Sam.)

7. (Uncle Sam) has been a national symbol ever since.

8. Illustrators started printing pictures of (Uncle Sam)

   in newspapers in 1820.

9. The most famous picture of (Uncle Sam) was painted

   by (James Montgomery Flagg.)

James Flagg's painting of Uncle Sam is still widely used today.

10. This painting was used on recruiting posters for the (U.S. Army) during (World War I.)

11. In striped pants and top hat, (Uncle Sam) is still seen in ads and political cartoons.

Part 2

Uncle Sam is a symbol used to represent the United States of America. Write four sentences about other symbols of our nation. Use nouns from the word bank or think of your own. Be sure to capitalize proper nouns.

bald eagle	Old Glory	the Liberty Bell
flag	Stars and Stripes	the White House

12. __Answers will vary._____

_____

13. _____

_____

14. _____

_____

15. _____

_____

Part 3

Circle the eight hidden nouns.
Write the proper nouns below.
Use proper capitalization.

Proper Nouns

16. _____ **Lincoln** _____

17. _____ **America** _____

18. _____ **Jefferson** _____

19. _____ **Washington** _____

I	J	S	B	F	R	O	P	Q	R
N	E	X	P	L	Q	G	U	G	W
D	F	S	A	S	X	P	K	Y	A
E	F	I	R	E	W	O	R	K	S
P	E	H	A	P	L	Q	U	X	H
E	R	Z	D	H	M	R	V	Y	I
N	S	C	E	I	K	S	W	Z	N
D	O	V	Q	J	O	F	L	A	G
E	N	B	R	K	P	T	M	P	T
N	L	I	N	C	O	L	N	R	O
C	Z	H	Z	D	V	N	A	Z	N
E	A	A	M	E	R	I	C	A	M

Name _____

Looking Back

The **Pilgrims'** first year in Plymouth had been hard. Many had died. But in the fall of 1621, the **survivors** had much to be thankful for.

Circle the part of the word *Pilgrims'* that shows possession.
Circle the part of the word *survivors* that shows it is talking about more than one person.

A **plural noun** names more than one person, place, thing, or idea. Most nouns add *s* to form the plural. Some nouns change spelling instead of adding *s* (*woman/women*). Some nouns have the same singular and plural form (*deer*). A **possessive noun** shows ownership. Most plural nouns add an apostrophe after the *s* to form the possessive (*boys'*). Plurals that don't end in *s*, such as *men*, add apostrophe and *s* to show possession (*men's*).

See Handbook Sections 25 and 26

Part 1

Draw a box around each noun that is both plural and possessive. For the remaining nouns, underline each plural noun and circle each possessive noun.

1. The colonists' Patuxet friend Squanto had helped them build houses and plant crops.

2. The colony's governor had made peace with Massasoit, chief of the Wampanoag.

3. The settlers' harvest was expected to be good.

4. The colonists planned to invite the Wampanoag to a celebration.

5. Four women and two teenagers cooked food for 147 people.

6. The group's celebration lasted three days.

7. Unfortunately, the next year's harvest was not as good.

8. The settlers did not hold another celebration.

9. Americans did not celebrate Thanksgiving again until 1777.

10. Sarah Josepha Hale tried for more than 30 years to make Thanksgiving a holiday.

11. President Lincoln's proclamation in 1863 made Hale's wish come true.

12. Americans celebrate Thanksgiving on the fourth Thursday of November.

Women ground corn to make bread and biscuits for the first Thanksgiving.

Looking Back

Part 2

If the boldfaced noun is singular, write its plural form. If the boldfaced noun is plural, write its plural possessive form.

13. The Wampanoag's **gift** to the feast included five **deer** and, perhaps, popcorn.

    gifts   deer's

14. The **celebration** probably began with a blare of **bugles** and a parade.

    celebrations   bugles'

15. Everyone feasted on wild **birds**, **pumpkins**, and cranberries.

    birds'   pumpkins'

16. For entertainment, the **men** competed in foot races and jumping **matches**.

    men's   matches'

17. The **friendship** lasted until 1675, when **war** broke out over land disputes.

    friendships   wars

18. Today, **visitors** to Plymouth can tour a village just like the one the **Pilgrims** built.

    visitors'   Pilgrims'

Part 3

See Handbook Section 32

Ask an adult to help you search the Internet to learn more about the first Thanksgiving. Write a paragraph telling what you learned. Use at least one plural noun and one possessive noun.

Answers will vary.

Name _____

Read and Discover

Personal and Possessive Pronouns
Lesson 13

In the early 1890s Katherine Lee Bates, a professor from Massachusetts, visited Colorado. While there, **she** climbed Pikes Peak. The view from the summit was so magnificent that Miss Bates was inspired to write a poem. **Its** first line was "O beautiful for spacious skies."

To whom does the word *she* refer? _____ Katherine Lee Bates _____

What word does *Its* stand for? _____ poem _____

A **pronoun** can take the place of a noun. Use the **personal pronouns** *I, me, we,* and *us* to speak or write about yourself. Use *she, her, it, he, him, you, they,* and *them* to refer to other people and things. The **possessive pronouns** *his, its, our, her, their, my,* and *your* show ownership.
◀ **Remember to use this information when you speak, too.**

See Handbook Section 16

Part 1

Circle each personal pronoun in the sentences below. Underline each possessive pronoun.

1. <u>Her</u> poem was matched with the melody of a hymn called "Materna."

2. (It) had been written by Samuel A. Ward thirteen years earlier.

3. <u>His</u> melody fit perfectly with the verses (she) had written.

4. The result of <u>their</u> creative talents was the song "America the Beautiful."

5. Some of (us) find that song easier to sing than "The Star-Spangled Banner."

6. (We) would prefer to have "America the Beautiful" become <u>our</u> national anthem.

7. (I) am not a good singer, but "The Star-Spangled Banner" is one of <u>my</u> favorite songs.

8. (It) was written by Francis Scott Key during the War of 1812 and quickly became the unofficial national anthem.

9. The sight of the American flag flying after a fierce battle was <u>his</u> inspiration for writing "The Star-Spangled Banner."

10. More than 100 years later, President Herbert Hoover made <u>its</u> status as national anthem official.

Bates's poem became
"America the Beautiful."

Looking Back

Part 2 Suggested answers appear below. Accept all reasonable responses.

Rewrite each sentence, replacing each underlined word with a pronoun from the box. More than one pronoun may be correct. Remember to capitalize a pronoun that begins a sentence.

| they | them | we | us | it | its | she | her | their |

11. <u>Katherine Lee Bates</u> would be pleased to know that <u>Katherine Lee Bates's</u> poem remains popular more than a century after <u>the poem</u> was written. **She would be pleased to know that her poem remains popular more than a century after it was written.**

12. Most of <u>the residents of the United States</u> know <u>the song's</u> first verse by heart. **Most of us know its first verse by heart.**

13. <u>School children across America</u> sing <u>this song</u> often. **They sing it often.**

14. <u>Patriotic songs</u> can help people express <u>people's</u> pride in <u>people's</u> country. **They can help people express their pride in their country.**

15. <u>America's national anthem</u> is played at most sports events. **It is played at most sports events.**

Part 3

Do you think that "America the Beautiful" should become our national anthem? Write two or three sentences to explain how you feel and why. Circle personal and possessive pronouns.

Answers will vary.

_____

_____

_____

Name _____

Looking Back

Read and Discover

Mississippi (means) "Big River." The Illinois, Kickapoo, Ojibway, and Santee Dakota peoples **lived** in the upper Mississippi Valley long ago. They **gave** the river its name.

Circle the boldfaced word that tells you something is happening right now or is true now.

The **present tense** of a verb indicates that something happens regularly or is true now. When the subject is *he, she, it,* or a singular noun, form the present tense by adding an *s* to most verbs. Add *es* to verbs ending in *s, ch, sh, x,* or *z*. Drop the *y* and add *ies* to verbs ending in a consonant and *y*. Most verbs that follow plural nouns do not end in *s*.
Remember to use this information when you speak, too.

See Handbook Section 17

Part 1
Circle each verb that is in the present tense. (1–13)

The first Europeans traveled on the Mississippi River in 1541. The river became vital to transportation and industry about 200 years ago.

Today important products (move) up and down the Mississippi on huge barges daily. Tugboats (guide) the barges north or south. Southbound barges usually (contain) agricultural products. Northbound barges (haul) coal and steel products. Each year barges (transport) about 300 million tons of freight on the Mississippi River.

Good farmland (surrounds) the southern Mississippi River. When the river (floods), it (adds) important nutrients to the soil. The river (carries) soil and minerals along with it. When it (floods), it (spreads) these minerals over the river valley. When the waters (recede), rich sediment (remains).

Minneapolis/St. Paul

St. Louis

New Orleans

Looking Back

39

Part 2

Complete each sentence. Use the present tense form of a verb in the word bank.

reach	pass	begin	make	flow

14. The Mississippi River ____begins____ as a small stream in northwestern Minnesota.

15. It ____flows____ southward at about 1.2 to 3 miles per hour.

16. The river's fast current ____makes____ the southbound journey more dangerous than the northbound journey.

17. A barge must be guided carefully so that it ____passes____ safely between bridge pillars.

18. The cargo is unloaded when the barge ____reaches____ port.

Part 3

Suppose you are the captain of a tugboat that hauls barges on the Mississippi River. Write a paragraph about what you typically see and do on a downriver run. Use present tense verbs from the word bank. You may want to include information about some of the ports on the map on page 39.

see	learn	share	discover	tell	receive

Answers will vary.

_____

_____

_____

_____

_____

_____

_____

Name _____

Looking Back

In the past, leukemia patients <u>had</u> no hope for survival. This lesson (will acquaint) you with the researcher responsible for some of the first effective leukemia treatments.

Underline the verb that tells about an event that happened in the past. Circle the verb that tells about something that will happen in the future.

A **past tense** verb tells about something that has already happened. Regular verbs form the past tense by adding -*ed*. Irregular verbs change their spelling in the past tense. A **future tense** verb tells what is going to happen in the future. Use the helping verb *will* plus the first-person present tense form of the verb to form the future tense.

🔊 **Remember to use this information when you speak, too.**

See Handbook Section 17

Part 1

Underline each verb that is in the past tense. Circle each verb that is in the future tense.

1. Gertrude B. Elion <u>was</u> born in 1918 in New York.

2. During her teenage years, her grandfather <u>died</u> of cancer.

3. "I will develop a cure for cancer," Gertrude <u>told</u> herself.

4. "I will study chemistry."

5. Elion <u>graduated</u> as the only woman in her master's degree program.

6. At that time, there <u>were</u> few jobs open for women chemists.

7. But during World War II, there <u>was</u> a shortage of chemists.

8. Then Elion <u>found</u> work in a research laboratory.

9. Later she and her partner <u>developed</u> some of the first treatments for leukemia.

10. They also <u>created</u> other important medications.

11. Elion <u>was</u> one of three winners of The Nobel Prize in Physiology or Medicine in 1988.

12. Her past discoveries will continue to help scientists in the future.

Gertrude B. Elion was a Nobel Prize winner.

Looking Back

Part 2

Write the past tense or future tense form of the verb in parentheses to complete each sentence correctly.

13. Amy _____**fell**_____ in love with science ten years ago, in first grade. (fall)

14. Two generations ago, very few women _____**became**_____ scientists. (become)

15. Nevertheless, women scientists _____**made**_____ important breakthroughs. (make)

16. For example, Gertrude Elion _____**developed**_____ leukemia treatments. (develop)

17. Barbara McClintock _____**discovered**_____ principles of genetics. (discover)

18. Grace Hopper _____**invented**_____ the compiler for computers. (invent)

19. Soon Amy _____**will go**_____ to college. (go)

20. She _____**will study**_____ very hard in the upcoming years. (study)

21. Perhaps someday Amy _____**will discover**_____ a new treatment for a serious illness. (discover)

Part 3

Write down five goals you have for the future. Use a future tense verb in each sentence.

_**Answers will vary.**_____

_____

_____

_____

_____

Name _____

Looking Back

For years many residents of Westminster, California, (have called) their business district "Little Saigon." Now a new freeway sign **announces** the location of this bustling commercial area.

Circle the boldfaced verb that tells about an action that began in the past and continues today.

The **present perfect tense** indicates action that started in the past and may still be happening. To form the present perfect tense, add the helping verb *has* or *have* to the past participle of a verb. The **past participle** of regular verbs is formed by adding *-ed* (*work/had worked*). Irregular verbs change their spelling when they form past participles (*build/have built*). **Remember to use this information when you speak, too.**

See Handbook Section 17

Part 1

Circle each verb in the present perfect tense. Be sure to include the helping verb. (1–10)

Since America's earliest days, immigrants (have shaped) the culture of the United States. Before the 1970s, few immigrants from Southeast Asia lived in the United States. People from many countries in the region (have moved) here since then.

Tens of thousands of Vietnamese people fled their country after it was taken over by North Vietnamese forces in 1975. Many of the refugees settled in California. Refugees (have established) in Orange County the world's largest Vietnamese community outside of Vietnam. There they (have maintained) many traditions of their homeland. For years the Orange County community of Westminster (has celebrated) Tet, the Vietnamese celebration of the lunar New Year. Little Saigon, as it is known, is decked out each February in the traditional good luck colors of red and yellow.

In Orange County, Vietnamese Americans also (have brought) their traditions into an American institution, the shopping mall. To remind shoppers of their homeland, the Vietnamese American owners of the Asian Garden Mall (have built) an entrance with red pillars joined by a curved tile roof. This style of architecture (has existed) in Asia for centuries, but it (has been) a rarity in the United States. In Little Saigon, Vietnamese and American cultures (have combined) to create a distinctive cultural experience.

Looking Back

Part 2

Write the present perfect form (*has* or *have* plus the past participle) of the verb in parentheses to complete each sentence correctly.

11. At the entrance to the Asian Garden Mall, the designer _____**has placed**_____ an

    enormous statue of Buddha. (place)

12. The drugstore _____**has lined**_____ its shelves with Vietnamese folk remedies. (line)

13. The tailor shops _____**have stocked**_____ plenty of silk for the Vietnamese women's

    ao dais, a traditional kind of clothing. (stock)

14. The supermarket _____**has filled**_____ its bins with Asian produce such as bamboo

    shoots, ginger, and persimmons. (fill)

15. Bookstores sell books that Vietnamese authors _____**have written**_____. (write)

16. The stores _____**have hired**_____ clerks who speak Vietnamese. (hire)

17. Travel agencies _____**have arranged**_____ trips to Vietnam for many people. (arrange)

18. The mall _____**has become**_____ an important center for Vietnamese people in the

    Los Angeles area. (become)

Part 3   Answers will vary.

Write an ad that will convince readers to shop at the Asian Garden Mall. The headline and first sentence have been started for you.

Have You Ever _____?

If you have _____

_____

_____

_____

Name _____

Looking Back

The Outer Banks of North Carolina are (beautiful), (sandy) islands. However, the (treacherous) currents of this region have challenged sailors for hundreds of years.

Circle the two words that tell what the islands are like. Circle one word that tells what the currents are like.

Adjectives describe nouns and pronouns. Some adjectives tell **what kind**. Others, like *many* and *six,* tell **how many**. The adjectives *this, that, these,* and *those* tell **which one**. These are called *demonstrative adjectives*. The articles *a, an,* and *the* are also adjectives.

See Handbook **Section 15**

Part 1

Some adjectives in these sentences appear in boldfaced type. Circle each boldfaced adjective that tells what kind. Underline each boldfaced adjective that tells how many. Draw a box around each boldfaced adjective that tells which one. Underline each boldfaced article (*a, an, the*) twice.

1. One of <u>the</u> United States' most (famous) historical sights was built to warn sailors of the (dangerous) waters of the Outer Banks.

2. <u>Two</u> currents collide near Cape Hatteras, causing (powerful) waves.

3. A (treacherous) reef called Diamond Shoals also lies in <u>the</u> area.

4. This combination has caused many shipwrecks over <u>the</u> centuries.

5. Hurricanes sometimes strike this area as well.

6. For <u>all</u> these reasons, it is known as <u>the</u> Graveyard of <u>the</u> Atlantic.

7. In 1870, <u>a</u> (striped) lighthouse was built on Cape Hatteras to warn ships.

8. At <u>208</u> feet, it is <u>the</u> (tallest) lighthouse in <u>the</u> United States.

9. This (historic) lighthouse still stands today, and it is visited by <u>many</u> tourists each year.

10. <u>The</u> Outer Banks are (beautiful) and (interesting) as well as (dangerous).

11. Tourists come to <u>the</u> Cape Hatteras National Seashore to visit <u>the</u> (gorgeous) beaches.

12. Nearby is Kitty Hawk, where <u>the</u> Wright brothers made their (famous) flight.

The Cape Hatteras Lighthouse is endangered by beach erosion.

Part 2 Possible answers appear below. Accept all reasonable responses.
Complete each sentence with an appropriate adjective from the word bank or use your own word.

that	ten	brave	modern	few	the	those	heroic

13. People have made _____**heroic**_____ efforts to help ships near the Outer Banks.

14. In 1899, Rasmus S. Midgett saved _____**ten**_____ men from a sinking ship during a hurricane.

15. _____**Those**_____ men would have died without him.

16. Mr. Midgett was a _____**brave**_____ member of the U.S. Life-Saving Service.

17. _____**That**_____ service joined the Coast Guard in 1915.

18. Today the Coast Guard uses _____**modern**_____ technology to find and help ships in trouble near Cape Hatteras.

19. As a result, _____**few**_____ ships have been wrecked in recent years.

Part 3
Use these clues to complete the puzzle.

Across
5. A __ adjective tells which one is being talked about.
6. The word __ is an article.
7. *This, that, these,* and __ are demonstrative adjectives.

Down
1. An adjective may __ a noun.
2. Adjectives such as *two* and *few* tell __ many.
3. *A* is a special kind of adjective called an __.
4. Most adjectives come __ the nouns they tell about.

Puzzle answers:
- 5 Across: DEMONSTRATIVE
- 6 Across: THE
- 7 Across: THOSE
- 1 Down: DESCRIBE
- 2 Down: HOW
- 3 Down: ARTICLE
- 4 Down: BEFORE

Name _____

Read and Discover

The whaling industry was **very** important to the United States in the early 1800s. During that time, whalers **expertly** hunted thousands of whales each year.

Which boldfaced word tells how people do something? **expertly**

Which boldfaced word describes an adjective and tells how much?
very

> **Adverbs** describe verbs or adjectives. They tell **how, when, where,** or **to what extent** (how much). Many adverbs end in *-ly*. Other common adverbs are *fast, very, often, again, sometimes, soon, only, however, too, later, first, then, far,* and *now.*

See Handbook Section 18

Part 1
Circle each adverb below.

1. American whalers (first) hunted sperm whales in the 1700s.

2. The oils from sperm whales were (extremely) valuable (then).

3. These oils were used (chiefly) for lamps.

4. Whaling voyages (sometimes) lasted for four or five years.

5. When the California gold rush started (suddenly) in 1849, many whalers (quickly) abandoned their ships to seek their fortunes on land.

Whalers like this one sailed the high seas in search of whales.

6. The American whaling industry declined (rapidly) after the Civil War.

7. (Soon) (only) a few whaling operations remained in the United States.

8. (However,) the whaling industries of other nations expanded (dramatically) in the late 1800s.

9. New technology helped whalers catch and process whales (efficiently.)

10. (Tragically,) the whalers killed many thousands of whales.

11. Many species were (nearly) made extinct.

12. (Now) commercial whaling is illegal in the United States and most other countries.

13. The population of many whale species has risen (significantly.)

Looking Back

Part 2

Circle the adverb that tells more about each underlined word or words. Then tell whether the adverb explains *how, when, where,* or *to what extent.*

14. Humpback whales <u>migrate</u> (yearly) between polar and tropical regions. ___when___

15. Because humpbacks <u>swim</u> (slowly,) they used to be easy prey for whalers. ___how___

16. The commercial whaling of humpbacks (finally) <u>ended</u> in the 1960s. ___when___

17. Many humpbacks (accidentally) <u>become</u> entangled in fishing nets. ___how___

18. If a whale <u>is caught</u> (there) it usually drowns or starves to death. ___where___

19. Whales that <u>struggle</u> (frantically) may tear an expensive net to shreds. ___how___

20. Experts cut a net so that the whale <u>can swim</u> (free) and the net can be fixed. ___how___

Part 3

Circle five adverbs in the puzzle. Then choose two of the adverbs. Use each in a sentence about whales or whaling.

```
Q F S X Y X W Q J
W G O C T C R T K
R V M D V V T S L
T R E C E N T L Y
Y J T B R B Y O N
P X I N Y N D W V
S L M Q R M G L Y
T H E R E S K Y W
D Z S Q W D Z K Z
```

21. __Answers will vary.__
_____

22. _____
_____

Name _____

Read and Discover

At dawn a lone hiker steps **onto** the trail. By ten o'clock she has descended four thousand feet. Her reward is a cool drink **of** water.

Which two boldfaced words begin phrases that tell _when_?
   At   By

Which boldfaced word begins a phrase that tells _where_? _____onto_____

Which boldfaced word begins a phrase that tells about a noun? _____of_____

A **preposition** shows a relationship between one word in a sentence and the noun or pronoun that follows the preposition. The noun or pronoun that follows the preposition is the **object of the preposition**. The preposition, the object of the preposition, and the words in between them make a **prepositional phrase**.

See Handbook Section 19

Part 1

In the sentences below, underline each prepositional phrase. Circle the preposition and draw a box around its object. There may be more than one prepositional phrase in each sentence.

1. The Grand Canyon is one (of) the world's most spectacular natural [formations].

2. It was carved (by) the Colorado River's rushing [waters].

3. The river has been carving this masterpiece (for) perhaps six million [years].

4. There are different climates (at) different [elevations].

5. Native Americans have lived (in) the [area] (for) thousands (of) [years].

6. Today, many members (of) the Havasupai [nation] live (in) a nearby [canyon].

7. The first European visitors (to) the [Grand Canyon] were a group (of) Spanish [explorers] led (by) [García López de Cárdenas].

8. They came (to) the [region] (in) [1540].

9. (In) [1869] John Wesley Powell led an expedition (through) the [area] and named it the Grand Canyon.

10. The Grand Canyon became a national park (in) [1919].

Tassel-eared squirrels like these live in Grand Canyon National Park.

Looking Back

Part 2   Possible answers appear below. Accept all reasonable responses.
Complete each sentence with an appropriate prepositional phrase from the word bank or use one of your own.

| along its trails | at sunset | above the Grand Canyon |
| to the bottom | over the Grand Canyon | down the Colorado River |

11. Most visitors drive or walk to viewing points _____**above the Grand Canyon**_____.

12. Some people like to hike _____**along its trails**_____.

13. Others ride rafts _____**down the Colorado River**_____.

14. Still others like to ride a mule _____**to the bottom**_____

and then back up.

15. Some have even flown _____**over the Grand Canyon**_____ in a plane.

16. Most people agree that the best time to see the canyon is _____**at sunset**_____.

Part 3
The South Rim of the Grand Canyon is filled with tassel-eared squirrels. Use prepositional phrases to describe the three squirrels on page 49. Write one sentence describing each squirrel. Then trade papers with a partner. Match each sentence with the squirrel it describes.

17. **Answers will vary.**
_____

_____

18. _____

_____

19. _____

_____

Name _____

Looking Back

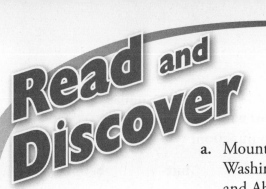

a. Mount Rushmore features enormous carvings of George Washington, Thomas Jefferson, Theodore Roosevelt, and Abraham Lincoln.

b. I recommend seeing it because it is so unusual.

Which word in sentence a. links several proper nouns? _____**and**_____

Which word in sentence b. links the first part of the sentence to the second part of the sentence? _____**because**_____

Coordinating conjunctions (*and, but, or*) connect words or groups of words (including independent clauses) that are similar. **Subordinating conjunctions,** such as *although, because, if,* and *before,* show how one clause is related to another clause. Subordinating conjunctions appear at the beginning of dependent clauses.

See Handbook Section 21

Part 1

Underline each coordinating conjunction and circle each subordinating conjunction.

1. Doane Robinson had the idea to carve sculptures into Mount Rushmore, <u>but</u> he didn't think of portraying American presidents.

2. His idea was to carve legendary Westerners, Kit Carson, Jim Bridger, <u>and</u> John Colter.

The faces of four American presidents stare across the prairies of South Dakota.

3. Gutzon Borglum wanted to make carvings of presidents (because) presidents are important.

4. Borglum was hired (because) he had already carved statues in the sides of mountains.

5. (If) Borglum had not had experience, the project probably would have failed.

6. The peak could be reached only by foot <u>or</u> horseback.

7. Equipment had to be hauled up thousands of feet <u>and</u> then lowered by ropes to work areas.

8. Dynamite <u>and</u> steam drills were used to blast away rock.

9. (Although) Borglum died before the project was finished, his son Lincoln did complete it.

10. It took 14 years <u>and</u> nearly one million dollars to complete the sculpture.

Looking Back

Part 2
Suggested answers appear below. Accept all reasonable responses.
Complete each sentence with a conjunction from the word bank. Write *C* if it is a coordinating conjunction and *S* if it is a subordinating conjunction.

although	and	or	because	but	before

11. __Although__ Americans do not often create giant monuments anymore, many still admire those created in the past. __S__

12. Borglum started out as a painter, __but__ he became a sculptor in later life. __C__

13. Visitors to Mount Rushmore are often surprised __because__ the carved heads are much paler than the uncarved rock around them. __S__

14. The heads are sixty feet high, __and__ the mouths are eighteen feet wide. __C__

15. Almost every visitor to Mount Rushmore takes photographs __or__ buys postcards of the huge monument. __C__

16. __Before__ I saw Mount Rushmore, I had no idea of its huge size. __S__

Part 3
Write the name of each president on Mount Rushmore next to the statement that describes him. Then circle the conjunction in each sentence.

17. (Before) he became America's first president, he was a surveyor. __George Washington__

18. People may admire him for crafting The Declaration of Independence (and) for bringing the recipe for ice cream to America. __Thomas Jefferson__

19. (Since) he once spared a bear cub during a hunting trip, a toy bear was named for him. __Theodore Roosevelt__

20. His Gettysburg Address contains only ten sentences, (yet) it is considered one of the greatest speeches of all time. __Abraham Lincoln__

Name _____

Looking Back

Proofreading
Practice

Read this report about Route 66 and find the mistakes. Use the proofreading marks below to show how each mistake should be corrected.

Suggested answers appear below. Accept all reasonable responses.

Proofreading Marks

Mark	Means	Example
ℛ	take away	America is made up up of many cultures.
∧	add	America *is* made up of many cultures.
≡	make into a capital letter	america is made up of many cultures.
⊙	add a period	America is made up of many cultures⊙
/	make into a lowercase letter	America is made up of many Cultures.
sp	fix spelling	America is maade up of many cultures.

The Main Street of America

Route 66 is *has* been called the "mother road" and the "main street of america." It represents adventure to many Americans'. The song "Get Your Kicks on Route 66" and a 1960s television series called Route 66 are two examples of the role this road has played in popular culture.

Route 66 is one of the most famous roads in the world. When it was completed, it was more than 2,400 miles long and ran between chicago and Los angeles. Route 66 cross *es* eight states and three time zones Before the Interstate Highway system was created, Route 66 was one of the most important roads linking the eastern and western parts of the United States.

In the 1930s, Route 66 carries *d* many families from oklahoma to California. They *ir* farmland had been ruined by severely droughts in Oklahoma. Oklahomans desperate *ly* needed work and food. Many of them found work on farms in California. The Oklahomans called Route 66 the "Dust Bowl Hiway." (sp)

Today, Interstate 40 has replaced Route 66 as the main Route across America's Southwest. But Route 66 is still a symbol of adventure, *and* many people are sorry it has been replaced.

Looking Back

Proofreading
Checklist

You can use the list below to help you find and fix mistakes in your own writing. Write the titles of your own stories or reports in the blanks on top of the chart. Then use the questions to check your work. Make a check mark (✓) in each box after you have checked that item.

Answers will vary.

Proofreading Checklist for Unit 2

	Titles			
Have I capitalized proper nouns?				
Have I used plural and possessive nouns correctly?				
Have I used adverbs correctly?				
Have I used adjectives correctly?				
Have I used the past, future, and present perfect tenses correctly?				
Have I used coordinating and subordinating conjunctions correctly?				

Also Remember . . .

Does each sentence begin with a capital letter?				
Does each sentence end with the right mark?				
Have I spelled each word correctly?				
Have I used commas correctly?				

Your Own List
Use this space to write your own list of things to check in your writing.

Name _____

Looking Back

Review

Nouns

Write whether the boldfaced word is a proper noun or a common noun. Then circle each boldfaced noun that is plural. Underline each one that is possessive.

1. **America's** first hard-surfaced road was the Lancaster Turnpike in Pennsylvania.

   proper noun   (11, 12)

2. Until the automobile became popular, few (roads) in America were paved.

   common noun   (11, 12)

3. More than four million miles of paved roads and highways now crisscross the

   United States.   proper noun   (11)

   (If necessary, explain that *United States* is singular because it is the name of a country.)

4. Americans have noticed in recent years that many of the **country's** roads need repair.

   common noun   (11, 12)

5. (Taxpayers') money is used to build and repair roads.   common noun   (11, 12)

Pronouns

Rewrite each sentence. Use a pronoun in place of each boldfaced word or phrase.

6. In 1820, **Major Stephen Long** said that Nebraska was nearly a desert and that **Nebraska** could not support crops.   In 1820, he said that Nebraska was nearly a desert and that it could not support crops.   (13)

7. **Major Long's** opinion about **Nebraska's** suitability for growing crops was wrong.   His opinion about its suitability for growing crops was wrong.   (13)

8. In Nebraska today, **farmers and ranchers** produce huge amounts of grain and meat for **you and me** to eat.   In Nebraska today, they produce huge amounts of grain and meat for us to eat.   (13)

Verbs

Write *present, past, future,* or *present perfect* to identify the tense of each boldfaced verb.

9. The Liberty Bell **hangs** in Philadelphia. _____ present (14)

10. Patriots **rang** the bell in 1776 to celebrate independence. _____ past (15)

11. The bell **has had** a crack in it since 1835. _____ present perfect (16)

12. Abolitionists **gave** the Liberty Bell its name in the 1830s. _____ past (15)

13. My family **will visit** Philadelphia this summer. _____ future (15)

Adjectives and Adverbs

Circle the boldfaced words that are adjectives. Underline the boldfaced words that are adverbs.

14. In (the) early 1800s, the Natchez Trace was a (dangerous), (rugged) trail between Natchez, Mississippi, and Nashville, Tennessee. (17)

15. Boats floated <u>swiftly</u> down the Mississippi River with goods from the (fertile) Ohio Valley. (17, 18)

16. The river currents flowed too <u>violently</u> for the boatmen to row upriver <u>safely</u>. (18)

17. They <u>wearily</u> rode the (long) way home on horseback along the Natchez Trace. (17, 18)

Prepositions

Underline each prepositional phrase. Circle the preposition. Draw a box around its object.

18. Nellie Bly was a famous reporter (in) the late 1800s. (19)

19. She exposed bad conditions (in) mental hospitals and reported mistreatment (of) prisoners. (19)

20. She wrote (about) these cruelties (in) her articles. (19)

Conjunctions

Circle each coordinating conjunction. Underline each subordinating conjunction.

21. <u>When</u> immigrants arrived in America in the 1800s, they went through an approval process. (20)

22. <u>If</u> they were declared healthy, they could settle in America. (20)

23. Some immigrants were sick, (and) they were sent back home. (20)

24. Europeans were examined at Ellis Island, (but) Asians were examined at Angel Island. (20)

Name _____

Looking Back

School 🏠 Home Connection

In Unit 2 of *G.U.M.* students are learning about the different parts of speech, such as nouns, verbs, adjectives, and adverbs. The activities on this page give extra practice with some of the concepts the students are learning. You can reinforce the information your child is learning in school by choosing one or more activities to complete with him or her at home.

Survey Says... (Personal and Possessive Pronouns)

Help your child conduct a survey. Together, list the names of family members on a sheet of paper. (Include friends and neighbors if you like.) Have your child ask the people individually whether they think the national anthem should be changed from "The Star-Spangled Banner" to "America the Beautiful" and why they think as they do. Have your child record each person's answer. Then have your child report the results to you, using personal and possessive pronouns in complete sentences. (Personal pronouns include *he, she, her, him, it, you, I, me, we, us, they,* and *them.* Possessive pronouns include *his, her, our, their, your, its,* and *my.*)

Example   **My** uncle thinks "America the Beautiful" should be the national anthem. **He** thinks **it** is easier to sing than "The Star-Spangled Banner."

Word Search (Adverbs)

Work with your child to find at least fourteen adverbs in the puzzle below. (Adverbs tell *how, when, where,* and *how much* and often describe actions. Many adverbs end in *-ly,* but some do not. *Slowly, quickly, often, not,* and *never* are adverbs.)

B	F	U	L	G	E	N	E	R	O	U	S	L	Y
E	D	T	R	N	O	U	L	Y	C	P	Q	Q	D
S	S	M	K	O	N	L	Y	U	C	B	C	S	A
P	S	M	O	O	T	H	L	Y	A	P	U	L	N
E	F	F	O	R	T	L	E	S	S	L	Y	O	G
C	X	G	U	Z	L	A	Z	C	I	F	R	W	E
I	O	F	T	E	N	R	X	N	O	T	M	L	R
A	W	S	S	R	A	H	B	W	N	A	O	Y	O
L	M	N	I	H	V	A	L	W	A	Y	S	T	U
L	T	X	D	N	E	V	E	R	L	D	V	R	S
Y	R	A	E	N	I	T	K	U	L	W	S	C	L
L	Y	P	K	W	E	L	L	J	Y	M	O	L	Y

Now invite your child to use each adverb from the puzzle in a sentence.

Example   The whale swam **effortlessly** through the water.

Looking Back

On the Move (The Present Tense)

Look through old magazines with your child to find pictures of people transporting goods by rail, truck, car, or boat. Ask your child to cut out at least three pictures and paste them on a large piece of paper. Then take turns asking and answering questions about each picture. Use present tense verbs in your questions and answers.

Example | How do people **transport** lumber?
A truck **carries** logs down the highway.

Mystery Guest (The Present Perfect Tense)

Ask your child to think of a member of your family, or a close friend you both know. Invite your child to write five clue sentences in the present perfect tense to help you guess the mystery person. (The present perfect tense describes events that first happened in the past and are still happening. The helping verb *has* or *have* is used in this tense.) Ask your child to reveal one clue at a time until you correctly name the mystery person. Then switch roles.

Example | The person **has lived** in Wichita for fifty years.
The person **has visited** New York City many times.

Our Hero (Coordinating and Subordinating Conjunctions)

Work with your child to research an admirable American such as Frederick Douglass, Mother Jones, a past president, or someone else. Have your child write a few short sentences about the person. Work together to see how many pairs of sentences you can combine. Use coordinating conjunctions (*and, but, or*) or subordinating conjunctions (*since, if, because, when, although*).

Example | George Washington Carver was a scientist. He was an artist. He was an inventor.
George Washington Carver was a scientist, an artist, **and** an inventor.

Example | He is responsible for many inventions. He is known for his work with peanuts.
Although he is responsible for many inventions, he is best known for his work with peanuts.

Silly Sentences (Plural and Possessive Nouns)

Give each player two index cards. Invite each player to write two nouns. (A noun names a person, place, thing, or idea.) One noun should be singular (*astronaut*) and one should be plural (*pancakes*). Put all the cards into one pile. Form teams of two people and take turns selecting two cards from the pile. Each team has one minute to come up with a sentence that includes both nouns and uses one noun as a possessive. (Possessive nouns, such as *girl's* or *women's,* show ownership.) Encourage the teams to make their sentences as silly as possible. Write all of the sentences on a piece of paper.

Example | The **crocodile's shoes** were red.

Name _____

Looking Back

"Who is your favorite Olympic athlete?" Don asked Angela.

"**They're** all great athletes. **Their** stamina is phenomenal."

"My favorite is Billy Mills, who won the 10,000 meter at the Tokyo Olympic games in 1964," said Don. "I wish I could have been **there**!"

Which boldfaced word means "belonging to them"? _____**their**_____

Which boldfaced word refers to a place? _____**there**_____

Which boldfaced word is a contraction of the words *they* and *are*?
_____**they're**_____

The words **their, there,** and **they're** sound alike, but have different spellings and meanings. *Their* is a possessive pronoun meaning "belonging to them." *There* is an adverb that usually means "in that place." *They're* is the contraction made from the words *they are*.

See Handbook Section 28

Part 1

Circle the word in parentheses that correctly completes each sentence.

1. "American spectators never thought (**their**/there/they're) countrymate could win," said Don.

2. "No American had ever won the 10,000 meter Olympic race before. (Their/**There**/They're) was an American silver medalist once, but that was back in 1912."

3. "The spectators must have been astounded," said Angela.

   "Who were (**their**/there/they're) favorites before the race?"

4. "(Their/There/**They're**) not so interesting to me," Don replied,

   "because those other runners had already won international medals."

5. "Here's how it happened," Don said, getting into the moment.

   "It's halfway through the race, and a few runners are ahead of

   the pack. (Their/There/**They're**) chasing Ron Clarke, the leader."

The movie *Running Brave* tells the story of Billy Mills.

6. "As they enter the last few laps, Mohammed Gammoudi pulls ahead. Clarke,

   then Mills, are right (their/**there**/they're) behind him. Then Mills begins losing ground."

7. "At the last minute, Mills sprints past both Clarke and Gammoudi to cross the finish line!

   People cannot believe (**their**/there/they're) eyes!"

Part 2

Imagine that you are an announcer describing a race. Write three sentences. Use *their* in one, *there* in another, and *they're* in the third.

8. __Answers will vary._____

_____

9. _____

_____

10. _____

_____

Part 3

Write *their, there,* or *they're* in each blank. When you have completed the clues, solve the riddle. (11–19)

_____They're_____ made of valuable material, but _____they're_____

worth more than _____their_____ weight in gold.

_____There_____ are a limited number of them in the world.

They cannot be bought. In fact, _____they're_____ given away.

Every two years _____there_____ is a chance to get one.

_____Their_____ owners hang them around _____their_____ necks

or on _____their_____ walls.

What are they?

They're __O__ __L__ __Y__ __M__ __P__ __I__ __C__ __M__ __E__ __D__ __A__ __L__ __S__.

Name _____

Unforgettable Folks

Read and Discover

It's hard to remain at the top in table tennis. Jan-Ove Waldner has proven himself one of **its** most consistent performers over the past twenty years.

Which boldfaced word means "belonging to something"? ___**its**___
Which is a contraction made from the words *it* and *is*? ___**It's**___

The words **its** and **it's** sound the same, but they have different spellings and meanings. *Its* is a possessive pronoun that means "belonging to it." *It's* is the contraction made from *it is* or *it has*.

See Handbook Section 28

Part 1
Underline the word in parentheses that correctly completes each sentence.

1. To be successful in table tennis, (<u>it's</u>/its) helpful to begin playing at a young age.

2. By the time Jan-Ove Waldner was nine, table tennis had worked (it's/<u>its</u>) charms on him.

3. Jan-Ove studied table tennis in China, where (<u>it's</u>/its) a very popular sport.

4. He began winning championships as a teenager, and continued to win in his 20s and 30s; eventually the world of table tennis honored Jan-Ove as one of (it's/<u>its</u>) greatest champions.

5. Some say that athletic success comes from natural talent, and some say (<u>it's</u>/its) due to practice and desire.

6. Waldner says that to excel at a sport, you must practice (<u>its</u>/it's) skills.

7. He tells table tennis players to work on hitting the ball on (<u>its</u>/it's) way up.

8. He says also to practice hitting the ball at the apex of (<u>its</u>/it's) flight.

9. (Its/<u>It's</u>) important to practice hitting downward-moving balls, too, in his opinion.

10. He says that (its/<u>it's</u>) particularly important to stay relaxed while competing.

Jan-Ove Waldner won two Olympic medals, one silver and one gold.

Unforgettable Folks

Part 2

Write *its* or *it's* to complete each sentence.

11. When table tennis was first invented, _____its_____ greatest appeal was that it could be played indoors.

12. Now _____it's_____ one of the world's most popular sports, with more than 40 million competitive players worldwide.

13. In 1988 table tennis was awarded _____its_____ status as a Summer Olympic sport.

14. Athleticism is a necessity for elite players, but _____it's_____ not a requirement for casual players.

15. Children, older people, and disabled people can all play table tennis. _____It's_____ recognized as an official sport of the Paralympics.

Part 3

Write *its* or *it's* in each blank. Remember to capitalize a word if it begins a sentence. Then use the finished clues to solve the riddle. (16–24)

_____It's_____ an important part of the game, but _____it's_____ not a player.

_____Its_____ job is at the table, but _____it's_____ not an athlete.

_____It's_____ at every game, but _____it's_____ not the property of either player.

_____It's_____ made of celluloid, the first plastic material.

_____It's_____ shaped like an eyeball and _____it's_____ just a little bigger than one.

What is it?

It's a table tennis __B__ __A__ __L__ __L__!

Name _____

Unforgettable Folks

Read and Discover

"Who is **your** favorite American figure skater?" Robin asked Simone. "**You're** looking at a poster of her," said Simone, pointing to a huge photo of Michelle Kwan.

Which boldfaced word means "belonging to you"? _____**your**_____

Which boldfaced word is a short form of *you are*? _____**You're**_____

The words **your** and **you're** sound the same, but they have different spellings and meanings. *Your* is a possessive pronoun. It means "belonging to you." *You're* is the contraction of the pronoun *you* and the verb *are*.

See Handbook Section 28

Part 1

Underline the word in parentheses that correctly completes each sentence.

1. "I hear that (your/<u>you're</u>) an elegant skater just like Michelle Kwan," Robin said to Simone.

2. "I will never be as elegant as she is, but (your/<u>you're</u>) kind to say that," said Simone.

3. Robin asked, "If (your/<u>you're</u>) going to be here awhile, would you mind watching my routine?"

4. Simone asked, "Do they have (<u>your</u>/you're) music cued up?"

5. Robin nodded and said, "I think (your/<u>you're</u>) going to like it."

6. When Robin finished skating, Simone said, "(<u>Your</u>/You're) form has definitely improved, and the music is great."

7. "(<u>Your</u>/You're) friend Lili says you love Michelle Kwan's autobiography," Robin said.

8. "Oh, (your/<u>you're</u>) talking about *Michelle Kwan: Heart of a Champion*," Simone answered.

9. She continued, "I have a copy signed by Michelle. (Your/<u>You're</u>) welcome to borrow it."

10. "I couldn't take (<u>your</u>/you're) copy; I'll borrow one from the library," Robin replied.

Michelle Kwan was a five-time World Figure Skating champion.

Unforgettable Folks

Part 2 Possible answers appear below. Accept all reasonable responses.

Imagine you are ice skating, and someone asks you these questions. Write an answer to each one. Use *your* or *you're* in each answer.

11. Is my coach here yet? _Yes, your coach is here._

12. Am I getting in the way? _No, you're not getting in the way._

13. Did you find my coat in the dressing area? _Yes, I found your coat in the dressing area._

14. Am I starting my jump on the correct foot? _No, you're starting your jump on the wrong foot._

15. Am I the greatest skater you've ever seen? _Yes, you're the greatest skater I've ever seen._

Part 3

Imagine you are the coach of a skater or another athlete who is about to compete. What can you say that will help him or her stay calm and perform well? What things should he or she remember? Write a pep talk you could give. Use *your* and *you're*.

Answers will vary.

Name _____

Unforgettable Folks

Read and Discover

Cat Osterman is ~~like~~ 6 feet 2 inches tall, and that's, ~~you know,~~ very tall! Cat is a **great** softball player.

Look at the boldfaced words above. Cross out the boldfaced words that interrupt the flow of communication.

Some people develop the habit of using **like** or **you know** in places where they don't belong. This habit is annoying to most listeners and readers, and it certainly does not help communicate ideas clearly. Unless you are using *like* or *you know* as a meaningful part of a sentence, do not say or write these expressions. **Remember to use this information when you speak, too.**

See Handbook Section 27

Part 1

Cross out *like* or *you know* when they are used incorrectly. Write *C* after each correct sentence.

1. Cat Osterman played softball for ~~like~~ only a year when she was in elementary school. ___

2. By fifth grade, she realized she did like softball and has played it ever since. _C_

3. Osterman is, ~~you know,~~ a star pitcher. ___

4. Perhaps you know that Osterman has very large hands. _C_

5. Her large hands allow her to ~~like~~ wrap her fingers all the way around a softball. ___

6. By holding the ball that way, ~~you know,~~ she can make it spin more than other pitchers. ___

7. In 2004 Osterman played for the U.S. Olympic softball team and performed like a true champion. _C_

8. You know that the team won gold that year, but did you know that it also broke 18 Olympic records? _C_

9. Osterman has recorded more than 2,000 strikeouts, which is, ~~like,~~ amazing! ___

10. Perhaps you know that it takes dedication to play a demanding sport and excel in your studies, too. _C_

The Women's Sports Foundation named Cat Osterman Sportswoman of the Year in 2005.

Unforgettable Folks

65

Part 2

Each sentence below is written incorrectly. Rewrite each sentence correctly.

11. Softball is, like, very similar to baseball, but there are some important differences between the two sports. <u>**Softball is very similar to baseball, but there are some important**</u> <u>**differences between the two sports.**</u>

12. Softball began as, you know, an indoor version of baseball. <u>**Softball began as an**</u> <u>**indoor version of baseball.**</u>

13. The ball used in softball is, like, larger and heavier than a baseball. <u>**The ball used in**</u> <u>**softball is larger and heavier than a baseball.**</u>

14. Softball pitchers, you know, throw underhand. <u>**Softball pitchers throw underhand.**</u>

Part 3

Help the announcer in the commercial below. He says *like* and *you know* in almost every sentence! Cross out these words when they are used incorrectly. Then write a commercial for an imaginary product of your own. Use *like* and *you know* correctly.

ANNOUNCER: Goofy Gumdrops make, ~~like,~~ a great half-time snack, because they're, ~~like,~~ really sweet and chewy, ~~you know,~~ and they taste just like real fruit. You know how hungry you can get watching your favorite sport on TV? Goofy Gumdrops are, ~~you know,~~ ~~like,~~ just the thing.

<u>**Answers will vary.**</u>

_____

_____

_____

_____

_____

Name _____

Unforgettable Folks

Baseball fans love to argue about whether this star or that star is **better**, and who was the (**best**) player ever at a position. They also like to debate which of two bad teams is **worse** and which manager is the (**worst**) of all.

Underline the boldfaced words that compare two people or things. Circle the boldfaced words that compare more than two people or things.

The words **good** and **bad** change form when they're used to compare. Use **better** and **worse** when you compare two people or things. Use **best** and **worst** when you compare three or more people or things. Avoid *gooder, goodest, bestest, more better, worser, worstest, badder,* and *baddest.* These are all nonstandard forms. **Remember to use this information when you speak, too.**

See Handbook Section 23

Part 1
Underline the form of *good* or *bad* that correctly completes each sentence.

1. Many people consider Ichiro Suzuki to be the (better/<u>best</u>) hitter playing today.

2. No hitter has ever had a (<u>better</u>/gooder) year than Ichiro had in 2004.

3. His total of 262 hits that year is the (bestest/<u>best</u>) single-year performance in major league history.

4. Ichiro also has the (<u>best</u>/most best) five-year hit total ever.

5. Unfortunately, his team, the Seattle Mariners, had the (worse/<u>worst</u>) record in its division in two of those years.

6. Many players feel it's (<u>worse</u>/worst) to be an all-star on a losing team than to be a decent player on a championship team.

7. Ichiro would have a (<u>worse</u>/worst) batting average than he does if he did not have blazing speed.

8. His time from home plate to first base is (gooder/<u>better</u>) than most players'.

9. Ichiro uses bats of Japanese blue tamo wood, which he believes are (<u>better</u>/more better) than bats made of maple or hickory.

Ichiro Suzuki was the first non-pitcher from Japan to play major league baseball in the United States.

Unforgettable Folks

Part 2

Write a form of *good* or *bad* from the word bank to complete each sentence.

best	better	worst	worse

10. The owner of the Brooklyn Dodgers, Branch Rickey, wanted only the

    _____**best**_____ players of all on his team.

11. He decided that baseball would be a much _____**better**_____ game with African

    American players than without them.

12. He signed Jackie Robinson to a contract because he thought Robinson was the

    _____**best**_____ person of all for the tough job of integrating the big leagues.

13. Robinson knew that being the first African American major league player would be hard,

    but his first year on the team was _____**worse**_____ than he had expected.

14. Prejudiced fans called Robinson the _____**worst**_____ names you could imagine.

15. Robinson had _____**better**_____ self-control than many other players, and he

    never let his anger show.

16. Robinson did the _____**best**_____ job he could despite the prejudice he faced.

17. Jackie Robinson was one of the very _____**best**_____ baseball players of his time,

    and he was certainly one of the bravest.

Part 3

Compare baseball with another sport. Tell which one you like better and why. Use the words
best, worst, better, and *worse*.

Answers will vary.

_____

_____

_____

Name _____

Unforgettable Folks

a. The Super Bowl, **which** is the championship game of the National Football League, has been played annually since 1967.

b. A quarterback **who** leads a team to a Super Bowl victory becomes famous for life.

c. Winning two Super Bowl championships is a feat **that** few quarterbacks have accomplished.

In which sentence does the boldfaced pronoun refer to a person? _b._

Use **who** to refer to people. Use **which** to refer to things. You may use **that** to refer either to people or to things. Use *that* instead of *which* to begin a clause that is necessary to the meaning of the sentence.
📢 **Remember to use this information when you speak, too.**

See Handbook Section 27

Part 1

Underline the word in parentheses that correctly completes each sentence.

1. Quarterback is a position (who/<u>that</u>) demands leadership as well as athletic talent.

2. Jim Plunkett, (<u>who</u>/which) became a great quarterback, possesses both qualities.

3. Plunkett grew up in a household (who/<u>that</u>) was a bit unusual: both his mother and his father were blind.

4. His parents were people (<u>who</u>/which) believed that education should be a young person's top priority.

5. They told Jim (<u>that</u>/which) he had to study hard and do well if he wanted to play sports.

6. A high school athlete (<u>who</u>/which) competes in football, basketball, baseball, track, and wrestling is a rarity.

7. Jim won a football scholarship to Stanford University, (who/<u>which</u>) is an outstanding academic school.

8. In his senior year, Jim won the Heisman Trophy, the award (who/<u>that</u>) is given to the top college football player each year.

Jim Plunkett led the Oakland Raiders to victory in Super Bowl XV.

Part 2

Write *who, which,* or *that* to complete each sentence correctly.

9. The success ___**that**___ Jim enjoyed in college was repeated in the pros during his

first five years as the quarterback of the New England Patriots.

10. The team never reached the Super Bowl, though, ___**which**___ disappointed Jim.

11. In 1978 Jim Plunkett, ___**who**___ had been let go by his second team, the San

Francisco 49ers, was signed by the Oakland Raiders.

12. Plunkett led the Raiders to the 1981 Super Bowl, ___**which**___ they won by a score of

27–10 over the Philadelphia Eagles.

13. Three years later Plunkett, ___**who**___ stepped back into the starting role in mid-year,

led the Raiders to another Super Bowl win!

Part 3

Complete the clues correctly by writing *who, which,* or *that.* Then answer the riddle. (14–18)

We are the targets ___**that**___ football kickers aim for.

A kick ___**that**___ sails through us adds to the score.

A kicker ___**who**___ sends balls through our uprights is a player who brings joy to

the team's fans!

A conversion, ___**which**___ is worth one point, caps a touchdown.

But we prefer field goals, ___**which**___ are always worth three points!

We are the __G__ __O__ __A__ __L__ __P__ __O__ __S__ __T__ __S__.

Name _____

Unforgettable Folks

a. Mario Lemieux was **real** young when he began to play hockey.

b. He played on a **very** small rink behind the neighborhood church.

c. Everyone believed that Mario had **real** talent.

In which sentence is the boldfaced word used incorrectly? __a.__

Real is an adjective and must describe a noun or a pronoun. It means "actual." **Very** is an adverb. It means "extremely." Do not use *real* in place of *very*. ◀ **Remember to use this information when you speak, too.**

See Handbook Section 27

Part 1

Draw *X* through each boldfaced word that is used incorrectly. Write *C* next to each sentence that uses the boldfaced word correctly.

1. In his **very** first season in the National Hockey League, Lemieux was chosen as the most valuable player in the All-Star Game. __C__

2. He became a **real** hero throughout Canada in 1987 when he scored the winning goal in Canada's victory over the Soviet Union in an international championship series. __C__

3. In the 1989–90 NHL season, Lemieux suffered a ~~real~~ painful back injury. ____

4. The next season, Lemieux led his team, the Pittsburgh Penguins, to their first league championship, symbolized by the ~~real~~ famous Stanley Cup. ____

5. In 1992, the Penguins again won the Stanley Cup, a **real** feat. __C__

6. Then Lemieux faced a **real** challenge: he was diagnosed with Hodgkin's disease. __C__

7. He missed a month of the 1992–93 season, but he played ~~real~~ well. ____

8. Later Lemieux missed almost two full seasons due to ~~real~~ serious health problems. ____

9. He surprised almost everyone by having one of his **very** best seasons when he returned. __C__

Mario Lemieux was one of the greatest hockey scorers of all time.

Unforgettable Folks

Part 2 Answers will vary.

Write a sentence about each topic below. Use *very* or *real* in each sentence you write.

10. your favorite sport _____

11. why you like that sport _____

_____

12. your favorite athlete _____

13. why you like that player _____

_____

14. the most exciting sporting event you have seen _____

_____

15. another topic that interests you _____

_____

Part 3

Complete this poem by writing *very* or *real* in each blank. Then answer the riddle. (16–22)

I'm _____very_____ small and I'm _____very_____ fast. If you close your eyes I'll shoot

right past!

I live on the ice, where it's _____very_____ cold. Or at least that's what I've been told.

I myself can't feel at all. I'm not a _____real_____ player—I'm more like a ball.

Although I don't bounce, I'm perfectly round. I'm _____very_____ important, though I stay on the ground.

I'm not _____very_____ modest, but why should I be? I am hockey's _____real_____ MVP!

What am I? I'm a H   O   C   K   E   Y   P   U   C   K !

Name _____

Unforgettable Folks

Tracy **set** her math book on the table. She **sat** down on the sofa and began watching a DVD of Olympic champion gymnast Carly Patterson.

Which boldfaced verb means "placed something somewhere"? ____set____

Which means "moved into a seat"? ____sat____

Set and **sit** are different verbs. *Set* takes a direct object and *sit* does not. If you're about to use *set,* ask yourself, *"Set* what?" If you can't answer that question, use *sit*. Also, remember that you can't *sit* anything down— you must *set* it down. The past tense form of *sit* is *sat. Set* is spelled the same in the present and past tenses. **Remember to use this information when you speak, too.**

See Handbook Section 27

Part 1

Underline the word in parentheses that correctly completes each sentence.

1. Carly (sat/<u>set</u>) her feet firmly on the balance beam.

2. Carly's fans in the bleachers (<u>sat</u>/set) silently and watched.

3. Her coach (sat/<u>set</u>) the clipboard on a chair and stared intently.

4. After she (sat/<u>set</u>) her hands exactly right, Carly slowly

   raised her body into a perfect handstand.

5. In the bleachers, Carly's fans couldn't (<u>sit</u>/set) still any longer.

6. They held their breath as Carly lowered her legs and (sat/<u>set</u>)

   her feet back on the balance beam.

7. Throughout Carly's routine, her coach (<u>sat</u>/set) on the

   sidelines, amazed by her calmness under pressure.

Carly Patterson says the balance beam is her favorite event.

8. Carly (sat/<u>set</u>) her feet perfectly for her final move.

9. After her signature beam dismount, the young athlete (<u>sat</u>/set) down.

10. Carly (<u>sat</u>/set) quietly until the judges scored her performance.

11. In local, regional, and international meets, Carly Patterson has (sat/<u>set</u>) a new standard

    for gymnastic excellence in the United States.

Part 2   Possible answers appear below. Accept all reasonable responses.

Rewrite each sentence using a form of *set* or *sit* correctly. There is more than one way to rewrite each sentence.

12. The members of the audience at the 2004 Summer Olympics took their seats.

    The members of the audience at the 2004 Summer Olympics sat down.

13. Gymnastic equipment had been carefully arranged in the arena. **Gymnastic equipment**

    had been carefully set up in the arena.

14. Gymnasts from all over the world were in chairs on the sidelines. **Gymnasts from all**

    over the world sat in chairs on the sidelines.

15. Sixteen-year-old Carly Patterson was with the U.S. women's gymnastics team.

    Sixteen-year-old Carly Patterson sat with the U.S. women's gymnastics team.

16. She always placed her feet perfectly in position on the balance beam. **She always set**

    her feet perfectly on the balance beam.

17. By the end of the competition, Carly Patterson had a gold medal in the Women's Individual

    All-Around to deposit in her trophy case. **By the end of the competition, Carly Patterson**

    had a gold medal in the Women's Individual All-Around to set in her trophy case.

    _____

Part 3   Answers will vary.

List three things you might set on a table. Then write three places you might sit down.

Things I Might *Set* Down   Places Where I Might *Sit* Down

_____   _____

_____   _____

_____   _____

Name _____

Unforgettable Folks

Maritza Correia **growed** up near the ocean, so she (**knew**) how to stay safe at the beach.

Circle the boldfaced verb that is correct. Write the correct form of the other boldfaced word. _____grew_____

Know and **grow** are **irregular verbs**. You cannot make the past tense of these verbs by adding *-ed*. These verbs have different forms.

📣 **Remember to use this information when you speak, too.**

Present	Past	With *have, has,* or *had*
know(s)	knew	known
grow(s)	grew	grown

See Handbook Section 17

Part 1
Underline the verb in parentheses that correctly completes each sentence.

1. When Maritza Correia was 6, doctors discovered that her spine had (grew/<u>grown</u>) curved.

2. If her parents had (knew/<u>known</u>) about her condition earlier, they probably

   would have acted sooner to correct it.

3. Correia's doctor (<u>knew</u>/known) that swimming could help, so Correia started to swim.

4. Her back condition improved, and she also

   (<u>grew</u>/growed) to be a strong swimmer.

5. Her skills (<u>grew</u>/grown), winning her medals at the

   World Championships in 2001, 2003, and 2004.

6. When Correia made the Olympic team in 2004,

   she (<u>knew</u>/knowed) she had made history.

7. Did you (<u>know</u>/known) that Correia was the first

   African American woman on a U.S. Olympic swim team?

8. Her reputation (<u>grew</u>/grown) when she won a silver medal at the 2004 Olympics.

9. She has swum so well that she has become (knowed/<u>known</u>) as "Relay Woman."

Maritza Correia overcame a physical challenge to become a champion swimmer.

Unforgettable Folks

Part 2 Answers will vary.
Write sentences to answer the following questions. Use a form of *know* or *grow* in each sentence.

10. When did you first know you liked the sport or hobby that is now your favorite? _____

_____

_____

11. How does someone grow more and more skilled at that sport or hobby? _____

_____

_____

12. How much have you grown in the last year? _____

_____

13. How long have you known your best friend? _____

_____

Part 3
Use the correct forms of *know* or *grow* to complete the puzzle.

Across
2. "That girl has __ to be a fine athlete," said her coach.
3. "I always __ she would," said her mother.
4. "I have always __ that I wanted to be a swimmer," said the girl.

Down
1. "I want to get better as I __ older," she added.
2. She __ more confident as she won more and more competitions.
3. "I __ you will achieve your goals," said her coach.

Crossword solution:
1 Down: G R O W
2 Across: G R O W N
2 Down: G R E W
3 Across: K N E W
3 Down: K N O W
4 Across: K N O W N

Name _____

Unforgettable Folks

Read and Discover

Learn and Teach

Lesson 30

Briana Scurry's parents **taught** her that she could succeed, but Briana **learned** for herself that success requires overcoming obstacles.

Which boldfaced word means "gained knowledge"? __learned__

Which means "gave knowledge"? __taught__

Both **learn** and **teach** are related to knowledge, so they are often confused. *Learn* means "to get knowledge" and *teach* means "to give knowledge." **Remember to use this information when you speak, too.**

Present	Past	With *have, has,* or *had*
learn(s)	learned	learned
teach(es)	taught	taught

See Handbook Section 27

Part 1

Underline the word in parentheses that correctly completes each sentence.

1. At twelve years old, Briana (<u>learned</u>/taught) that there were no girls' soccer leagues in the Minneapolis area, so she joined a boys' league.

2. The coach (learned/<u>taught</u>) Briana to be a goalkeeper because he thought that was the safest position.

3. He soon (<u>learned</u>/taught) that Briana could take care of herself; the next three years she played in the field.

4. Then Briana became goalie again because she had (<u>learned</u>/taught) that she could control the game from there.

5. Briana (<u>learned</u>/taught) a lot in high school, where she played both soccer and basketball.

6. At the University of Massachusetts, coach Jim Rudy (learned/<u>taught</u>) her the fine points of goaltending.

7. After she graduated, she (<u>learned</u>/taught) that the U.S. Women's National Team wanted her.

8. From 1994 to 1999, Scurry started 95 international matches and posted 54 shutouts; she (learned/<u>taught</u>) the world how to be a great goalie.

Briana Scurry was a member of the gold medal-winning 2004 Olympic soccer team.

Unforgettable Folks

77

Part 2 Answers will vary.

Answer each question. Use the boldfaced word in your answer.

9. What do you want to **learn** in high school? _____

_____

10. What important skill would you like to **teach** to a younger family member or friend?

_____

_____

11. What is the most important thing you have **learned** in the past year? _____

_____

_____

12. Think of a sport or hobby you like. What is the first thing a beginner should be **taught**

about this sport or hobby? _____

_____

_____

Part 3

Write a paragraph about something you learned from an important person in your life. Use *learn* and *teach* correctly.

Answers will vary. _____

_____

_____

_____

_____

_____

Name _____

Unforgettable Folks

Proofreading
Practice

Read this passage about bike tours and find the mistakes. Use the proofreading marks below to show how each mistake should be fixed.

Suggested answers appear below.
Accept all reasonable responses.

Proofreading Marks

Mark	Means	Example
℘	take away	Riders climbs France's highest peaks.
∧	add	Riders ∧climb France's highest peaks.
≡	make into a capital letter	Riders climb france's highest peaks.
/	make into a lowercase letter	Riders Climb France's highest peaks.
⊙	add a period	Riders climb France's highest peaks⊙
(sp)	fix spelling	Riders climb France's hiest peaks.

Tour de France? Sure!

Nelson wasn't a professional cyclist. He was, like, a regular cycling enthusiast who happened to be sixty-one years old. Still, Nelson had just completed six days of the Tour de France bicling route.

Just hours ahead of the real Tour de France, nelson's tour group had cycled the same steep roads the professional riders would cycle later in the day. His tour group was made up of amateur cyclists which wanted to experience the challenges of the Tour de France.

The tour guides provided the hotels, meals, transportation, and medical support. The tour members even had they're own van following them, ready with food, advice, doctors, and, you know, a comfortable place to set down and catch a breath.

Do you think you'll ever want to ride in you're own Tour de France? By joining a group like this, nearly anyone can Anyone, that is, which can cycle a grooling 50 miles or more in a day, up and down mountains that are real steep. Do you think you might be interested? Then its time to start training!

Proofreading
Checklist

You can use the list below to help you find and fix mistakes in your own writing. Write the titles of your own stories or reports on the blanks on top of the chart. Then use the questions to check your work. Make a check mark (✔) in each box after you have checked that item.

Answers will vary.

Proofreading Checklist for Unit 3

	Titles			
Have I used *your* and *you're* correctly?				
Have I used *its* and *it's* correctly?				
Have I used *their, there,* and *they're* correctly?				
Have I avoided using *like* and *you know* incorrectly?				
Have I used *very* and *real* correctly?				
Have I used *sit* and *set* correctly?				
Have I used past tense forms of irregular verbs correctly?				

Also Remember . . .

Does each sentence begin with a capital letter?				
Does each sentence end with the correct end mark?				
Have I spelled each word correctly?				
Have I used commas correctly?				

Your Own List

Use this space to write your own list of things to check in your writing.

Name _____

Unforgettable Folks

Review

(Numbers in parentheses identify related lessons.)

Usage

Underline the word in parentheses that correctly completes each sentence.

1. The exhausted surfers stuck (their/there/they're) surfboards in the sand. **(21)**

2. Then they sat down to catch (their/there/they're) breath. **(21)**

3. "That was the (bestest/best) surfing I've done in weeks," said Alyssa. **(25)**

4. "Not I," said Gustavo. "I did (gooder/better) yesterday." **(25)**

5. "Look at that wave over (their/there/they're)!" Lani exclaimed. **(21)**

6. "(It's/Its) at least twenty feet high!" **(22)**

7. "A yacht would fit in (it's/its) curl!" she cried. **(22)**

8. "Aren't you glad (you're/your) not out there?" Gustavo asked. **(23)**

9. "Look at the lifeguards! (Their/There/They're) calling everyone in to shore," he continued. **(21)**

10. "I (knew/knowed) it was a good time to quit," said Lani. **(29)**

Write *who, which,* or *that* on the line to complete each sentence correctly.

11. Edson Arantes do Nascimento may be the greatest soccer player _____who____ **(26)**

    has ever lived.

12. You may be more familiar with this star's nickname, ____which___ **(26)** is Pelé.

13. It was Pelé's exploits as a member of the Brazilian national team ____that___ **(26)**

    made him famous.

14. Soccer, ____which___ **(26)** is popular throughout the world, is especially popular

    in Brazil.

Underline the word in parentheses that correctly completes each sentence.

15. If you want to learn to ski well, (you're/your) going to have to train hard. **(23)**

16. First you must find a coach who will (learn/teach) you the right techniques. **(30)**

17. It is also (real/very) important to eat a healthy diet. **(27)**

18. Your training schedule won't leave you much time to (set/sit) on the sofa watching TV. **(28)**

19. When your coach sees that you have (growed/grown) stronger and have developed good technique, you'll be allowed to compete in more challenging events. **(29)**

20. Slalom racing is a (real/very) difficult event. **(27)**

21. Slalom skiers are (know/known) for their strength, agility, and speed. **(29)**

22. Bowling is a (very/real) popular sport. **(27)**

23. Since bowlers spend much of their time (setting/sitting) down and waiting for their turns, this sport usually does not provide aerobic exercise. **(28)**

24. My uncle wants to (learn/teach) me how to deliver a bowling ball correctly. **(30)**

25. Uncle Mike says, "Hold the ball slightly above (your/you're) waist." **(23)**

26. He (taught/learned) me to keep my eyes on the pins when I roll the ball. **(30)**

Write *C* next to each sentence that is written correctly and *I* next to each incorrect sentence. Cross out the error in each incorrect sentence.

27. Did you know that *duckpins, candlepins, boccie,* and *ninepins* are all names for bowling games? __C__ **(24)**

28. Lawn bowling is, ~~like,~~ popular in Canada and England. __I__ **(24)**

29. In the United States more people compete, ~~you know,~~ in bowling than in any other sport. __I__ **(24)**

30. Bowling leagues are, ~~like,~~ very popular in communities across America. __I__ **(24)**

Name _____

School 🏠 Home Connection

In Unit 3 of *G.U.M.* students are learning how to use words that are often confused in writing, such as *its* and *it's*. The activities on these pages give extra practice with some of the concepts they are learning. You can help reinforce this information by choosing one or more activities to complete with your child at home.

Crossword Puzzle (Irregular Verbs: *Know* and *Grow*)

Work with your child to complete this crossword puzzle. Each missing word is a form of the word *know* or *grow*.

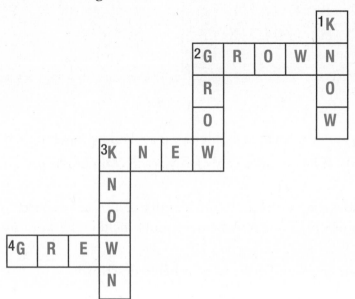

Across

2. Eli has ___ stronger by doing exercises.

3. Even before yesterday's victory, I ___ we'd win.

4. I ___ more and more excited each time we scored.

Down

1. I ___ it's not easy to become a professional soccer player.

2. When I ___ up, I want to keep playing soccer on weekends.

3. I've ___ for a long time that soccer is my favorite sport.

They're Over There with Their Sister (*Their, There, They're*)

With your child, write some sentences that describe family photos. Use the words *their, there,* and *they're* in your sentences. Have your child make sure each of these words is used correctly.

Example

This photo shows Rosie and Eileen. **They're** my aunts.
In this photo, our family is posing with the Ortiz family and **their** dog.

Grab Bag (*Its* and *It's*; *Their, There, They're*; *Your* and *You're*)

You can play this game with several family members. Write these words on slips of paper: *its, it's, their, there, they're, your,* and *you're*. Put the slips into a paper sack. Take turns drawing a word and using it in a sentence. Ask listeners to decide which spelling of each word is being used in the sentence and how they know.

Word Search (Comparing with *Good* or *Bad*; *That, Which, Who*; *Real* and *Very*; *Set* and *Sit*)

There are 13 words hidden in the puzzle. Work with your child to find them all. Then ask your child to use each word in a sentence.

```
V  W  H  O  S  S  R  V  W
X  O  K  B  E  T  T  E  R
N  R  P  T  T  Q  C  R  P
R  S  Q  G  R  R  W  Y  S
G  E  W  O  R  S  T  Z  Q
K  M  Q  O  Z  K  R  P  J
F  B  A  D  Q  B  E  S  T
A  L  S  K  L  K  A  K  H
W  H  I  C  H  G  L  X  A
P  S  T  X  M  N  Z  J  T
```

Guessing Game (*Its* and *It's*)

Work with your child to create a guessing game your whole family can play. Follow these steps:

1. Cut thick paper into six 3" x 5" cards. (Or use index cards.) Give each team of players two cards.

2. On each card, team members should write four clues to the identity of a piece of sports equipment or one part of a sports uniform. Some of the clues should include the word *its* or *it's*.

3. Ask teams to exchange cards, read the clues, and guess what is being described.

> 1. It's made of wood or metal.
> 2. It's long and thin.
> 3. Its surface is smooth.
> 4. It's a little thicker at one end than it is at the other.
>
> **(a baseball bat)**

You might enjoy making up more categories, such as *animals*, *birds*, or *food*.

Name _____

84   Unforgettable Folks

Read and Discover

Auto racing fans admire the sleek cars before the race. **They** watch **them** closely during the warm-up period.

Which boldfaced word replaces the phrase *auto racing fans*? __They__

Which boldfaced word replaces the phrase *the sleek cars*? __them__

Which boldfaced word is the subject of the sentence? __They__

A pronoun can be the subject or the object in a sentence. **Subject pronouns** include *I, he, she, we,* and *they*. **Object pronouns** can be used after an action verb or a preposition. Object pronouns include *me, him, her, us,* and *them*. The pronouns *it* and *you* can be either subjects or objects. **Remember to use this information when you speak, too.**

See Handbook | Section 16

Part 1

Circle each boldfaced word that is a subject pronoun. Underline each boldfaced word that is an object pronoun.

1. My friends and (I) watch the Indy 500 every year on TV.

2. The speed, the noise, and the excitement thrill <u>us</u>.

3. (You) might know that only three drivers have four Indy victories to their credit.

4. Can (you) name <u>them</u>?

5. (They) are A.J. Foyt, Jr., Al Unser, Sr., and Rick Mears.

6. (I) have an autographed photo of Al Unser and

   his brother Bobby, another Indy winner.

7. My aunt Dinah gave <u>it</u> to <u>me</u>.

Racecars are custom built for stability and speed.

8. (I) keep <u>it</u> next to a photograph of Janet Guthrie.

9. Many fans remember <u>her,</u> because (she) was the first woman to race at Indy.

10. Today more women are competing at Indy, and (they) are well prepared.

11. Indy competitor Sarah Fisher started racing a quarter-midget car when (she) was five.

Grab Bag

Part 2

Rewrite each sentence. Replace each boldfaced phrase with a pronoun.

12. **Janet Guthrie** had to quit **the 1977 race** after 27 laps because of mechanical problems.

    She had to quit it after 27 laps because of mechanical problems.

13. Sometimes **a driver's crew** can solve **mechanical problems** during a race.

    Sometimes they can solve them during a race.

14. **The crew** must often change **two or more tires** in just a few seconds. They must often

    change them in just a few seconds.

15. **The driver** watches for **colored flag signals.** He/She watches for them.

16. **Safety** must be strictly maintained to prevent **accidents.** It must be strictly maintained

    to prevent them.

Part 3

Imagine that you were at an Indy 500 car race. Write two or three sentences about what you saw, heard, and felt at the racetrack. Use subject and object pronouns in your sentences.

Answers will vary.

Name _____

Grab Bag

Read and Discover

a. Tyrin and me went to the drag races last weekend.
b. My cousin Phil introduced Tyrin and me to his racing partner, Betty.

If you remove "Tyrin and" from each sentence, which sentence sounds correct? **b.**

Use the pronouns *I, we, he, she,* and *they* as **subjects** in sentences. Use the pronouns *me, us, him, her,* and *them* as **objects** in sentences.
📢 **Remember to use this information when you speak, too.**

See Handbook Sections 16 and 27

Part 1

Circle the correct pronoun in each pair. Write *S* if you chose a subject pronoun and *O* if you chose an object pronoun.

1. Betty and (he/him) take turns driving their dragster. __S__

2. They showed Tyrin and (I/me) a picture of a dragster with an open parachute behind it. __O__

3. Tyrin asked (they/them) why the parachute was there. __O__

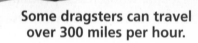

Some dragsters can travel over 300 miles per hour.

4. (She/Her) and Phil explained that parachutes help the dragsters stop after they cross the finish line. __S__

5. Betty took Tyrin and (I/me) to the drag strip. __O__

6. Phil took a picture of (she/her) and me standing in front of the dragster. __O__

7. Then Tyrin and I watched Phil and (her/she) on their practice runs. __O__

8. Phil told Tyrin and (I/me) that race car drivers need great concentration. __O__

9. Now Tyrin and (I/me) want to learn how to drive a dragster. __S__

10. (He/Him) and I will begin by reading more about drag racing. __S__

11. Phil gave Tyrin and (I/me) a book about drag racing. __O__

12. Tyrin and (I/me) can't wait to read it. __S__

Grab Bag

87

Part 2

Rewrite the sentences. Substitute a pronoun for each boldfaced noun.

13. **Betty** and **Phil** drive a "funny car." <u>She and he drive a "funny car."</u>

_____

14. A mechanic helped **Betty** and **Phil** build the car and perfect its engine. <u>A mechanic</u> <u>helped her and him build the car and perfect its engine.</u>

15. **Tyrin** and **Lorene** laughed when they heard the name of the car, <u>Betty, Set, Go!</u> <u>He and</u> <u>she laughed when they heard the name of the car, <u>Betty, Set, Go!</u></u>

16. Then Phil told **Lorene** and **Tyrin** that the car goes 200 miles per hour! <u>Then Phil told</u> <u>her and him that the car goes 200 miles per hour!</u>

17. Tyrin told **Phil** and **Betty** he wouldn't laugh anymore. <u>Tyrin told him and her he</u> <u>wouldn't laugh anymore.</u>

Part 3

Decide whom each pronoun refers to. (The answers appear in the sentences above.) Use the names to complete the puzzle.

Across
2. **She** drives a "funny car."
3. Tyrin told **him** he wouldn't laugh anymore.
5. Phil told **him** that the car goes 200 miles per hour.
6. **She** laughed at the name of the car.

Down
1. **He** helped Betty and Phil improve the car.
4. **He** laughed at the name of the car.

Name _____

_____ Me and Vera went to the demolition derby.

___X___ Vera's dad drove her and me to the event.

Write *X* in front of the sentence in which the pronouns are used correctly.

I is a subject pronoun. It can be used as the subject of a sentence. **Me** is an object pronoun. It is used after an action verb or a preposition. When you talk about yourself and another person, always name the other person first. **Remember to use this information when you speak, too.**

See Handbook Sections 16 and 27

Part 1

Circle the group of words in parentheses that will complete each sentence correctly.

1. (Me and Vera/**Vera and I**) thought the beat-up cars were going to race, but we were wrong.

2. Her dad told (me and her/**her and me**) that the point of the demolition derby was to be the last car running.

3. (I and her/**She and I**) couldn't believe that people fixed up cars just to smash them up!

4. Vera pointed out to (me and her father/**her father and me**) that the cars had no windows.

5. Her father explained to (me and her/**her and me**) that the teams removed parts that could injure drivers.

6. (**Vera and I**/Me and Vera) asked what other changes had been made.

7. (She and me/**She and I**) learned that the cars did not use regular gas tanks, to reduce the risk of fire.

8. When the derby started, (**Vera and I**/me and Vera) noticed cars going backward.

9. Vera's dad told (her and I/**her and me**) that the drivers wanted to protect their engines, so they used their tail ends to ram other cars.

10. As the cars plowed across the wet dirt, they splattered (Vera and I/**Vera and me**).

11. Vera's dad laughed at (me and her/**her and me**) and said, "A demolition derby can get messy!"

Part 2

Write the name of a friend of yours here: _____ Answers will vary. _____.
Now complete each sentence by writing pronouns. One pronoun in each pair should stand for your friend's name. The other should refer to you.

12. ____He/She____ and ____I____ were looking at the cars before the demolition

    derby.

13. A mechanic asked ____him/her____ and ____me____ which car we liked best.

14. ____He/She____ and ____I____ both pointed to a zebra-striped car.

15. Both ____he/she____ and ____I____ want to drive in a demolition derby.

16. The mechanic introduced ____him/her____ and ____me____ to the driver of the

    zebra-striped car.

Part 3

Draw a picture of you and a friend doing your favorite activity. Then write three sentences about the picture. Use a subject pronoun pair or an object pronoun pair in each sentence.

17. __Answers will vary._____

    _____

    _____

18. _____

    _____

    _____

19. _____

    _____

    _____

Name _____

Grab Bag

Lesson 34

The 1908 New York-to-Paris auto race began as a test of the automobiles. **It** ended as a test of the drivers.

Circle the word that the boldfaced pronoun replaces. Draw an arrow from the pronoun to the circled word.

An **antecedent** is the word or words a pronoun refers to. The antecedent is almost always a noun. When you write a pronoun, be sure its antecedent is clear. Pronouns must also **agree** with their antecedents. An antecedent and pronoun agree when they have the same number (singular or plural) and gender (male or female).

See Handbook Section 16

Part 1

Circle the antecedent for each boldfaced pronoun.

1. Six teams left New York City on February 12. Not all of **them** would finish the race.

2. The first leg of the journey took drivers across the United States.

   It was a distance of more than 3,000 miles.

3. Before long, two French teams dropped out

   of the race. **They** had run out of money.

4. The Americans drove their automobile along the

   transcontinental train tracks. **Its** tires blew out from

   the rough ride.

The 1908 race took drivers across three continents and 22,000 miles.

5. The teams became famous. Fans greeted **them** as they

   drove across the United States.

6. In Utah the German car broke down, so the team sent **it** to Seattle on a train.

7. The Germans solved the problem but broke a race rule. **They** would pay for this later.

8. The other teams drove from San Francisco to Seattle. **They** met harsh winter conditions.

9. The sponsors could not drive across the ice to Russia as planned. They reached **it** by ship

   instead.

Grab Bag

Part 2

Write the pronoun that could replace each boldfaced word or phrase.

10. After the boat trip, the **Americans and Germans** raced across Russia. _____**They**_____ found

    it a hard country to cross.

11. The **Italians,** meanwhile, were nearly lost in a flood. It put _____**them**_____ so far behind

    that they had no hope of winning.

12. The **German team** beat the Americans to Paris, but _____**they**_____ were in for a surprise.

13. The Americans were named the winners, not the **Germans**. Breaking the race rule had

    cost _____**them**_____ the prize.

14. The **Italian team** never gave up, even though _____**they**_____ had no chance of winning.

15. About six weeks after the Americans had won, the **Italians** crossed the finish line.

    _____**They**_____ had driven around the world in 219 days.

Part 3

Circle the pronoun in each riddle. Then find the antecedent of each pronoun in the puzzle.
Use the antecedents to solve the riddles.

```
T R A I N F G
H R M U I W H
T W E O T Y S
G E R M A N S
F K I R L J T
N B C J I N I
T X A L A P R
Y X N Y N O E
R J S C S L S
```

16. The Americans blew (them) out by driving on

    railroad tracks. _____**tires**_____

17. (They) finished first but didn't win the race.

    _____**Germans**_____

18. The German car rode on (it). _____**train**_____

19. (They) were declared the winners. _____**Americans**_____

20. (They) never gave up. _____**Italians**_____

Name _____

Grab Bag

Read and Discover

Making the Subject and Verb Agree

Lesson 35

A [pack] of growling (autos) approaches the village at top speed.

Draw a box around the boldfaced noun that is the simple subject.
Circle the boldfaced noun that is the object of the preposition *of*.
Is the subject singular or plural? ___singular___
Now underline the verb.

The **subject** and its **verb must agree**. Add *s* or *es* to a regular verb in the present tense when the subject is a singular noun or *he, she,* or *it*. Do not add *s* or *es* to a regular verb in the present tense when the subject is a plural noun or *I, you, we,* or *they*. Be sure that the verb agrees with its subject and not with the object of a preposition that comes before the verb. ◀ **Remember to use this information when you speak, too.**

See Handbook | Section 17

Part 1

Circle the simple subject in each sentence. Underline the correct verb in parentheses.

1. Many (types) of racecars (<u>compete</u>/competes) in races today.

2. Most (experts) (<u>say</u>/says) that Formula One cars are the costliest to build and race.

3. (Engineers) (<u>create</u>/creates) Formula One cars using some principles of airplane design.

4. A long, tubelike (body) and (tires) without fenders (<u>make</u>/makes) these cars easy to recognize.

5. Two (pairs) of wings attached to the car's body (<u>keep</u>/keeps) the car on the ground.

6. The (downforce) from the wings (enable/<u>enables</u>) the car to go fast around turns.

7. The (engine) (release/<u>releases</u>) much power to make the car move fast.

8. The (engines) (<u>make</u>/makes) a deafening roar.

9. (People) close to the track often (<u>cover</u>/covers) their ears.

10. (Fans) worldwide (<u>follow</u>/follows) Formula One racing.

11. Many (fans) (<u>believe</u>/believes) that Formula One competitions are more exciting than any other form of racing.

Some Formula One races are still held on roads and highways.

Grab Bag

93

Part 2 Possible answers appear below. Accept all reasonable responses.

Write a verb to complete each sentence correctly. You may use words from the word bank.

reach	earn	range	compete	win
reaches	earns	ranges	competes	wins

12. Formula One cars _____compete_____ in a series called the Grand Prix.

13. Grand Prix races _____range_____ from about 150 to about 200 miles long.

14. The leader in a typical race _____reaches_____ speeds above 200 mph.

15. The top eight drivers to finish a Grand Prix race _____earn_____ points.

16. At the end of the year, the driver with the most points _____wins_____ the World Drivers' Championship.

Part 3

Use the clues to complete the puzzle. Each answer is a verb that appears in this lesson.

Across
1. When the cars race by, I __ my ears.
3. A boy in my class __ money washing cars.
4. The driver of the car must __ the parking brake before driving.
6. Winning this race will __ him a champion.
7. The car in that showroom __ speeds of 200 miles per hour.

Down
1. The woman in these pictures __ in auto races.
2. Will the man in that car __ the race?
5. A victory in this race will __ him to enter the finals.

Crossword solution:
1 Across: COVER
1 Down: COMPETES
2 Down: WINS
3 Across: EARNS
4 Across: RELEASE
5 Down: ENABLE
6 Across: MAKE
7 Across: REACHES

Name _____

Grab Bag

Read and Discover

a. Stock car races <u>are</u> very popular in the United States.
b. My dad (is) going to the Southern 500 this year.

Which sentence has a singular subject? _b._ Circle the boldfaced verb in that sentence.
Which has a plural subject? _a._ Underline the verb in that sentence.

Am, is, was, are, and *were* are forms of the verb *be*. Use *am* after the pronoun *I*. Use *is* or *was* after a **singular subject** or after the pronouns *he, she,* or *it*. Use *are* or *were* after a **plural subject** or after the pronouns *we, you,* or *they*. ◄ **Remember to use this information when you speak, too.**

See Handbook Sections 17 and 27

Part 1

Underline the correct form of *be* in each sentence.

1. Stock car racing (<u>was</u>/were) first popular in the southern United States.

2. NASCAR (<u>is</u>/are) the association that governs stock car racing in the United States.

3. Once, only American cars (was/<u>were</u>) contestants in NASCAR races.

4. Today, cars of other nations (is/<u>are</u>) among the cars that compete.

5. Stock cars (is/<u>are</u>) similar in appearance to regular passenger cars.

6. Regular car engines (is/<u>are</u>) required in NASCAR autos.

7. However, a stock car (<u>is</u>/are) different from an ordinary car in many ways.

8. The car's engine (<u>is</u>/are) modified to make it more powerful.

9. The inside of the car (<u>is</u>/are) empty, except for the driver's seat and the controls.

10. Because stock cars have regular steel bodies, they (is/<u>are</u>) much heavier than most racecars.

11. The first NASCAR race (<u>was</u>/were) on a beach in Daytona, Florida, in 1948.

The banked corners of a stock car track help cars go around curves at over 200 mph.

12. Today, the Daytona 500 (<u>is</u>/are) a famous stock car race.

Grab Bag

Part 2

Write a form of the verb *be* from the word bank to complete each sentence correctly. Make sure the first word in each sentence begins with a capital letter. (13–20)

am	is	was	were	are

_____**Were**_____ you at the NASCAR races last Saturday? I _____**was**_____ there with my family.

My sisters and I _____**are**_____ big fans of car racing. My parents _____**are**_____ fans, too. We

_____**were**_____ in the front row.

I _____**am**_____ also a fan of drag racing. The races _____**are**_____ very exciting! What

_____**is**_____ your favorite kind of car race?

Part 3

Imagine that you and a friend are auto racers. Write four sentences about yourselves. Use a form of the verb *be* in each sentence.

21. _**Answers will vary.**_____

_____

22. _____

_____

23. _____

_____

24. _____

_____

Name _____

Grab Bag

Drivers **have competed** in the 24 Hours of Daytona since 1966. These drivers cover as many miles as they can in 24 hours. Who (**has won**) the race next year?

Circle the boldfaced verb or verb phrase above that does not give a correct sense of time.

All the words in a sentence must work together to give an accurate sense of time. Make sure each **verb** is in the **proper tense** for the time period being discussed. **Remember to use this information when you speak, too.**

See Handbook Section 17

Part 1
Underline the verb or verb phrase that gives the correct sense of time.

1. Until the 1960s, Ferraris (had been/have been) among the fastest racecars in the world.

2. In the late 1960s, Porsches (won/have won) race after race.

3. In 1970, Ferrari engineers (believe/believed) their cars were superior once again.

4. They (choose/had chosen) Mario Andretti to drive their best car in the upcoming race.

5. Mario Andretti (had moved/moves) to the United States in 1955.

6. He (had become/becomes) famous for his driving ability.

7. Ferrari executives and engineers (hope/hoped) Andretti would prove their car's superiority.

8. Andretti (agrees/agreed) to test the Ferrari's ability in a race.

9. The starter (waves/waved) the green flag.

10. The sound of screeching tires (has filled/filled) the air.

11. Everyone (was/has been) excited.

12. Sixty-five cars (roar/roared) down the track.

13. In the end, the Porsche (had covered/covers) the most distance.

14. In 1972, however, Mario Andretti finally (drove/will drive) a Ferrari to victory.

Grab Bag

Part 2

Rewrite the following sentences to indicate that the events took place in 1970.

15. Cars race around the track for 24 hours. _Cars raced around the track for 24 hours._

    _____

16. Pedro Rodriguez drives the winning Porsche. _Pedro Rodriguez drove the winning_

    Porsche.

17. Andretti finishes third in a Ferrari. _Andretti finished third in a Ferrari._

    _____

The Porsche retained its racing crown at Daytona in 1970.

Part 3

Write three sentences using the characters and verbs below. Use a different verb tense in each sentence. Check to make sure the verb tenses are correct.

Characters	Action verb	Tense/time
Laura, Polly	race	future
Zeon	watch	present
Ira	win	past

18. _Answers will vary._

    _____

    _____

19. _____

    _____

20. _____

    _____

Name _____

Read and Discover

___X___ Piero Taruffi hadn't never won the famous Mille Miglia.

_____ The Silver Fox didn't stop trying, however.

Write *X* in front of the sentence that has two negative words.

A **negative** is a word that means "no" or "not." The words *no, not, nothing, none, never, nowhere,* and *nobody* are negatives. The negative word *not* is often found in contractions like *don't* or *wasn't.* Use only one negative word in a sentence to express a negative idea.

◀ **Remember to use this information when you speak, too.**

See Handbook   Section 22

Part 1
Write *X* next to each sentence with two negative expressions.

1. Taruffi wouldn't never have another chance to win this race. __X__

2. After 1957, the race wouldn't ever be run no more. __X__

3. Racing experts thought Taruffi had almost no chance of beating the great British driver Stirling Moss. ____

4. Moss wasn't no threat after his brake pedal broke. __X__

5. He wasn't in the race no more. __X__

6. Late in the race, a young English driver named Collins held a large lead, but Taruffi would not give up. ____

7. Taruffi didn't never believe he would finally win the race. __X__

8. "It wouldn't be so bad to come in second," he thought. ____

9. Collins had pushed his Ferrari too hard earlier, and it wasn't running well no more. __X__

10. Taruffi flew past; he didn't have nobody in front of him. __X__

11. There wasn't no one happier than the Silver Fox when he finally won the Mille Miglia after trying for so long. __X__

12. His family and friends couldn't have been happier for him. ____

Mille Miglia means "thousand miles" in Italian.

Grab Bag

99

Part 2 Possible answers appear below. Accept all reasonable responses.
Rewrite these sentences correctly. There is more than one way to correct each sentence.

13. After 1957, the Mille Miglia wasn't held no more. __After 1957, the Mille Miglia wasn't__ __held anymore.__

14. Fans along the racing route wouldn't never see the racecars zooming through their towns again. __Fans along the racing route would never see the racecars zooming through__ __their towns again.__

15. Italian authorities had complained that there weren't no safety precautions.
__Italian authorities had complained that there were no safety precautions.__

16. They didn't want no fans to get hurt. __They didn't want any fans to get hurt.__

17. Anyone who saw the final race wouldn't never forget it. __Anyone who saw the final race__ __wouldn't ever forget it.__

Part 3
Circle the hidden negatives and write them on the lines. Add apostrophes where they belong.

Note: Answers can be in any order.

18. __NOT__
19. __NOWHERE__
20. __ISN'T__
21. __DON'T__
22. __DOESN'T__
23. __WEREN'T__
24. __NEVER__

Name _____

Read and Discover

Lou was determined to create the [fastest] soap box racer in all of St. Louis this year. He needed to find a (more effective) type of axle grease than the one he had been using.

Circle the boldfaced adjective that compares something with one other thing. Draw a box around the boldfaced adjective that compares something with more than one other thing.

The **comparative form** of an **adjective** compares two people, places, or things. It is often followed by the word *than*. Add *-er* to short adjectives to create the comparative form. Use the word *more* before long adjectives to create this form. The **superlative form** of an adjective compares three or more people, places, or things. The superlative form usually follows the article *the*. Add *-est* to short adjectives to create the superlative. Use the word *most* before long adjectives to create this form.

📣 **Remember to use this information when you speak, too.**

See Handbook Sections 15 and 23

Part 1

Think about how many things are being compared in each sentence. Then underline the correct form of the adjective in parentheses.

1. Last year, Lou had worked to make his car the (more beautiful/<u>most beautiful</u>) in the race.

2. He had used the (brighter/<u>brightest</u>) paints he could find.

3. He had used (<u>brighter</u>/brightest) colors for the sides than the top because a racer's sides are more visible than its top is.

4. When Lou and his friend Bill had compared their racers, Bill had admitted that Lou's was definitely (<u>more colorful</u>/the most colorful).

5. But Lou's pride faded when his car proved to be (slower/<u>the slowest</u>) of all the racers.

6. Lou knew he would have to work (<u>harder</u>/hardest) this year to build a better racer.

7. "Use (<u>lighter</u>/lightest) building materials than you used last year," said Lou's mom.

8. Lou decided to use a(n) (efficienter/<u>more efficient</u>) design for his new racer.

9. He was determined to build the (more streamlined/<u>most streamlined</u>) racer in the derby.

Grab Bag

Part 2

On the blank, write the correct form of the adjective in parentheses. You will need to add *more, most, -er,* or *-est* to each adjective.

10. Soap box racers have no engine, so Lou had looked in hundreds of books to find the

    _____**most efficient**_____ design. (efficient)

11. He had bought lightweight materials to make sure the new car would be

    _____**faster**_____ than last year's model. (fast)

12. Today he would test his new car against Bill's car,

    the _____**swiftest**_____ soap box

    racer in the neighborhood. (swift)

Soap box races start on a downhill ramp.

13. He thought his racer was the _____**sleekest**_____ car in the world. (sleek)

14. For Lou, driving his newly designed racer was _____**more exciting**_____ than

    beating Bill. (exciting)

Part 3

Circle six hidden adjectives. If an adjective is a comparative, write its superlative form. If an adjective is a superlative, write its comparative form. Note: Answers can be in any order.

```
M C N X Q C S S C H
L D G J T B O J P I
S N T K X D F K M G
W I L D E S T N G H
V R O C R H E L K E
N Z W Q B S R D B S
J K E A R L I E S T
X S S P K N L J P G
P T T F A S T E R K
```

15. _____**WILDER**_____

16. _____**EARLIER**_____

17. _____**FASTEST**_____

18. _____**LOWER**_____

19. _____**SOFTEST**_____

20. _____**HIGHER**_____

Name _____

Grab Bag

Read and Discover

The racers drove their midget racecars (more carefully) when it started to rain. Hank drove the [most carefully] of all the racers.

Circle the boldfaced adverb that compares two actions. Draw a box around the boldfaced adverb that compares three or more actions.

The **comparative form** of an adverb compares two actions. Adverbs that end in *-ly* are preceded by *more* for the comparative form (*more carefully*) and are often followed by the word *than*. The **superlative form** of an adverb compares three or more actions. Adverbs that end in *-ly* are preceded by *most* for the superlative form (*most carefully*). Some adverbs add *-er* for the comparative form (*faster*) and *-est* for the superlative form (*fastest*).

See Handbook   Sections 18 and 23

Part 1
Underline the correct form of the adverb.

1. After skidding on the first turn, Adrian approached the next corner (more cautiously/
   most cautiously).

2. Jayne drove the last lap (faster/fastest) than the first.

3. Kesara drove the last lap (more quickly/most quickly) than anyone else.

4. When Kesara crossed the finish line, her sister cheered (louder/loudest) of all.

5. Reza's midget car moved (more quickly/most quickly) than Anthony's car.

6. Tuan's engine ran (more smoothly/most smoothly) in the first race than in any other race.

7. Vera took the turns (more swiftly/most swiftly) than Reza.

8. Reza drives (most carefully/more carefully) than Vera.

9. Adrian drives (more cautiously/most cautiously) than Kesara.

10. Out of all the racers, Vera drives the
    (most boldly/more boldly).

11. Vera wins (more often/most often) than Reza.

Midget cars are very small racecars with very powerful engines.

Grab Bag

Part 2

Complete each sentence by writing the correct form of the adverb in parentheses. You will need to add *more, most, -er,* or *-est* to each adverb.

12. Vito's bright yellow car ran the _____**most smoothly**_____ of all the midget race-

    cars. (smoothly)

13. Kathy had thought she would be bored, but she ended up cheering

    _____**more enthusiastically**_____ than any of her friends. (enthusiastically)

14. Now she is thinking that she could drive a midget car _____**more skillfully**_____

    than any driver on the track. (skillfully)

15. "After all, I ride my mountain bike downhill the _____**fastest**_____ of all,"

    she said to herself. (fast)

16. She watched the drivers _____**more closely**_____ during the second race than she

    did during the first. (closely)

Part 3

Write three sentences comparing the contestants in a competition you have recently seen. Use comparative and superlative adverbs.

17. **Answers will vary.**_____

    _____

18. _____

    _____

19. _____

    _____

Name _____

104

Grab Bag

Proofreading
Practice

Read this report about racecar driver Kelly Sutton and find the mistakes. Use the proofreading marks below to show how each mistake should be fixed. **Suggested answers appear below. Accept all reasonable responses.**

Proofreading Marks

Mark	Means	Example
⊙	add a period	Kelly Sutton is a NASCAR driver⊙
/	make into a lowercase letter	Kelly Sutton is a NASCAR Ⅾriver.
℘	take away	Kelly Sutton s̶h̶e̶ is a NASCAR driver.
∧	add	Kelly Sutton ∧is a NASCAR driver.
(sp)	fix spelling	Kelly Sutton is a NASCAR dryver.(sp)

Kelly Sutton: NASCAR Driver

Kelly Sutton grew up wanting to be a racecar driver. L̶ike her grandfather and her father.
When Kelly i̶s̶ *was* sixteen, doctors gave her father and s̶h̶e̶ *her* some bad news. They said Kelly had multiple sclerosis, or MS. That disease attacks the nervous system m̶o̶s̶t̶ *more* vigorously than many other illnesses do. People with MS may have trouble controlling their movements. The disease can get b̶a̶d̶d̶e̶r̶ *worse* over time. Some people with MS must use wheelchairs⊙

Kelly Sutton was determined to pursue her goals. She would not let n̶o̶t̶h̶i̶n̶g̶ *anything* keep her down.
She told her father she still wanted to drive a racecar. She b̶e̶g̶i̶n̶s̶ *began* racing when she was nineteen years old. She proved herself to be a skillful driver, and she worked hard to get even better. Her determanation(sp) paid off. She became a NASCAR racer, just as h̶e̶r̶ *she* had hoped. Sometimes she has to take time off because of her illness. As soon as she can, tho(sp), she returns to the track.

When she isn't busy racing, Kelly helps other people with MS. She tells t̶h̶e̶y̶ *them* about treatment options. She and t̶h̶e̶m̶ *they* share experiences. Kelly w̶a̶n̶t̶ *wants* people with MS to know that they can make their dreams come true. M̶e̶ ̶a̶n̶d̶ ̶y̶o̶u̶ *You and I* can learn much from this inspiring person.

Proofreading
Checklist

You can use the list below to help you find and fix mistakes in your own writing. Write the titles of your own stories or reports in the blanks on top of the chart. Then use the questions to check your work. Make a check mark (✔) in each box after you have checked that item.

Answers will vary.

Titles

Proofreading Checklist for Unit 4

Have I used subject pronouns correctly? (*I, you, he, she, it, we, they*)				
Have I used object pronouns correctly? (*me, you, him, her, it, us, them*)				
Have I used *I* and *me* correctly when naming myself and another person?				
Do the subject and verb in every sentence agree?				
Have I used comparative and superlative forms of adverbs and adjectives correctly?				
Have I avoided extra negatives?				

Also Remember . . .

Does each sentence begin with a capital letter?				
Does each sentence end with the right mark?				
Have I spelled each word correctly?				
Have I used commas correctly?				

Your Own List

Use this space to write your own list of things to check in your writing.

Name _____

Grab Bag

Review

Pronouns

Circle each boldfaced word that is a subject pronoun. Underline each boldfaced word that is an object pronoun. (1–4)

Barney Oldfield brought speed to racing. (He) **(31)** was the first person to drive a car one mile per minute. In 1902 Henry Ford built a racecar for **him**. **(31)** Oldfield drove **it** **(31)** in Detroit and won his first race in that car. In 1910 (he) **(31)** set a world speed record of 131 mph.

Circle the correct pronoun or pronouns in parentheses.

5. Last weekend Grandma and Grandpa took my sister and (I/me) to the drag races. **(31, 32, 33)**

6. They told (her and me/me and her) how they first became interested in drag racing. **(31, 32, 33)**

7. She and (he/him) went to see Shirley "Cha-Cha" Muldowney race in 1969. **(31, 32)**

8. They told (Lani and me/Lani and I) all about Shirley Muldowney. **(31, 32, 33)**

Circle the antecedent or antecedents of each boldfaced pronoun.

9. "(Shirley) and her (husband) loved fast cars," Grandpa said. "**They** worked together on dragsters."

10. (Lani) is interested in cars. **She** wants to be a mechanic. **(34)**

11. (Lani) and (I) wanted to hear more, so Grandma and Grandpa told **us** another story. **(34)**

Verb Tenses

Circle the correct form of each verb in parentheses.

12. "In those days people really (wanted/will want) to see Shirley succeed," Grandma said. **(37)**

13. "Shirley Muldowney (was/were) one of the first female racecar drivers," Grandpa added. **(36)**

14. "Thousands of fans (cheer/cheered) her at the Hot Rod Nationals in 1971," Grandpa said.

15. "As long as I live, I (remembered/will remember) Shirley's Mustang on the track," he added. **(37)**

16. "Many people (was/were) fans of Shirley," Grandma said. **(36)** **(37)**

17. "Articles about that 1971 race (is/are) still in my scrapbook," she continued. **(36)**

18. My sister and I (like/likes) to hear those stories. **(35)**

Grab Bag

Negatives Possible answers appear below. Accept all reasonable responses.

Rewrite each sentence so it has only one negative term.

19. Great racecar drivers never do nothing foolish. <u>Great racecar drivers never do</u>

    <u>anything foolish.   (38)</u>

20. None of them would never drive no unsafe car in a race. <u>None of them would ever</u>

    <u>drive an unsafe car in a race.   (38)</u>

21. Some racecar drivers believe the racetrack isn't no more dangerous than the freeway.

    <u>Some racecar drivers believe the racetrack is no more dangerous than the freeway.   (38)</u>

22. On freeways, many drivers don't pay no attention to what they're doing. <u>On freeways,</u>

    <u>many drivers don't pay any attention to what they're doing.   (38)</u>

Adjectives and Adverbs

Complete each sentence by writing the correct form of the adjective or adverb in parentheses.

23. A person who has a new car drives the <u>most carefully   (40)</u> of all. (carefully)

24. Bruce's hot rod is <u>noisier   (39)</u> than his brother's sedan. (noisy)

25. After reading about different models, Gord decided that the new Remarka was the

    <u>safest   (39)</u> car of all. (safe)

26. Gord believes the Remarka is <u>prettier   (39)</u> than the Afforda. (pretty)

27. He was surprised to learn that the Remarka handles <u>more precisely   (40)</u> than

    the Afforda. (precisely)

28. Dan's car is the <u>quietest   (39)</u> of all. (quiet)

Name _____

Grab Bag

School 🏫 Home Connection

In Unit 4 of *G.U.M.* students are learning how different kinds of words are used in sentences. The activities on these pages give extra practice with some of the concepts we're learning. You can help reinforce the information your child is learning in school by choosing one or more activities to complete at home.

Guess What? (Subject and Object Pronouns)

Have your child think of an object that is familiar to both of you. Then have your child write three sentences about that object using pronouns; ask him or her not to tell what the object is.

> **Example** Aunt Sarah gave **it** to **you**. **You** wear **it** on your wrist. **It** ticks.

Read the sentences and guess what the secret object is. After you have guessed, work with your child to circle each pronoun he or she used.

Capture the Caption (Forms of *Be*)

With your child, flip through old magazines or a family photo album. Have your child select three or four pictures and write captions for them using forms of the verb *be,* such as *am, is, are, was,* or *were.*

> **Example** Grandma **is** in front of the piano. All the kids **are** in the kitchen.

Interview (Pronouns in Pairs)

Have your child interview you (or another adult) about what you did with your best friend when you were in the fifth grade. Encourage your child to take notes during the interview. Then have your child write four sentences describing what you and your friend did, using pronouns in some of the sentences.

> **Example** Mom and Greta were best friends. **She and Mom** used to play on the soccer team together.

Read the completed sentences together to make sure the pronouns have been used correctly.

Grab Bag

Silly Sentences (Making the Subject and Verb Agree)

Work with your child to think of three subjects, three verbs, and three locations. (Or, use the list below.) Write these in three columns, like this:

A bright red apple	roll	the sky
Three blue bikes	skid	the barn
The gray clouds	twist	the aisle

Then have your child choose one word or phrase from each column and write a sentence.

Example   A bright red apple rolls down the aisle.

What's Wrong with These Pictures? (Negatives)

Look at these pictures with your child. Talk together about what is wrong with each picture. Then have your child use negatives to write one sentence about each picture. Make sure each sentence has only one negative word. Negatives include *no, not, nothing, none, never, nowhere,* and *nobody*.

Example   The car has no tires.

Compare/Contrast (Comparative and Superlative Adjectives)

Have your child think of something that both of you have, such as a jacket, a closet, a hairbrush, or a bicycle. Then have your child write three sentences comparing the two things.

Example   Your closet is <u>bigger</u> than mine. My closet is <u>messier</u> than yours.

In each sentence, have your child underline the word that compares.

Name _____

Grab Bag

What is the largest turtle alive today? It is the leatherback turtle. Look at this picture of a leatherback. Wow, the caption says some leatherbacks weigh 1,400 pounds!

Which sentence gives a command? Circle its end mark.
Which sentence shows excitement? Circle its end mark.
Which sentence asks a question? Circle its end mark.
Which sentence makes a statement? Circle its end mark.

Begin every **sentence** with a capital letter. A **declarative** sentence makes a statement and ends with a **period**. An **interrogative** sentence asks a question and ends with a **question mark**. An **imperative** sentence gives a command and ends with a **period** or an **exclamation point**. An **exclamatory** sentence shows excitement and ends with an **exclamation point**.

See Handbook Section 9

Part 1 Suggested answers appear below. Accept all reasonable responses.

Correct each capitalization or punctuation error. Then label each sentence *declarative, interrogative, imperative,* or *exclamatory*.

1. Tell me all about leatherback turtles. _____imperative_____

2. Leatherbacks range over an extremely wide area. _____declarative_____

3. they can live in icy seas as well as tropical waters. _____declarative_____

4. Why are they called leatherbacks? _____interrogative_____

5. These huge turtles do not have a hard shell! _____exclamatory_____

6. How big is a leatherback's shell? _____interrogative_____

7. some shells are about six feet long. _____declarative_____

8. do you know another way leatherbacks are unusual? _____interrogative_____

9. a leatherback can't pull its head into its shell. _____declarative_____

10. Don't try to eat the leatherback's favorite food, the man-of-war. _____imperative_____

11. These jellyfish are deadly to humans. _____declarative_____

12. Wow, the leatherback in that photograph is huge! _____exclamatory_____

Beasts & Critters

Part 2 Answers will vary.

Look at the picture below. Write four sentences about it, one of each kind.

13. Imperative: _____

   _____

   _____

   _____

Leatherbacks have been found as far north as Norway and as far south as Australia.

14. Interrogative: _____

   _____

15. Declarative: _____

   _____

16. Exclamatory: _____

   _____

Part 3

Add end punctuation to each clue. Then solve the riddle.

17. I am round and smooth .

18. Female sea turtles bury me on the beach .

19. Please don't break me . or !

20. I can't wait until a tiny turtle comes out of me . or !

21. What am I ?

   Answer: I am an ___E___ ___G___ ___G___ .

Name _____

Beasts & Critters

Read and Discover

The babies were scaly and rough. The zoologists at the (Bronx Zoo) in (New York City) thought they were adorable, however.

Circle the words that name specific people, places, or organizations.

A common noun names a person, place, or thing. A **proper noun** names a specific person, place, or thing. All the important words in proper nouns are **capitalized**. The names of months and days of the week are proper nouns. **Proper adjectives** are descriptive words formed from proper nouns. They must be capitalized. A **title of respect** is used before a person's name. Titles of respect include *Chairperson* and *Mr.* They are also capitalized.

See Handbook Sections 1, 14, and 15

Part 1

Circle lowercase letters that should be capital letters. Draw a line through capital letters that should be lowercase letters.

1. In the early 1980s, roughly 500 chinese alligators lived in the wild in china.

2. The Alligators' natural habitat in the Anhui province of china was being destroyed.

3. An american zoologist named doctor John L. behler wanted to help.

4. He brought chinese alligators to the bronx Zoo to create a breeding program.

5. On august 21, 1984, the Zoologist's effort finally paid off.

6. Four baby chinese alligators hatched from their shells.

7. The Zoo became the leader in captive breeding of Chinese alligators in the united states.

8. Another american reptile specialist, doctor myrna Watanabe, studied the alligators in China.

9. Chinese officials and scientists worked hard to study and protect the Alligators, too.

10. Today there are about 10,000 Chinese alligators at a Research Center in anhui.

11. In april 2003, the bronx zoo sent three alligators to Shanghai to introduce into protected wetlands.

12. researchers were heartened when the Animals survived and one female had hatchlings.

Beasts & Critters

Part 2

Rewrite these sentences to correct the errors.

13. The rockefeller Wildlife Refuge in louisiana is also working to protect chinese alligators.

   The Rockefeller Wildlife Refuge in Louisiana is also working to protect Chinese

   alligators.

14. Parts of louisiana are like the alligators' home in the yangtze river in china.

   Parts of Louisiana are like the alligators' home in the Yangtze River in China.

15. Researchers in new york and louisiana work together to determine how captive-bred chinese alligators can be introduced into the wild.

   Researchers in New York and Louisiana work together to determine how captive-bred

   Chinese alligators can be introduced into the wild.

Part 3

Circle eight proper nouns, proper adjectives, or titles of respect. (All the hidden words appear in this lesson.) Write a sentence using two words you found. Use correct capitalization.

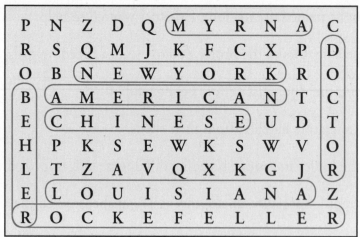

16. **Answers will vary.**

Name _____

Our teacher, <u>Mr.</u> Miles, sent Dr. Marilyn <u>C.</u> Winters an invitation to talk to our class about snakes next Friday. Dr. Winters wrote herself a note that read, "(Fri.), (Jan.) 12—talk to class."

Underline a short way to write *Mister*. Draw a square around a short way to write *Doctor*. Circle short ways to write *Friday* and *January*. Underline a single letter that stands for a name.

An **abbreviation** is a shortened form of a word. **Titles of respect** are usually abbreviated. So are words in **addresses** like *Street* (*St.*) and *Avenue* (*Ave.*). **Days,** most **months,** and **kinds of businesses** are often abbreviated in e-mail and informal notes. Abbreviations usually begin with a capital letter and end with a period. An **initial** takes the place of a name. It is written as a capital letter followed by a period.

See Handbook Section 2

Part 1

In the sentences below, circle each lowercase letter that should be a capital letter. Draw a line through each capital letter that should be a lowercase letter. Add periods where they are needed.

1. Mr. Miles gave dr. Winters directions to u.s. Grant Middle School.

2. He told her to drive east on Elm Blvd. and make a right on Oak st.

3. Dr. Winters owns the most unusual business on Franklin ave.

4. Her company, Snakes inc., supplies snakes for films.

5. She showed us the feeding schedule for the boa constrictors.

    It read, "Feb. Feeding Schedule: Feed boas every wed."

Boa constrictors use powerful muscles to squeeze and kill their prey.

6. Dr. Winters explained that she sometimes orders the food from Hungry Reptile corp.

7. She also feeds the boas mice from mrs. Joy g. Wong's pet store on Maple blvd.

8. Dr. Winters said that boa constrictors do not lay eggs. Their babies are born live.

9. Mrs. wong's assistant, ms. Brown, had a big surprise last week.

10. When she got to the office on Franklin Ave., she found fifty newborn boas.

11. She told mrs. Wong, "I hope you have plenty of mice because we're going to need them!"

Beasts & Critters

Part 2

Rewrite the items below. Use abbreviations and initials where you can.

12. Mister Michael Edward Cleveland _____ Mr. M. E. Cleveland _____

13. Reverend Marcia Ann Fong _____ Rev. M. A. Fong _____

14. 1055 West Lincoln Boulevard _____ 1055 W. Lincoln Blvd. _____

15. Reptile Research Incorporated _____ Reptile Research Inc. _____

16. Tuesday, January 3 _____ Tues., Jan. 3 _____

17. Doctor Duane Estaris _____ Dr. D. Estaris _____

18. today's date (include the day of the week) _____ Answers will vary. _____

19. your date of birth _____ Answers will vary. _____

Part 3

Imagine you are addressing an envelope to your teacher. Write your teacher's name and the name and the address of your school. Then write your name and address in the top left corner. Check the capitalization and punctuation of the abbreviations you use in each address.

Answers will vary.

_____

_____

Answers will vary.

_____

_____

_____

Name _____

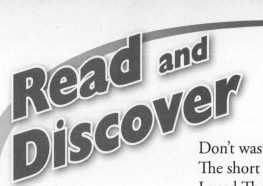

Don't waste your money on the movie (Temple of the Turtles)
The short story "Froggy's Fandango" is quite funny.
I used The Reptile Encyclopedia when I wrote my science report.

Circle the movie title. Draw a box around the story title. Tell how they are written differently. The movie title is underlined. The story title is in quotation marks.

Underline **book titles** and **movie titles** in handwritten work. Italicize book titles and movie titles when you write with a word processor. Use quotation marks around the titles of **songs, stories,** and **poems.** Capitalize the first word and last word in every title you write. Capitalize all other words except articles, prepositions, and conjunctions. Remember to capitalize forms of the verb *be,* such as *is* and *are.*

See Handbook Sections 1 and 3

Part 1

Circle each lowercase letter that should be a capital letter. Draw a line through capital letters that should be lowercase letters. Underline or add quotation marks to the titles.

1. Sagit lent Jorge a book called cobra capers.

2. Sagit thought "spitting mad" was the best story in the book.

3. Lu loved the movie the ghosts of rattlesnake ranch.

4. The movie's theme song is called "spurs are jingling."

5. Mark Twain wrote a short story called "the celebrated jumping frog of calaveras county."

6. After reading that story, Tran got the book teaching your frog to leap farther.

7. Nola wrote a poem called "notes to a newt."

8. Brad set the poem to music, and he called the song "amphibian rhapsody."

9. Joelle read the book the adventures of Leroy the lizard three times.

10. After dinner, Anya read us a poem from the book Odes to Toads.

11. The poem was titled "a toad is a beautiful thing."

12. Then I read my poem titled "A frog makes a Better pet than A hog."

Part 2

Read the titles below. Then write a title to answer each item. Be sure to write each title correctly.

13. Which book would tell you how to treat a snake bite? __First Aid__

14. Make up a title for a short story that might appear in <u>Reptile Tales</u>. **Answers will vary but should be in quotation marks.**

15. Which movie is likely to be a horror film? __The Monster of Gila Bend__

16. Which book might give you information about painted turtles? __Turtle Territory__

Part 3

Draw a line to match each title in the first column with the item that best describes it in the second column.

17. "Ferdinand Frog's Life at the Plaza"   a movie about the life cycle of a turtle

18. <u>Larry Lizard's Loud Act</u>   a poem about a snake shedding its skin

19. "Marvin's Miraculous Molting"   a short story about a frog that lives in a fancy hotel

20. "Dot, the Silly Salamander"   a book about a singing lizard

21. <u>The Life and Times of Tommy Turtle</u>   a song about a spotted salamander

Name _____

Read and Discover

Most **amphibians'** lives are spent partly in water and partly on land. **They're** descendants of the first vertebrates that crawled on land long ago.

Which boldfaced word shows ownership? _____ amphibians'

Which boldfaced word combines two words? _____ They're

To form the **possessive** of a singular noun, add an **apostrophe** and **s** (*snake's fangs*). For plural nouns that end in *s,* add an apostrophe. For plural nouns that do not end in *s,* add an apostrophe and *s* (the *children's snake*). **Apostrophes** are also used in **contractions,** two words that have been shortened and combined.

See Handbook Sections 7, 24, and 26

Part 1

Underline the correct word in parentheses. If the answer is a possessive, write *P*. If the answer is a contraction, write *C*.

1. (Ive/<u>I've</u>) read that amphibians stay the same temperature as their surroundings. <u>C</u>

2. (<u>That's</u>/Thats') why we say they are "cold-blooded." <u>C</u>

3. An (<u>amphibian's</u>/amphibians') body tells a lot about how it lives and moves. <u>P</u>

4. Sticky disks on a tree (frogs'/<u>frog's</u>) fingers and toes help it grip and climb. <u>P</u>

5. The spade-like shape of an African (bullfrogs'/<u>bullfrog's</u>) feet help it burrow into the ground. <u>P</u>

6. Water (<u>dwellers'</u>/dweller's) webbed feet help them swim. <u>P</u>

7. Some amphibians are colored to match their surroundings so that predators (<u>won't</u>/wo'nt) see them. <u>C</u>

Most amphibians absorb much of the water they need through their skin.

8. An (<u>amphibian's</u>/amphibians') color may help it stay warm or cool. <u>P</u>

9. A (<u>tadpole's</u>/tadpoles') form changes as it grows into a frog. <u>P</u>

10. Tadpoles (<u>don't</u>/do'nt) breathe air. <u>C</u>

11. They (cant/<u>can't</u>) live out of water until they have changed form and become frogs. <u>C</u>

12. Frogs (<u>don't</u>/dont) flip out their tongues at their prey unless the prey is moving. <u>C</u>

Part 2

Rewrite the sentences below. Replace the boldfaced words with possessives or contractions.

13. The **gills of some salamanders** let them breathe underwater. <u>Some salamanders' gills</u>

<u>let them breathe underwater.</u>

14. **Do not** expect a short-legged frog to make long jumps. <u>Don't expect a short-legged</u>

<u>frog to make long jumps.</u>

15. The **skin color of a poison-dart frog** warns other creatures to stay away. <u>The poison-dart</u>

<u>frog's skin color warns other creatures to stay away.</u>

_____

16. **It is** a little known fact that some amphibians have no legs. <u>It's a little known fact that</u>

<u>some amphibians have no legs.</u>

17. **They are** called caecilians, and they look like worms. <u>They're called caecilians, and</u>

<u>they look like worms.</u>

Part 3

Circle the five hidden words in the puzzle. Then write the possessive form of each noun and the contraction of the negative expression. (Hint: Two of the nouns are plural.)

Y	D	L	T	A	D	P	O	L	E
W	C	K	X	G	M	B	S	K	F
S	A	L	A	M	A	N	D	E	R
Q	N	B	J	M	K	Q	F	B	O
X	N	G	U	S	S	E	R	P	G
Z	O	X	K	J	G	N	V	R	S
V	T	O	N	G	U	E	S	D	B

Note: Answers can be in any order.

18. _____ TADPOLE'S

19. _____ SALAMANDER'S

20. _____ TONGUES'

21. _____ FROGS'

22. _____ CAN'T

Name _____

Beasts & Critters

Read and Discover

Commas in a Series

Lesson 46

Salamanders may look like (lizards,) (geckos,) or even (snakes.)

In the sentence above, circle three items in a series. What punctuation mark follows each of the first two items? __comma__

They are related to (frogs,) (toads,) and other (amphibians,) however.

Circle three items in a series in this sentence. What punctuation mark should follow each of the first two items? __comma__

A **series** is a list of three or more words or phrases. **Commas** are used to separate the items in a series. The last comma in a series goes before the word *and* or the word *or*.

See Handbook Section 8

Part 1

Add commas where they are needed below. Cross out commas that should not be there.

1. An adult spotted salamander has~~,~~ four legs, a tail, black skin, and yellow spots.

2. Spotted salamanders~~,~~ hatch, mate, and lay eggs underwater.

3. A female lays her eggs, attaches them to a stick, covers them with a jelly-like substance, and~~,~~ leaves them.

4. Grubs, mold, or acid rain~~,~~ can kill the salamander eggs.

5. The larvae that hatch from the eggs have long tails, no legs, and feathery gills.

6. The spotted salamander larvae~~,~~ eat fleas, shrimps, and grubs.

7. Beetles, salamanders, or giant water bugs might eat~~,~~ the larvae.

8. As adults, the spotted salamanders leave the pool, crawl on land, and find hiding places.

9. Adult spotted salamanders~~,~~ live under rocks, in holes, or~~,~~ in rotten logs.

10. Every spring they follow a scent, the slope of the ground, or even the stars to return to the pool where they hatched.

11. Other kinds of salamanders are the tiger salamander and the Japanese giant salamander.

12. These salamanders are found in streams, ponds, and lakes.

The life cycle of the spotted salamander

Beasts & Critters

121

Part 2 Possible answers appear below. Accept all reasonable responses.

Use what you read on page 121 to write a sentence to respond to each item. Include items in a series in each answer.

13. List three creatures that spotted salamander larvae eat.

   Spotted salamander larvae eat fleas, shrimps, and grubs.

   _____

14. List three places where you might find a spotted salamander.

   You might find a spotted salamander under rocks, in holes, or in rotten logs.

   _____

15. List three dangers for spotted salamander eggs and larvae.

   Three dangers for spotted salamander eggs and larvae are grubs, mold, and acid rain.

   _____

16. List three kinds of amphibians.

   Three kinds of amphibians are salamanders, frogs, and toads.

   _____

Part 3 Answers will vary.

Imagine that you have discovered a new species of salamander. Complete the sentences below to describe your salamander. Use at least three adjectives in each answer. (Use words from the word bank or your own words.) Be sure to use commas correctly. Then draw your salamander.

| green | long | striped | bumpy | spotted | wrinkled |
| red | smooth | slimy | yellow | shiny | short |

17. Its body is _____

18. Its tail is _____

19. Its legs are _____

Name _____

Beasts & Critters

Yes, we decided to have a frog jumping contest. Ms. Li helped us catch the bullfrogs, but she said that we'd have to let them go later. "Be careful not to squeeze your frog, Celia!" she said sharply.

Find the word that introduces the first sentence. What punctuation mark follows it? __comma__

Find the conjunction that joins the two parts of the second sentence. What punctuation mark comes before it? __comma__

Find the name of the person being spoken to in the third sentence. What punctuation mark comes before it? __comma__

Commas tell a reader where to pause. A comma is used to separate an **introductory word** from the rest of a sentence. It is used to separate **independent clauses** in a compound sentence. It is also used to separate a **noun of direct address** from the rest of a sentence. A noun of direct address names a person who is being spoken to.

See Handbook Sections 8 and 21

Part 1

A comma is missing from each sentence. Add the missing comma. Then decide why each comma is needed. Write *I* for introductory word, *C* for compound sentence, or *D* for direct address.

1. "Ms. Li, what species of frog is the best jumper?" asked Jules. __D__

2. "Well, the African sharp-nosed frog can jump 65 times the length of its body," she said. __I__

3. "Wow, look at how long its legs are!" said Raj. __I__

4. Ms. Li said, "Yes, frogs' powerful legs make them good jumpers." __I__

5. "Do you know another way frogs use their legs, Ali?" Ms. Li asked. __D__

6. "Yes, they use them to swim," Ali answered. __I__

7. "Many frogs have webbed feet, and that helps them swim faster." __C__

8. We lined up with our frogs at the start, but some got away. __C__

9. "Hey, follow that frog!" shouted Jenny. __I__

10. Ms. Li gave the signal, and we urged our frogs to jump. __C__

11. "Alexis, your frog is winning!" Jules cried. __D__

12. "Hooray, my frog won first prize!" Ali said. __I__

Bullfrogs can jump up to nine times the length of their bodies.

Part 2 Possible answers appear below. Accept all reasonable responses.
Rewrite the sentences so they include a word in parentheses. Be sure to use commas correctly.

13. Some frogs live near water. (but) Some are tree dwellers. <u>**Some frogs live near water,**</u>

   <u>**but some are tree dwellers.**</u>

14. Many frogs capture insects with their long, sticky tongues. (and/but) Others gulp food
   directly into their mouths.

   <u>**Many frogs capture insects with their long, sticky tongues, but others gulp food**</u>

   <u>**directly into their mouths.**</u>

   _____

15. Put your frog back in the pond. (James) <u>**Put your frog back in the pond, James.**</u>

   _____

16. (Well) The frog will be happier there. <u>**Well, the frog will be happier there.**</u>

   _____

Part 3
Amphibians can live on land or water. The words *amphibian* and *amphibious* come from two
Greek roots: *amphi,* meaning "both," and *bios,* meaning "life." Write a paragraph explaining how
amphibians live a double life. Use commas to separate elements in your sentences.

<u>Answers will vary.</u>

_____

_____

_____

_____

_____

Name _____

Beasts & Critters

a. The chameleon crouched on a branch; an unsuspecting butterfly landed nearby.

    b. Chameleons don't like each other, they must be kept in separate enclosures.

In which sentence do you think the two clauses are separated correctly? _____a._____

A **semicolon** can be used instead of a comma and a conjunction to separate the **independent clauses** in a compound sentence.

See Handbook Section 8

Part 1

Write a semicolon to separate the clauses in each sentence.

1. The chameleon is a very quiet lizard; it sits perfectly still.

2. The chameleon's name comes from two Greek words; the words mean "dwarf lion."

3. Some chameleons have horns on their heads; they use the horns for fighting.

4. Chameleons are adapted for living in trees; they can grasp branches with their tails.

5. Chameleons' feet are shaped like hands; they have thumbs and fingers.

6. A chameleon's eyes move independently; they can focus on two different objects at once.

7. Some chameleons eat insects; others eat grasses.

8. Chameleons also change colors; a chameleon can make itself gray, black, green, or brown.

9. A chameleon doesn't change color to match its background; it can change color as its mood changes.

10. A chameleon that's won a fight for territory might turn bright green; the loser might turn gray.

11. Sometimes temperature affects a chameleon's color; a chameleon might turn pale when it gets cold.

A chameleon's powerful tongue can grow as long as its body.

12. Chameleons aren't the only lizards that change color; many lizards have this ability.

Beasts & Critters

Part 2

Each sentence on the left can be matched with a sentence on the right to make a compound sentence. Draw a line to connect each pair of sentences that have related information. Then rewrite each pair of sentences as one sentence. Use a semicolon to separate the independent clauses.

Chameleons are usually green or brown.
Chameleons move very slowly when hunting.
A chameleon's tongue is long and powerful.
A chameleon's tongue is also very sticky.

Insects get trapped on the end of it.
It can shoot out far and fast.
They are hard to see against the leaves.
They lift one foot at a time.

13. **Chameleons are usually green or brown; they are hard to see against the leaves.**

14. **Chameleons move very slowly when hunting; they lift one foot at a time.**

15. **A chameleon's tongue is long and powerful; it can shoot out far and fast.**

16. **A chameleon's tongue is also very sticky; insects get trapped on the end of it.**

Part 3 Answers will vary.

Use what you have read about chameleons to answer the questions below. Each answer should include two independent clauses separated by a semicolon.

17. What are two interesting features of a chameleon's appearance? _____

18. How does a chameleon move? _____

19. How does a chameleon eat? _____

Name _____

Beasts & Critters

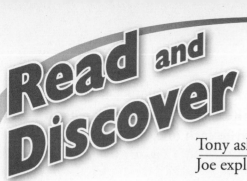

Tony asked, "How will we know where the rattlesnakes are?"
Joe explained that he knew where to look for timber rattlers.

Which sentence shows a speaker's exact words? Underline it.
Circle the marks that begin and end the quotation. Then circle the first letter of the quotation.

A **direct quotation** is a speaker's exact words. Use **quotation marks** around the beginning and end of a direct quotation. Use a comma to separate the speaker's exact words from the rest of the sentence. Begin a direct quotation with a capital letter, and add end punctuation before the last quotation mark. An **indirect quotation** retells a speaker's words. Do not use quotation marks when the words *that* or *whether* come before a speaker's words.

See Handbook Section 4

Part 1

Write *I* after each indirect quotation and *D* after each direct quotation. Add quotation marks, commas, and end marks to direct quotations. Circle lowercase letters that should be capitalized.

1. Nico asked whether timber rattlesnakes are easy to find. __I__

2. "They spend more than half the year hibernating in holes and rock cracks," Joe said. __D__

3. Joe commented that snakes are cold-blooded and need the sun to warm them. __I__

4. "Timber rattlers warm up on sunny rocks for a few days every spring," Joe said. __D__

5. "That's the best time to see them," he added. __D__

6. Joe said that rattlesnakes hibernate in groups and return to the same spot each year. __I__

7. He said, "this is an area where I saw snakes sunning themselves last year." __D__

8. "What's that buzzing sound?" Tony asked nervously. __D__

9. "Look! It's a rattlesnake!" Nico shouted. __D__

10. Joe said that we should stay calm and stand back. __I__

11. "These snakes are poisonous," he warned. __D__

12. Tony said, "look at that one's beautiful stripes." __D__

Timber rattlesnakes are found in the forests of the eastern United States.

Beasts & Critters

Part 2   Possible answers appear below. Accept all reasonable responses.

Rewrite each indirect quotation as a direct quotation. Rewrite each direct quotation as an indirect quotation. There is more than one right way to rewrite each one. Be sure to use punctuation marks correctly.

13. "Joe, how does a rattlesnake make its rattling sound?" Nico asked.

    Nico asked Joe how a rattlesnake makes its rattling sound.

14. Joe said that a rattlesnake sheds its skin a few times every year.

    Joe said, "A rattlesnake sheds its skin a few times every year."

15. "Each time the snake sheds its skin, a loose, hardened piece of skin stays on the end of its tail," Joe explained.

    Joe explained that each time the snake sheds its skin, a loose, hardened piece of skin

    stays on the end of its tail.

16. He said that these hardened pieces click together when the snake shakes its tail.

    He said, "These hardened pieces click together when the snake shakes its tail."

Part 3

Will Joe, Nico, and Tony meet more rattlers? Draw pictures in these boxes to show what will happen to these characters next. Under each box write a direct quotation to tell what a character is saying.

Answers will vary.

Answers will vary.

Name _____

Beasts & Critters

Camp Iguana
Box B-755
Yuma, AZ 85364
August 10, 2012

(Dear Miguel,)

Today is the hottest day of the year! Tomorrow we're supposed to go on a nature hike in the Yuma Desert. If it's as hot as today, I'll bet the hike will be cancelled. Write soon.

(Your buddy,)

(Ron)

This letter has five parts. Two have been circled. Circle each of the others.

A **friendly letter** has five parts. The **heading** gives your address and the date. The **greeting** includes the name of the person you are writing to. It begins with a capital letter and ends with a comma. The **body** gives your message. The **closing** is a friendly way to say good-bye. It begins with a capital letter and ends with a comma. The **signature** is your name. An **e-mail** should also include five parts. Like a letter, it contains a greeting, a body, a closing, and your name. An e-mail header contains your **e-mail address,** the e-mail address of the person you are writing to, the date, and a **subject line**.

See Handbook Sections 29 and 30

Part 1

Label the five parts of the letter below. Write the name of each part on the line next to the number that matches it.

1. 116 Hope St.
   Baltimore, MD 21210
   August 15, 2012

2. Dear Ron,

3.   Nestor and I visited the Taylor Natural History Museum this morning. The snake keeper let me hold a humongous boa constrictor. Its body felt cool and dry. Did you get to take that desert hike? Well, that's all for now.

4.   Your pal,

5.   Miguel

1. ____heading____

2. ____greeting____

3. ____body____

4. ____closing____

5. ____signature____

Part 2

Rewrite this friendly letter correctly on the lines below. (6–10)

Your friend, Camp Livingston July 10, 2012 Today at camp we caught tadpoles for the aquarium. Ross Springs, OH 43210 I'll write to tell you when they grow into frogs. Dear Sandra, Denise

Camp Livingston

Ross Springs, OH 43210

July 10, 2012

Dear Sandra,

Today at camp we caught tadpoles for the aquarium. I'll write to tell you when they

grow into frogs.

Your friend,

Denise

Part 3   Answers will vary.

See Handbook Section 32

Ask an adult to help you use the Internet to research a state or national park you would like to visit. Then write a formal e-mail to the park in which you request information. For example, you might ask whether the park offers tours or what wildlife might be seen at a particular time of year. Use correct e-mail form and proper netiquette.

Name _____

Beasts & Critters

Proofreading
Practice

Find the mistakes in the letter below. Use proofreading marks to show how to fix each mistake.

Proofreading Marks

Mark	Means	Example
∧	add	Iguanas ∧have long tails.
≡	make into a capital letter	iguanas have long tails.
/	make into a lowercase letter	Iguanas Have long tails.
⊙	add a period	Iguanas have long tails⊙
⌄	add a comma	Yes⌄ iguanas have long tails.
⌄⌄	add quotation marks	Iguanas have long tails, he said.
(sp)	fix spelling	Igwanas have long tails.
⌄	add apostrophe	Iguanas tails are long.

224 Hummingbird st⊙

Los Angeles, CA 90012

May 11⌄2012

dear Max,

Last weekend my dad and I drove into the mojave Desert⊙ I was looking for lizards. I borrowed my mom's binoculars. I also brought along a book, the story of reptiles, by dr R L Jackson.

We hiked into a canyon. All of a sudden, Dad shouted "Kevin⌄ look there?" A lizard skittered by⌄ but I got a good look at it. I found a picture of the lizard in my book⊙ it was a chuckwalla.

Chuckwallas store water in sacs under their skin⊙ they are able to survive in temperatures of up to 113° F. The chuckwalla is a species of iguana.

I've learned some amazing facts about iguanas. Most iguanas eat fruit, leafs, or insecs. One species in South america can run across the Surface of a pool of water without sinking. Another one in Fiji turns from bright green to black when it's frightened. I wrote a poem called i want to be an iguana.

Would you like to visit next month⌄ we could look for lizards in my yard.

Your friend⌄

Kevin

Beasts & Critters

Proofreading
Checklist

You can use the list below to help you find and fix mistakes in your own writing. Write the titles of your own stories or reports in the blanks on top of the chart. Then use the questions to check your work. Make a check mark (✓) in each box after you have checked that item.

Answers will vary.

Proofreading Checklist for Unit 5

	Titles			
Have I capitalized proper nouns, proper adjectives, and all the important words in titles?				
Have I placed quotation marks around direct quotations?				
Have I used commas to separate items in a series?				
Have I joined each compound sentence with a comma followed by a conjunction or with a semicolon?				

Also Remember . . .

Does each sentence begin with a capital letter and end with the right end mark?				
Do all abbreviations begin with a capital letter and end with a period?				
Have I used possessives correctly?				
Have I used contractions correctly?				

Your Own List

Use this space to write your own list of things to check in your writing.

Name _____

Beasts Critters

Review

(Numbers in parentheses
identify related lessons.)

Quotation Marks and Apostrophes

Write *D* after each direct quotation and *I* after each indirect quotation. Add quotation marks and other punctuation marks to direct quotations. Draw three lines (≡) under letters that should be capitalized.

1. Mr. Chi said that we were going to see a movie about how lizards defend themselves. __I__ (49)

2. "The dog has caught a skink by the tail!" said Paula. __D__ (49)

3. "Watch what the skink does now," said Mr. Chi. __D__ (49)

4. Trinh shouted, "the skink broke off its own tail and got away!" __D__ (49)

5. Mr. Chi told us that this is an unusual kind of defense. __I__ (49)

Underline the correct word in each pair. Write *C* if the answer is a contraction. Write *P* if the answer is a possessive.

6. Many people (<u>can't</u>/cant') tell the difference between salamanders and lizards. __C__ (45)

7. (<u>Salamanders'</u>/Salamander's) bodies look like the bodies of lizards. __P__ (45)

8. A (lizards'/<u>lizard's</u>) skin is dry and scaly, but salamanders have moist skin. __P__ (45)

9. (<u>They're</u>/There) not closely related to each other. __C__ (45)

Commas and Semicolons

Add commas and semicolons where they are needed. Cross out commas that are not needed.

10. Some of~~,~~ the largest lizards can be found in Africa, India, and Australia. (46)

11. "Which lizard is the biggest, Ms. Kaplan?" Katie asked. (47)

12. "Well, the world's largest lizard is~~,~~ the Komodo dragon," said Ms. Kaplan. (47)

13. These lizards hatch from small eggs, but they grow to be over ten feet long. (47)

14. Komodo dragons are very rare; they live only on a few islands in Indonesia. (48)

15. The zoo had a special display of Komodo dragons; I saw it. (48)

16. I watched Komodo dragons eat, walk, and sleep. (46)

Beasts & Critters

Punctuation and Capitalization

Use proofreading marks to correct each capitalization or punctuation error. Then label each sentence *declarative, interrogative, imperative,* or *exclamatory.*

17. did you know that some snakes are called "flying snakes"?   interrogative   (41)

18. Look at the snake in this picture.   imperative   (41)

19. It can glide through the air for short distances.   declarative   (41)

20. wow, that's amazing!   exclamatory   (41)

21. Its belly scales act like a parachute.   declarative   (41)

Use proofreading marks to correct each capitalization or punctuation error. Add underlines and quotation marks where they are needed.

22. professor starsky said that japanese giant salamanders can grow to be over five feet long. (42)

23. These huge amphibians live only on the island of honshu in japan. (42)

24. mr. f. b. Baker's Enterprise Productions inc. is making a movie about giant salamanders. (43)

25. His studio is on Main st. near the shoe factory. (43)

26. The movie will be called salamanders are super. (44)

27. It is based on a book titled the japanese giant salamander. (44)

Note: Students may refer to the list of proofreading marks on page 131.

28. The movie's theme song will be dance of the amphibians. (44)

29. I like the poem "salamander soup." (44)

Letters

Rewrite this friendly letter correctly on a separate sheet of paper.

30. Camp Komodo Markland, NJ 07902 June 22, 2012 Dear Matt, I can't wait for your visit. We're going to have a great time! Wait until you see my pet salamander. I'll see you next week. Your friend, Daniel

Camp Komodo
Markland, NJ 07902
June 22, 2012

Dear Matt,
     I can't wait for your visit. We're going to have a great time! Wait until you see my pet salamander. I'll see you next week.

Your friend,
Daniel   (50)

Name _____

Beasts & Critters

School 🏠 Home Connection

In Unit 5 of *G.U.M.* students are learning which letters to capitalize and how to use punctuation marks such as periods, apostrophes, commas, and quotation marks. The activities on this page give extra practice with some of the concepts in this unit. You can help your child use the information he or she is learning in school by choosing one or more activities to complete with him or her at home.

Word Search (Apostrophes)

Work with your child to find the eleven words hidden in the word search. Then ask your child to write as many contractions as possible by combining these words in different ways.

Example   The word *don't* is formed by combining *do* and *not*.

Postcard (Proper Nouns and Proper Adjectives; Initials and Abbreviations)

Help your child use a 4" x 6" blank card to design his or her own postcard. First have your child draw a picture on one side of the card. Then have him or her draw a line down the middle of the back of the card and write a message on the left side of the line. Help your child write the address of a friend or family member on the right side. Encourage your child to capitalize proper nouns and use abbreviations (*St., Ave.*).

Thumbs Up/Thumbs Down (Titles)

Ask your child to write a short review of a favorite book, movie, or song. Then ask him or her to write a review of a book, movie, or song he or she did not enjoy. Invite your child to be specific about what he or she liked or disliked. Remind your child to capitalize all important words in any title. He or she should underline the titles of books and movies and use quotation marks around titles of songs.

The Envelope, Please (Titles)

Ask each member of your family to write the title of a favorite movie, book, and story on a slip of paper. Put all the slips in a hat or bag. Then work with your child to use the slips and create a poster of these favorites. Make sure your child underlines movie titles and book titles and puts quotation marks around story titles. Decorate the poster and give it to another family you know.

The Li Family's Picks

Favorite Movie
<u>Ratatouille</u>

Best Book
<u>George Washington's Teeth</u>

Greatest Story
"The Gold Coin"

Traveling Game (Apostrophes; Commas in a Series)

Play a game with your child in which you plan an imaginary trip. Have your child write a list of objects he or she will borrow to bring on the trip. Encourage your child to use apostrophes to show possession (*Lucia's, students'*) and to separate the items in his or her list with commas.

Example	I'm going on a trip to Africa, and I will borrow my **sister's** tent, my **teacher's** map, **Alex's** cowboy boots, and my **grandparents'** camera.

Pen Pal (Friendly Letters and E-mails)

Encourage your child to begin writing to a pen pal. Help him or her find a pen pal through an organization such as KidsCom (www.kidscom.com). If your child uses e-mail to correspond, remind him or her to use proper e-mail netiquette. If your child writes a friendly letter, remind him or her to include all five parts.

The Show Must Go On! (Commas)

Invite your child to write a very short play. Suggest that he or she use introductory words (such as *Yes, No,* and *Well*) and direct address (for example, *Carl, come here!*) in the dialogue. Make sure your child uses commas to separate these elements from the rest of a sentence. Then read the play out loud with your child. Point out to him or her the way commas make a reader pause.

Example	SCENE ONE
	Ballet Dancer: Ouch, my ankle!
	Stage Hand: Hurry, we have to find a doctor!
	SCENE TWO
	Ballet Dancer: Will I ever dance again, Dr. Woo?
	Doctor: Well, you've had a bad sprain, but with some rest you'll be fine.

Name _____

Beasts & Critters

Appendix Table of Contents

Unit Assessments 139

Extra Practice 159

Unit Tests 185

Grammar, Usage, and Mechanics Handbook 195

    Mechanics 196

    Sentence Structure and Parts of Speech 200

    Usage 206

    Letters and E-mails 211

    Research 212

    Guidelines for Listening and Speaking 214

Topic Index 215

Language Index 216

TEST TIP: Read all four answer choices carefully before choosing and marking the answer you think is correct.

(Numbers in parentheses identify related lessons.)
Read each item carefully. Select the best answer and fill in the circle on the answer sheet below.

1. Read this sentence.

   Farm ponds attract wildlife of many kinds.

   What is the complete subject of this sentence? **(1)**

   A ponds
   B farm ponds
   C farm ponds attract
   D attract wildlife of many kinds

2. Read this sentence.

   Some farmers make their ponds attractive to wildlife.

   What are the simple subject and simple predicate of this sentence? **(2)**

   A some; farmers
   B ponds; attractive
   C make; ponds
   D farmers; make

3. Which of the following sentences has a compound predicate? **(3)**

   A Some farmers build sediment traps and ponds.
   B The traps and ponds receive irrigation water.
   C Irrigation water carries fertilizer and pesticides.
   D The traps absorb the water and remove chemicals.

4. Read this sentence.

   Farm ponds provide a habitat for frogs.

   What is the direct object in this sentence? **(4)**

   A farm
   B provide
   C habitat
   D frogs

5. Read this sentence.

   Frogs give farmers <u>help</u> with pest control.

   The direct object in this sentence is underlined. What is the indirect object? **(5)**

   A frogs
   B farmers
   C pest
   D control

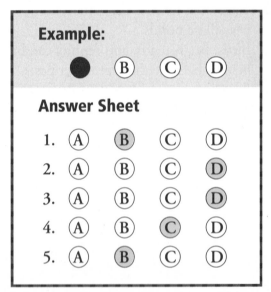

Example:

● Ⓑ Ⓒ Ⓓ

Answer Sheet

1. Ⓐ Ⓑ Ⓒ Ⓓ
2. Ⓐ Ⓑ Ⓒ Ⓓ
3. Ⓐ Ⓑ Ⓒ Ⓓ
4. Ⓐ Ⓑ Ⓒ Ⓓ
5. Ⓐ Ⓑ Ⓒ Ⓓ

Read each item carefully. Select the best answer and fill in the circle on the answer sheet below.

6. Read these sentences.

   Frogs are hungry creatures.
   Flies are yummy to frogs.

   Which statement tells about the sentences? (6)

   A The first sentence contains a predicate noun, and the second contains a predicate adjective.
   B The first sentence contains a predicate adjective, and the second contains a predicate noun.
   C Both sentences contain predicate nouns.
   D Both sentences contain predicate adjectives.

7. Which sentence has a prepositional phrase underlined? (7)

   A <u>Hawks and owls</u> may hunt near a farm pond.
   B An egret <u>or a heron</u> may take up residence.
   C Native grasses <u>provide cover</u> for birds.
   D Helpful insects can thrive <u>in grassy areas</u>.

8. Which sentence is a compound sentence? (8)

   A Flocks of migratory birds stop and rest at farm ponds.
   B Toads and reptiles make their homes near these ponds.
   C Birds, frogs, toads, and reptiles can be helpful because they eat insect pests.
   D Fewer pests mean healthier crops, and healthier crops mean more money for the farmer.

9. Read this sentence.

   Although farm ponds take up space, they can make farms more productive.

   What is the dependent clause in this sentence? (9)

   A although farm ponds take up space
   B farm ponds take up space
   C they can make farms more productive
   D make farms more productive

10. Read this item.

    Students help with some farm pond projects, they plant wild shrubs and grasses.

    How should this sentence be rewritten? (10)

    A Change **Students help** to **Students, they help**.
    B Insert the word **although** after the comma.
    C Change the comma to a period, and capitalize the word **they**.
    D It should not be rewritten. It is written correctly.

Answer Sheet

	A	B	C	D
6.	(A)	B	C	D
7.	A	B	C	(D)
8.	A	B	C	(D)
9.	(A)	B	C	D
10.	A	B	(C)	D

Read each item carefully. Select the best answer and fill in the circle on the answer sheet below.

11. Read this sentence.

    Some giant bluefin tuna live for thirty years.

    What is the complete subject of this sentence? **(1)**

    A some giant bluefin tuna
    B bluefin tuna
    C tuna live
    D for thirty years

12. Read this sentence.

    These huge fish range from Arctic waters to tropical regions.

    What are the simple subject and simple predicate of this sentence? **(2)**

    A huge; fish
    B fish; range
    C range; from
    D Arctic; waters

13. Which of the following sentences has a compound predicate? **(3)**

    A The meat of this fish is prized for its texture and its taste.
    B Ancient peoples caught bluefin and painted pictures of them on cave walls.
    C Today fishing crews search for bluefin tuna with high-tech equipment.
    D Large numbers of bluefin have been caught, and these fish are now rare in many areas.

14. Read this sentence.

    Fishing crews chase bluefin at high speeds.

    What is the direct object in this sentence? **(4)**

    A crews
    B chase
    C bluefin
    D speeds

15. Read this sentence.

    A large catch of bluefin brings a crew a huge <u>profit</u>.

    The direct object in this sentence is underlined. What is the indirect object? **(5)**

    A bluefin
    B brings
    C crew
    D huge

Answer Sheet

11. (A) B C D
12. A (B) C D
13. A (B) C D
14. A B (C) D
15. A B (C) D

Read each item carefully. Select the best answer and fill in the circle on the answer sheet below.

16. **Read these sentences.**

    Bluefin tuna are swift swimmers.
    Adults are very large.

    Which statement tells about the sentences? (6)

    A The first sentence contains a predicate noun, and the second contains a predicate adjective.
    B The first sentence contains a predicate adjective, and the second contains a predicate noun.
    C Both sentences contain predicate nouns.
    D Both sentences contain predicate adjectives.

17. **Which sentence has a prepositional phrase underlined?** (7)

    A Bluefin tuna are <u>warm-blooded fish</u>.
    B They live in icy waters and can <u>dive deeply</u>.
    C These fish once were numerous <u>in the Mediterranean Sea</u>.
    D Overfishing <u>has greatly reduced</u> the number of bluefin tuna there.

18. **Which sentence is a compound sentence?** (8)

    A Bluefin are protected by laws in some areas, but not all fishing crews obey the laws.
    B Scientists count bluefin populations and study their behavior.
    C The extinction of this remarkable and valuable fish seems a possibility.
    D Protection of this species requires international cooperation and greater enforcement of laws.

19. **Read this sentence.**

    Giant bluefin still flourish near Alaska because that state effectively manages fishing there.

    What is the dependent clause in this sentence? (9)

    A giant bluefin still flourish near Alaska
    B still flourish near Alaska
    C that state effectively manages fishing there
    D because that state effectively manages fishing there

20. **Read this sentence.**

    New Zealand protects its bluefin tuna population effectively Iceland does, too.

    How should this sentence be rewritten? (10)

    A Change **protects** to **protect**.
    B Change **its** to **it's**.
    C Insert a comma and the word **and** between **effectively** and **Iceland**.
    D Insert a comma between **effectively** and **Iceland**.

Answer Sheet

16. (A) (B) (C) (D)
17. (A) (B) (C) (D)
18. (A) (B) (C) (D)
19. (A) (B) (C) (D)
20. (A) (B) (C) (D)

Name _____

(Numbers in parentheses identify related lessons.)
Read each item carefully. Select the best answer and fill in the circle on the answer sheet below.

1. Which of the following sentences has a proper noun underlined? (11)

   A Let me show you this <u>timeline</u>.
   B It shows the dates of early voyages to our <u>continent</u>.
   C Not all dates are <u>exact</u>.
   D No one knows exactly when <u>Leif Ericson</u> sailed to North America.

2. Which of the following sentences has a possessive noun in it? (12)

   A Christopher Columbus moved to Lisbon, Portugal, at the age of 25.
   B In that city he learned to read and write.
   C Christopher Columbus's brother taught him mapmaking skills.
   D These skills helped him prepare for his historic voyage.

3. Read this sentence.

   Many New England colonists built their homes out of logs.

   Which word in the sentence is a possessive pronoun? (13)

   A many
   B New England
   C their
   D of

4. Which of the following sentences has a present tense verb in it? (14)

   A Some colonists built homes out of whole logs.
   B Wind often blows through cracks between logs.
   C Many more colonists shaped logs into square timbers.
   D They used broadaxes and other hand tools for this task.

5. Which sentence has both a past tense verb and a future tense verb in it? (15)

   A Ida finished her history report last night, and I will finish mine today.
   B My friends always start reports late, and they often finish them late, too.
   C Ida starts reports on time; she started this one last week.
   D I will submit my report on time, but my friends will miss the deadline.

Example:

● Ⓑ Ⓒ Ⓓ

Answer Sheet

1. Ⓐ Ⓑ Ⓒ **Ⓓ**
2. Ⓐ Ⓑ **Ⓒ** Ⓓ
3. Ⓐ Ⓑ **Ⓒ** Ⓓ
4. Ⓐ **Ⓑ** Ⓒ Ⓓ
5. **Ⓐ** Ⓑ Ⓒ Ⓓ

Read each item carefully. Select the best answer and fill in the circle on the answer sheet below.

6. Which of the following sentences has a present perfect tense verb in it? **(16)**

   A We will now study the colonies of New York, New Jersey, Delaware, and Pennsylvania.
   B Some historians call these the breadbasket colonies.
   C Farmers in these colonies raised grain and livestock.
   D Farms in these areas have prospered for centuries.

7. Read this sentence.

   Travelers in colonial America generally depended on horses for transportation.

   Which of these words is an adjective in the sentence? **(17)**

   A colonial
   B generally
   C depended
   D for

8. Read this sentence.

   On a trip from Boston to New York in 1704, Sarah Knight narrowly avoided a tragic fall into a river.

   Which of these words is an adverb in the sentence? **(18)**

   A from
   B 1704
   C narrowly
   D tragic

9. Which of the following sentences has a prepositional phrase underlined? **(19)**

   A Most roads <u>in the colonies</u> were very bad then.
   B <u>Muddy roads</u> slowed horses, and dusty roads choked riders.
   C Rocks littered the main roads; fallen trees <u>sometimes blocked them</u>.
   D Steep hills caused problems for horses with <u>heavily loaded wagons</u>.

10. Which of the following sentences has a subordinating conjunction in it? **(20)**

   A Benjamin Franklin traveled to Philadelphia at age 17.
   B He worked as a printer, but he also invented devices.
   C One of his inventions was the lightning rod.
   D Before he invented this device, lightning caused many house fires.

Answer Sheet

6. Ⓐ Ⓑ Ⓒ **Ⓓ**
7. **Ⓐ** Ⓑ Ⓒ Ⓓ
8. Ⓐ Ⓑ **Ⓒ** Ⓓ
9. **Ⓐ** Ⓑ Ⓒ Ⓓ
10. Ⓐ Ⓑ Ⓒ **Ⓓ**

Name _____

Read each item carefully. Select the best answer and fill in the circle on the answer sheet below.

11. **Which of the following sentences has a proper noun underlined?** (11)

   A Where can we go to see <u>totem poles</u>?
   B The Indians of the <u>Northwest Coast</u> carved them.
   C That totem pole commemorates an important <u>event</u> in a person's life.
   D A few Northwest Indian <u>artists</u> still carve these poles today.

12. **Which of the following sentences has a possessive noun in it?** (12)

   A We are studying America's mountain ranges.
   B Mountain ranges are barriers to travel.
   C Daniel Boone led settlers across the Appalachian Mountains.
   D Lewis and Clark had difficulty crossing the Rockies.

13. **Read this sentence.**

   I need to borrow this atlas to use its relief maps.

   Which word in the sentence is a possessive pronoun? (13)

   A this
   B use
   C its
   D relief

14. **Which of the following sentences has a present tense verb in it?** (14)

   A New England colonists caught large numbers of fish.
   B They usually had a surplus of fish.
   C People with surplus items often exchange them.
   D These colonists traded dried fish to people in the West Indies and Europe.

15. **Which sentence has both a past tense verb and a future tense verb in it?** (15)

   A Some early American settlers had hard lives, but others prospered.
   B We studied Plymouth Colony last week, and I learned a lot.
   C I saw a film about the Puritans, and I read an article about them, too.
   D I wrote notes about them, and I will use those notes tonight.

Answer Sheet

11. Ⓐ **Ⓑ** Ⓒ Ⓓ
12. **Ⓐ** Ⓑ Ⓒ Ⓓ
13. Ⓐ Ⓑ **Ⓒ** Ⓓ
14. Ⓐ Ⓑ **Ⓒ** Ⓓ
15. Ⓐ Ⓑ Ⓒ **Ⓓ**

Read each item carefully. Select the best answer and fill in the circle on the answer sheet below.

16. **Which of the following sentences has a present perfect tense verb in it?** (16)

  A Last year our family visited colonial Williamsburg.
  B We have begun an American history scrapbook.
  C Next month we will visit Mount Vernon.
  D Many Americans visit this historic residence.

17. **Read this sentence.**

  Thanks to its fine harbor, Charleston, South Carolina, is an important city.

  Which of these words is an adjective in the sentence? (17)

  A thanks
  B fine
  C South Carolina
  D city

18. **Read this sentence.**

  Ships could dock safely and be protected from stormy seas.

  Which of these words is an adverb in the sentence? (18)

  A could
  B dock
  C safely
  D stormy

19. **Which of the following sentences has a prepositional phrase underlined?** (19)

  A Farmers grew rice in the swampy land near Charleston.
  B Rice fields must be flooded in spring and summer.
  C The hot summer weather in the area is ideal for growing rice.
  D The fields must be drained before the rice can be harvested.

20. **Which of the following sentences has a subordinating conjunction in it?** (20)

  A Ships carried rice from Charleston to distant ports.
  B Rice planters in the Charleston area became prosperous.
  C Field workers suffered, though; the work was hard and unhealthy.
  D Because these workers were enslaved people, they could not leave their jobs.

Answer Sheet

16. Ⓐ ⬤B Ⓒ Ⓓ
17. Ⓐ ⬤B Ⓒ Ⓓ
18. Ⓐ Ⓑ ⬤C Ⓓ
19. ⬤A Ⓑ Ⓒ Ⓓ
20. Ⓐ Ⓑ Ⓒ ⬤D

Standardized Test Format

TEST TIP: Eliminate answer choices that you know are incorrect.

(Numbers in parentheses identify related lessons.)

Read each item carefully. Select the best answer and fill in the circle on the answer sheet below.

1. **Read this sentence.**

   Those athletes want to avoid injury, so ___ warming up carefully.

   Which word would complete the sentence correctly? (21)

   A their
   B there
   C they're
   D theyre

2. **Which of the following sentences has *its* or *it's* used *incorrectly*?** (22)

   A It's important to stretch your muscles before competing.
   B I am going to the gym to use it's exercise machines.
   C The gym has its schedule posted on the door.
   D I think it's fun to try new machines.

3. **Which of the following sentences has *your* or *you're* used *incorrectly*?** (23)

   A Do you like you're gymnastics coach?
   B I am amazed at your improvement!
   C You're the best of anyone on the balance beam.
   D Perhaps you have improved because you're a hard worker.

4. **Read each sentence. Look at the underlined word or words in it. Which sentence is written *incorrectly*?** (24)

   A Which indoor sport do you <u>like</u> best?
   B I think bowling is, <u>like</u>, the most fun sport of all.
   C Do <u>you know</u> how to keep score?
   D Tell me everything <u>you know</u> about that sport.

5. **Read this sentence.**

   These drills will help me become a ___ soccer player.

   Which choice would complete the sentence correctly? (25)

   A more good
   B gooder
   C more better
   D better

Example:

● Ⓑ Ⓒ Ⓓ

Answer Sheet

1. Ⓐ Ⓑ Ⓒ Ⓓ
2. Ⓐ Ⓑ Ⓒ Ⓓ
3. Ⓐ Ⓑ Ⓒ Ⓓ
4. Ⓐ Ⓑ Ⓒ Ⓓ
5. Ⓐ Ⓑ Ⓒ Ⓓ

Read each item carefully. Select the best answer and fill in the circle on the answer sheet below.

6. Read this sentence.

   The fishing rod ___ I use is old but effective.

   Which word would complete the sentence correctly? (26)

   A that
   B which
   C who
   D None of the above

7. **Read each sentence. Look at the underlined word in it. Which sentence is written *incorrectly*?** (27)

   A We cannot play with a <u>real</u> baseball here.
   B We would be <u>very</u> likely to break a window.
   C This hollow plastic ball is <u>very</u> safe.
   D It's <u>real</u> good for backyard ball games.

8. **Read each sentence. Look at the underlined word in it. Which sentence is written *incorrectly*?** (28)

   A Please <u>set</u> your bag on the floor.
   B <u>Sit</u> on the bench while I explain the rules.
   C My sister has <u>sat</u> the paddles on the table.
   D We have <u>sat</u> long enough; let's play!

9. **Read each sentence. Look at the underlined word in it. Which sentence is written *incorrectly*?** (29)

   A My aunt is <u>known</u> throughout the world as a champion.
   B Her fame <u>grown</u> when she won a race last year.
   C Few people <u>knew</u> how hard she had trained.
   D She has <u>grown</u> stronger through exercise.

10. Read this sentence.

    Saleem has ___ a lot about sports from his older brother.

    Which word would complete the sentence correctly? (30)

    A learn
    B teach
    C learned
    D taught

Answer Sheet

6. (A) B C D
7. A B C (D)
8. A B (C) D
9. A (B) C D
10. A B (C) D

Read each item carefully. Select the best answer and fill in the circle on the answer sheet below.

11. **Read this sentence.**

    Many pitchers do exercises to strengthen ___ legs.

    Which word would complete the sentence correctly? (21)

    A their
    B there
    C they're
    D theyre

12. **Which of the following sentences has *its* or *it's* used *incorrectly*?** (22)

    A This city is proud of its athletic fields.
    B It's important for students to get exercise.
    C Our school opens it's fields to the public.
    D They are filled with people, except when it's raining.

13. **Which of the following sentences has *your* or *you're* used *incorrectly*?** (23)

    A What is your favorite sport?
    B You're lucky to live near a soccer field.
    C How often do you play there with your friends?
    D Call me the next time your going to play there.

14. **Read each sentence. Look at the underlined word or words in it. Which sentence is written *incorrectly*?** (24)

    A I <u>like</u> sports that you can play barefoot.
    B Badminton is, <u>you know</u>, such a fun summer game!
    C Badminton is <u>like</u> tennis in some ways.
    D Did <u>you know</u> that badminton is an Olympic sport?

15. **Read this sentence.**

    Our team has played hard, but we have the ___ record of all.

    Which choice would complete the sentence correctly? (25)

    A worse
    B baddest
    C most bad
    D worst

Answer Sheet

11. (A) B C D
12. A B (C) D
13. A B C (D)
14. A (B) C D
15. A B C (D)

149

Read each item carefully. Select the best answer and fill in the circle on the answer sheet below.

16. Read this sentence.

    Myra is the batter ___ hit the home run.

    Which word would complete the sentence correctly? (26)

    A that
    B which
    C who
    D None of the above

17. **Read each sentence. Look at the underlined word in it. Which sentence is written *incorrectly*?** (27)

    A Is this a <u>real</u> golf club?
    B It isn't <u>very</u> heavy, and it's quite short.
    C It's for a young golfer; kids need <u>real</u> equipment to develop skills.
    D I will pay <u>real</u> careful attention to the instructor.

18. **Read each sentence. Look at the underlined word in it. Which sentence is written *incorrectly*?** (28)

    A I <u>sat</u> near mid-court at the basketball game.
    B I carelessly <u>sat</u> my sunglasses on the bench.
    C When Cici <u>sat</u> next to me, she broke them.
    D I should have <u>set</u> those glasses on my locker shelf.

19. **Read each sentence. Look at the underlined word in it. Which sentence is written *incorrectly*?** (29)

    A The home crowd <u>growed</u> quiet.
    B They <u>knew</u> that the next free throw could decide the game.
    C The star player swished the shot, and the home team's lead <u>grew</u>.
    D The fans all said they had <u>known</u> she'd make that free throw.

20. **Read this sentence.**

    Yesterday the coach ___ me how to run hurdles.

    Which word would complete the sentence correctly? (30)

    A learn
    B teach
    C learned
    D taught

Answer Sheet

16.	Ⓐ	Ⓑ	**Ⓒ**	Ⓓ
17.	Ⓐ	Ⓑ	Ⓒ	**Ⓓ**
18.	Ⓐ	**Ⓑ**	Ⓒ	Ⓓ
19.	**Ⓐ**	Ⓑ	Ⓒ	Ⓓ
20.	Ⓐ	Ⓑ	Ⓒ	**Ⓓ**

Unit 4 Assessment

 TEST TIP: Be sure to fill in the whole circle on the answer sheet.

(Numbers in parentheses identify related lessons.)

Read each item carefully. Select the best answer and fill in the circle on the answer sheet below.

1. Read this sentence.

   When my dad saw me in the stands, he waved.

   Which word in the sentence is an object pronoun? **(31)**

   A my
   B dad
   C me
   D he

2. Read each sentence. Look at the underlined word. Which sentence is written *incorrectly*? **(32)**

   A My dad takes my sister and <u>I</u> to the racetrack.
   B <u>He</u> and my uncle are part of a pit crew.
   C My sister and <u>I</u> are learning about auto mechanics.
   D You may see <u>her</u> or me in a pit crew someday.

3. Read each sentence. Look at the underlined words. Which sentence is written *incorrectly*? **(33)**

   A <u>Kenji and I</u> draw cars of the future.
   B You will often find <u>me and him</u> with our sketch pads.
   C "You are both talented car designers!" Kenji's mom said to <u>him and me</u>.
   D Kenji likes black cars, but <u>his mom and I</u> prefer bright colors for cars.

4. Read this sentence.

   My go-kart has speed and style. <u>Its</u> design is totally original.

   Which is the antecedent for the underlined pronoun? **(34)**

   A go-kart
   B style
   C design
   D original

5. Read each sentence. Look at the underlined verb. Which sentence is *not* correct? **(35)**

   A Drivers on a track always <u>have</u> smooth pavement ahead.
   B An off-road race for trucks <u>test</u> the drivers' reflexes.
   C Only durable vehicles <u>enter</u> this type of race.
   D A long race on dirt roads <u>punishes</u> vehicles and drivers.

Example:

● Ⓑ Ⓒ Ⓓ

Answer Sheet

1. Ⓐ Ⓑ **Ⓒ** Ⓓ
2. **Ⓐ** Ⓑ Ⓒ Ⓓ
3. Ⓐ **Ⓑ** Ⓒ Ⓓ
4. **Ⓐ** Ⓑ Ⓒ Ⓓ
5. Ⓐ **Ⓑ** Ⓒ Ⓓ

Read each item carefully. Select the best answer and fill in the circle on the answer sheet below.

6. Read each sentence. Look at the underlined verb. Which sentence is *not* correct? **(36)**

   A That screeching noise <u>is</u> a warning.
   B Your car's brake pads <u>are</u> ready for replacement.
   C The mechanics in this shop <u>are</u> skillful.
   D Repairs on an auto <u>is</u> never cheap.

7. Read this sentence.

   My mom ___ our old car last Saturday.

   Which verb would complete the sentence correctly? **(37)**

   A sells
   B will sell
   C sold
   D has sold

8. Read each sentence. Which sentence has too many negatives? **(38)**

   A There isn't no room for any more decals on that car!
   B I don't think it's possible to count all the decals.
   C No one knows what that decal stands for.
   D I would never drive a car covered with ads!

9. Read this sentence.

   My model racecar is ___ than my cousin's new model racecar.

   Which choice would complete the sentence correctly? **(39)**

   A beautifuler
   B more beautiful
   C beautifulest
   D most beautiful

10. Read this sentence.

    This car uses fuel the ___ of any car I've tested.

    Which choice would complete the sentence correctly? **(40)**

    A more efficient
    B more efficiently
    C most efficient
    D most efficiently

Answer Sheet

6. (A) (B) (C) ●D
7. (A) (B) ●C (D)
8. ●A (B) (C) (D)
9. (A) ●B (C) (D)
10. (A) (B) (C) ●D

Read each item carefully. Select the best answer and fill in the circle on the answer sheet below.

11. **Read this sentence.**

My brother and I bring our car magazines with us on vacation.

Which word in the sentence is an object pronoun? (31)

A I
B our
C magazines
D us

12. **Read each sentence. Look at the underlined word. Which sentence is written *incorrectly*?** (32)

A Tara and I went to a drag race with her parents.
B The noise didn't bother Tara or I.
C Tara shared her snack with her parents and me.
D She and her parents knew which cars would be the fastest.

13. **Read each sentence. Look at the underlined words. Which sentence is written *incorrectly*?** (33)

A My dad showed Iris and me an old Trans Am racecar.
B She and I saw that parts had been removed.
C "This car has no headlights!" Iris said to me and Dad.
D "They were removed to make the car lighter," Dad said to her and me.

14. **Read this sentence.**

My brother and I invited Rob and Jen to the movies, but they wanted to watch a NASCAR race on TV.

Which is the antecedent for the underlined pronoun? (34)

A brother, I
B Rob, Jen
C movies
D race

15. **Read each sentence. Look at the underlined verb. Which sentence is *not* correct?** (35)

A Drivers in this class learn racing techniques.
B The instructor demonstrates the correct position for hands on the steering wheel.
C The eyes of a racecar driver looks ahead, to the sides, and in the mirrors.
D Any race with other cars requires concentration on the part of the driver.

Answer Sheet

	A	B	C	D
11.	A	B	C	**D**
12.	A	**B**	C	D
13.	A	B	**C**	D
14.	A	**B**	C	D
15.	A	B	**C**	D

Read each item carefully. Select the best answer and fill in the circle on the answer sheet below.

16. Read each sentence. Look at the underlined verb. Which sentence is *not* correct? **(36)**

    A   A slick tire <u>is</u> unsafe in wet weather.
    B   An inspection of your tires <u>are</u> a good idea.
    C   Two tires on my car <u>were</u> bald.
    D   Fortunately, a tire sale <u>was</u> in progress.

17. Read this sentence.

    In the future, Brian ___ better care of his car.

    Which verb would complete the sentence correctly? **(37)**

    A   will take
    B   takes
    C   took
    D   has taken

18. Read each sentence. Which sentence has too many negatives? **(38)**

    A   I haven't never ridden in such a big car!
    B   I don't think it will fit in our garage.
    C   It isn't easy to drive a big car on a narrow road.
    D   Nobody in our neighborhood owns a car this size.

19. Read this sentence.

    Enrique's soap box racer has the ___ time of all, but he is still proud of it.

    Which choice would complete the sentence correctly? **(39)**

    A   slower
    B   more slow
    C   slowest
    D   most slow

20. Read this sentence.

    Clete drives ___ now than he did last year.

    Which choice would complete the sentence correctly? **(40)**

    A   more careful
    B   more carefully
    C   most careful
    D   most carefully

Answer Sheet

16. (A) ●B● (C) (D)
17. ●A● (B) (C) (D)
18. ●A● (B) (C) (D)
19. (A) (B) ●C● (D)
20. (A) ●B● (C) (D)

Unit 5 Assessment

Standardized Test Format

TEST TIP: Mark your answers neatly. If you erase, erase completely and clearly without smudging.

(Numbers in parentheses identify related lessons.)

Read each item carefully. Select the best answer and fill in the circle on the answer sheet below.

1. Read this sentence.

   What is the largest amphibian alive today!

   How should the sentence be changed to make it correct? (41)

   A Change the exclamation point to a period.
   B Change the exclamation point to a question mark.
   C Make the first letter in **amphibian** a capital letter.
   D Make no change. It is correct as written.

2. Read this sentence.

   The japanese salamander is the largest amphibian on our planet.

   Which underlined word should be capitalized? (42)

   A japanese
   B salamander
   C amphibian
   D planet

3. Read this sentence.

   Mister Niles Eugene Klein teaches us biology.

   How should the underlined name be written with abbreviations? (43)

   A Mr N E Klein
   B Mstr. n. e. Klein
   C Mr. N.E. Klein
   D Mstr. N.E. Klein

4. Read each sentence. Which sentence has the title in it written correctly? (44)

   A The book "Prehistoric Amphibians and Their Ancestors" is amazing.
   B Have you read the short story called *Don't Pet That Frog*?
   C I just saw the movie "Revenge of the Reptiles."
   D I am looking for the article titled "Stay Safe Around Snakes."

5. Read each sentence. Look at the underlined word. Which sentence is written *incorrectly*? (45)

   A One local park's ponds are filled with frogs.
   B Those frog's croaks are loud and deep.
   C Frogs are many birds' favorite food.
   D Some snakes feed on that park's frogs.

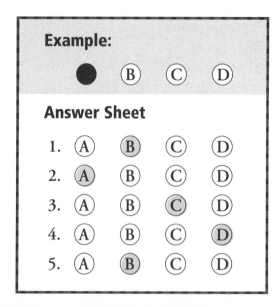

Example:

● Ⓑ Ⓒ Ⓓ

Answer Sheet

1. Ⓐ Ⓑ Ⓒ Ⓓ
2. Ⓐ Ⓑ Ⓒ Ⓓ
3. Ⓐ Ⓑ Ⓒ Ⓓ
4. Ⓐ Ⓑ Ⓒ Ⓓ
5. Ⓐ Ⓑ Ⓒ Ⓓ

Read each item carefully. Select the best answer and fill in the circle on the answer sheet below.

6. Read each sentence. Look at the commas. Which sentence is written correctly? **(46)**

   A Snakes live on the ground, in trees, and in caves.
   B Whiptales, racers, and whipsnakes, are fast-moving reptiles.
   C Alligators crocodiles, and caimans are large, dangerous reptiles.
   D Snakes have distinctive eyes, tongues, and, tails.

7. Read this sentence.

   "Would you like to be a reptile watcher Sandra?" asked Mr. Tran.

   Where should a comma be placed in this sentence? **(47)**

   A after **you**
   B after **be**
   C after **reptile**
   D after **watcher**

8. Read this sentence.

   He told her to bring a notebook and a pencil he warned her to keep a safe distance from any snake she observed.

   Where should a semicolon be placed in this sentence? **(48)**

   A after **notebook**
   B after **pencil**
   C after **distance**
   D after **snake**

9. Read each sentence. Which sentence needs to have quotation marks added to it? **(49)**

   A Ariel said that she saw an Eastern hognose snake yesterday.
   B Rich asked her what the snake did when it noticed her.
   C It hissed and puffed itself up, Ariel replied.
   D She said that the snake then flipped on its back and stuck out its tongue.

10. Read this friendly letter.

    Dear Amy,

    Did you borrow my reptile book? If so, please give it back. I need it for the nature hike next week.

    Your friend,

    Louis

    Which part of the letter is missing? **(50)**

    A heading
    B greeting
    C closing
    D signature

Answer Sheet

6.	(A)	B	C	D
7.	A	B	C	(D)
8.	A	(B)	C	D
9.	A	B	(C)	D
10.	(A)	B	C	D

Read each item carefully. Select the best answer and fill in the circle on the answer sheet below.

11. **Read this sentence.**

    do most amphibians live in moist habitats?

    How should the sentence be changed to make it correct? (41)

    A Change the question mark to an exclamation point.
    B Change the question mark to a period.
    C Make the first letter in **do** a capital letter.
    D Make no change. It is correct as written.

12. **Read this sentence.**

    Central <u>america</u>, a warm, humid <u>area</u>, is home to many <u>species</u> of <u>salamanders</u>.

    Which underlined word should be capitalized? (42)

    A america
    B area
    C species
    D salamanders

13. **Read this sentence.**

    I asked <u>Professor Jamal Lester Darby</u> about caecilians.

    How should the underlined name be written with abbreviations? (43)

    A Pro. J L Darby
    B Prof. JL. Darby
    C Pro JL Darby
    D Prof. J.L. Darby

14. **Read each sentence. Which sentence has the title in it written correctly?** (44)

    A Larkin taught us the song <u>The Toad on the Road</u>.
    B The movie titled <u>Jungle Squeeze</u> is about boa constrictors.
    C "How to Raise Frogs" is a book I will not read.
    D My poem <u>Turtle Journey</u> is the best one I've written.

15. **Read each sentence. Look at the underlined word. Which sentence is written *incorrectly*?** (45)

    A An <u>amphibian's</u> skin has no scales.
    B This <u>newt's</u> skin is smooth.
    C Those <u>amphibians'</u> glands produce mucus, which covers the skin.
    D That <u>toads'</u> skin feels like leather.

Answer Sheet

11. Ⓐ Ⓑ **Ⓒ** Ⓓ
12. **Ⓐ** Ⓑ Ⓒ Ⓓ
13. Ⓐ Ⓑ Ⓒ **Ⓓ**
14. Ⓐ **Ⓑ** Ⓒ Ⓓ
15. Ⓐ Ⓑ Ⓒ **Ⓓ**

Read each item carefully. Select the best answer and fill in the circle on the answer sheet below.

16. Read each sentence. Look at the commas. Which sentence is written correctly? (46)

    A Snakes, lizards, and iguanas, are reptiles.
    B Eastern fence lizards can be seen on rocks, fences, and, trees.
    C Many lizards eat tadpoles frogs and small fish.
    D Female iguanas have brown, white, and black markings.

17. Read this sentence.

    "No the glass lizard does not have legs," the ranger said to us.

    Where should a comma be placed in this sentence? (47)

    A after **no**
    B after **lizard**
    C after **not**
    D after **said**

18. Read this sentence.

    Spectacled caimans now live in southern Florida scientists believe they were brought from South America and released.

    Where should a semicolon be placed in this sentence? (48)

    A after **caimans**
    B after **Florida**
    C after **brought**
    D after **America**

19. Read each sentence. Which sentence needs to have quotation marks added to it? (49)

    A Ron asked Kesh to tell him which reptile has the longest tail.
    B Kesh said that the saltwater crocodile is the reptile with the longest tail.
    C He explained that a large saltwater crocodile's tail can be 13 feet long.
    D Ron said, I wonder how big its jaws are.

20. Read this friendly letter.

    125 Key Court
    Joliet, IL 60431
    March 12, 2012

    Dear Mrs. Elliot,

    I understand that you have a pet iguana. Would it be possible for me to come over and observe it? I am doing a report on that reptile for school.

    David Jefferson

    Which part of the letter is missing? (50)

    A heading
    B greeting
    C closing
    D signature

    Answer Sheet

    16. Ⓐ Ⓑ Ⓒ 🅓
    17. 🅐 Ⓑ Ⓒ Ⓓ
    18. Ⓐ 🅑 Ⓒ Ⓓ
    19. Ⓐ Ⓑ Ⓒ 🅓
    20. Ⓐ Ⓑ 🅒 Ⓓ

Lesson 1 Underline the complete subject in each sentence once. Underline the complete predicate twice.

1. Hot sand covered Zoe's feet.

2. She rested beside a pile of driftwood.

3. This hidden beach was her favorite place.

4. Zoe fell asleep.

5. A noisy sea gull landed at her feet.

6. Someone's radio blasted loud music.

7. Some teenagers set up a volleyball net.

8. A crowd gathered.

9. Everyone cheered the players.

10. A quiet place is hard to find.

Lesson 2 In each sentence, draw one line under the simple subject and two lines under the simple predicate.

1. My alarm rang at 6:30 this morning.

2. I looked out the window.

3. Heavy black clouds threatened rain.

4. I dressed in warm clothes.

5. My father prepared a hot breakfast for everyone.

6. My mother packed an umbrella in my backpack.

7. A crowd waited impatiently for the bus.

8. The first raindrops were huge.

9. My umbrella snapped in the wind.

10. Randy shared his umbrella with me.

Name _____

Lesson 3 Each sentence below has either a compound subject or a compound predicate. Write *S* next to each sentence with a compound subject. Circle the two subjects. Write *P* next to each sentence with a compound predicate. Underline the two verbs.

1. The travelers <u>stopped</u> at the edge of the plateau and <u>looked</u> across the desert plain. **P**

2. (Grasses) and (shrubs) grew in clumps. **S**

3. The travelers <u>saw</u> a small oasis and <u>headed</u> in that direction. **P**

4. A (salamander) and a (lizard) slithered across their path. **S**

5. The lizard <u>crawled</u> onto a rock and <u>sat</u> warming itself in the sun. **P**

6. The (boy) and his (father) smiled at each other. **S**

7. The boy <u>grabbed</u> at the lizard and <u>missed</u>. **P**

8. (Trees) and green (grasses) grow in an oasis. **S**

9. The travelers <u>stopped</u> at the oasis and <u>rested</u> for a while. **P**

10. The fresh (water) and cool (shade) attract many travelers. **S**

Lesson 4 Circle the direct object in each sentence below.

1. The diver stretched her (muscles).

2. The announcer called her (name).

3. Her parents watched their (daughter) anxiously.

4. She quickly climbed the (ladder).

5. She focused her (concentration).

6. She executed the (dive) perfectly.

7. She entered the (water) smoothly.

8. The announcer called out a perfect (score).

9. The diver's fans clapped their (hands).

10. The girl hugged her (parents).

Lesson 5 The direct object in each sentence is printed in bold type. Circle the indirect object in each sentence.

1. Bif sent his (cousin) a **bag** of marbles.

2. His cousin sent (Bif) a thank you **note**.

3. She also sent (Bif) an **invitation** to her birthday party.

4. Bif's father gave (him) **permission** to drive to the party.

5. He mailed his (cousin) a **postcard** saying he could come.

6. Bif's mother handed (him) the **keys** to the car.

7. He gave his (family) one last **wave** and headed for Spokane.

8. He handed the (toll taker) a five dollar **bill** and waited for change.

9. When Bif arrived, his cousin gave (him) a big **hug**.

10. At the party Bif sang his (cousin) a special birthday **song** he wrote for her.

Lesson 6 Draw a box around the linking verb in each sentence. Then circle each boldfaced word that is a predicate noun. Underline each boldfaced word that is a predicate adjective.

1. Martin Luther King Jr. [was] an important (leader) of the civil rights movement in the United States.

2. He [was] a Baptist (minister).

3. He [was] the (leader) of a bus boycott in Montgomery, Alabama, in 1955–1956.

4. Dr. King's demonstrations [were] **nonviolent**.

5. Some Montgomery residents [were] **angry** about segregation.

6. The boycott [was] **successful** in ending segregated seating on public buses.

7. Dr. King [was] an eloquent (speaker).

8. His "I Have a Dream" speech [is] still an (inspiration).

9. Dr. King's assassination in 1968 [was] **tragic**.

10. People across the United States [were] **upset** by his death.

Lesson 7 Underline the prepositional phrase in each sentence. Circle the preposition that begins the prepositional phrase.

1. It had rained (for) 11 days.

2. Water gushed (into) creeks and streams.

3. We went (to) the river's edge.

4. The river carried huge logs (in) its current.

5. Many river residents spent the night (in) hotels.

6. We listened (to) the radio report.

7. The flood waters crested (at) midnight.

8. The next day, many people returned (to) their homes.

9. Our house had thick mud (on) the floor.

10. Perhaps we should move (to) higher ground.

Lesson 8 Write *S* next to each simple sentence and *C* next to each compound sentence. Then circle each conjunction or semicolon in each compound sentence.

1. Danny and Alicia went rafting on the Colorado River. __S__

2. The first day the water was calm, (and) Danny and Alicia enjoyed the scenery. __C__

3. At night they camped along the river bank, (and) the guides made a delicious dinner. __C__

4. The next morning the weather had turned cloudy. __S__

5. The river still looked calm, (but) the guides warned of dangerous rapids ahead. __C__

6. The rafters entered a very difficult part of the river. __S__

7. The raft shot past huge boulders and down small waterfalls(;) Danny and Alicia held on tightly. __C__

8. The wild roller-coaster ride lasted only 30 seconds, (but) it was long enough for them. __C__

9. Finally the raft reached calmer waters(;) everyone breathed a sigh of relief. __C__

10. Danny and Alicia loved the experience. __S__

Lesson 9 Each sentence below has one independent clause and one dependent clause. Draw one line under each independent clause and two lines under each dependent clause. Then circle the subordinating conjunction that begins each dependent clause.

1. Many people don't visit the desert (because) they are worried about its intense heat.

2. (If) you take proper precautions, you can enjoy a desert vacation.

3. (Because) summer heat is quite intense, you should plan your trip for the spring or fall.

4. (Because) it is hottest at noon, you should begin your desert exploration in the morning.

5. (After) the sun has set, the desert air grows cooler.

6. (As) the temperature drops, nocturnal animals come out in search of food.

7. (Although) most desert creatures are harmless, you must be cautious in open terrain.

8. Startled rattlesnakes sometimes attack, (though) they generally avoid people.

9. (When) you hike in the desert, you should always carry a snake-bite kit.

10. A desert vacation can be fun and safe (when) you put safety first.

Lesson 10 Write *F* next to each fragment, *RO* next to each run-on sentence, and *CS* next to each comma splice.

1. While driving across Montana one dry summer. **F**

2. We saw a herd of buffalo, we were amazed. **CS**

3. In 1889 only 551 buffalo remained in the United States most had been killed by hunters. **RO**

4. Extinction of the entire species. **F**

5. Today more than fifteen thousand buffalo. **F**

6. Most live on game preserves some run wild in national parks. **RO**

7. The buffalo we saw in Montana lived on a private ranch, they are raised for meat. **CS**

8. I have never eaten buffalo stew I'd like to try it. **RO**

9. The animals we saw are called American bison, most people call them buffalo. **CS**

10. These powerful, majestic animals. **F**

Name _____

Lesson 11 Circle the common nouns. Underline the proper nouns.

1. <u>Langley Park</u> is always crowded on (holidays).

2. The (fireworks) attract (people) on the <u>Fourth of July</u>.

3. The <u>Smiths</u> arrive early at the (park).

4. <u>Janis</u> and <u>Nestor</u> play (baseball).

5. <u>Savannah</u> practices (karate).

6. The outdoor (pool) opens in <u>May</u>.

7. My (brother) won the <u>Best Swimmer Award</u>.

8. His (strength) has helped make him the best (swimmer) in <u>Nashville</u>.

9. <u>Labor Day</u> signals that (summer) is over.

10. In <u>September</u>, we go back to (school).

Lesson 12 First put a box around each noun that is both plural and possessive. For the remaining nouns, underline each plural noun and circle each possessive noun.

1. The <u>dancers</u> practiced for the Lunar New Year for many <u>months</u>.

2. <u>Volunteers</u> sewed the ornate red <u>costumes</u>.

3. The (group's) leader gave the signal to drum loudly.

4. The [firecrackers'] smoke filled the air.

5. The [women's] <u>movements</u> were graceful.

6. <u>Boys</u> and <u>girls</u> crowded closer to see the dancing <u>lions</u>.

7. One father tried to hush his (baby's) cries.

8. The [lions'] <u>heads</u> seemed to roar.

9. Several <u>photographers</u> ran out in front of the crowd.

10. Then the [acrobats'] performance began.

Name _____

Lesson 13 Write a pronoun from the word bank that could take the place of the underlined word or phrase in each sentence. Remember to capitalize a word that begins a sentence.

her	him	he	she	they	them	we

1. <u>Kate</u> always sings off key. ____She____

2. Kate's brothers and sisters complain about <u>Kate's</u> singing. ____her____

3. <u>Nora, Emily, Carl, and Matt</u> asked for ear plugs. ____They____

4. "<u>Your father and I</u> enjoy her singing," their mother replied. ____We____

5. "Then you share a room with her!" <u>Nora and Emily</u> said. ____they____

6. Kate's music teacher encouraged her to practice with <u>Luisa and Dawn</u>. ____them____

7. On the day of the spring concert <u>Kate's</u> family sat in the front row. ____her____

8. <u>Mr. Higashi</u> gave a welcoming speech to the students and guests. ____He____

9. A baby girl screamed happily at <u>Mr. Higashi</u>. ____him____

10. "<u>That baby</u> will be a member of our chorus someday!" said Mr. Higashi with a smile. ____She____

Lesson 14 Write the present tense form of the verb in parentheses to complete each sentence correctly.

1. The ship ____sails____ toward the shore. (sail)

2. Its captain ____shouts____ orders to the crew. (shout)

3. Storms ____bring____ high winds and rain. (bring)

4. The captain ____sees____ the lighthouse and knows the ship is in safe waters. (see)

5. Families ____wait____ on the dock. (wait)

6. A little girl ____waves____ to her father. (wave)

7. Her mother ____tells____ her that he is too far away to see them. (tell)

8. Tugboats ____spray____ water to celebrate the ship's arrival. (spray)

9. One sailor ____receives____ flowers from a friend. (receive)

10. People ____leave____ the ship. (leave)

Name _____

Lesson 15 Circle the word or words in parentheses that will show time correctly in each sentence.

1. Last year I (**borrowed**/borrow) my sister's new roller skates.

2. She promised, "You (**will have**/had) the ride of your life!"

3. She (know/**knew**) how fast the skates were.

4. I (start/**started**) skating on my street right away.

5. Then I (will head/**headed**) for the beach.

6. I (**tripped**/trip) on a dog's leash just a few yards from the beach.

7. The dog (barks/**barked**) at me, and I fell.

8. Luckily, the dog (**decided**/will decide) to lick me instead of bite me!

9. When I skate to the beach next week, I (wear/**will wear**) kneepads.

10. I (**will stay**/stayed) away from dog leashes, too!

Lesson 16 Complete each sentence by writing the present perfect form of the verb (*has* or *have* plus the past participle) in parentheses. Watch for irregular verbs!

1. Jessie _____**has flown**_____ model airplanes since she was eight. (fly)

2. Her dad _____**has loved**_____ model airplanes since he was a little boy. (love)

3. Their neighbors _____**have asked**_____ them how to fly model planes. (ask)

4. Jessie's mom _____**has packed**_____ a picnic lunch for the flying lesson. (pack)

5. "I _____**have heard**_____ that it may rain this morning," Jessie's mom warned. (hear)

6. "It _____**has rained**_____ every Saturday!" Jessie complained. (rain)

7. "You _____**have waited**_____ a long time to fly your plane," her father said. (wait)

8. "The neighbors _____**have left**_____ for the park already," her mother added. (leave)

9. "Everyone _____**has wanted**_____ to do this for a long time," Jessie pointed out. (want)

10. "I _____**have reached**_____ my decision," Jessie's mother said. "Let's go!" (reach)

Lesson 17 Underline each adjective (including *a, an,* and *the*) in the sentences below.

1. Sam has <u>a</u> <u>small</u>, <u>shady</u> garden.

2. <u>Three</u> <u>golden</u> carp swim in <u>a</u> pond.

3. <u>The</u> cat stares at them with <u>sharp</u> eyes.

4. <u>Many</u> flowers bloom in pots.

5. <u>Some</u> flowers are <u>white</u> and <u>blue</u>; others are <u>yellow</u> and <u>red</u>.

6. Butterflies land on <u>the</u> <u>tall</u> grass.

7. Sam digs in <u>the</u> <u>dark</u>, <u>moist</u> earth.

8. <u>Slimy</u> earthworms curl into <u>tiny</u> balls.

9. <u>Hungry</u> robins dive at <u>the</u> <u>slithery</u> worms.

10. Sam enjoys <u>this</u> <u>tiny</u> garden.

Lesson 18 Circle the adverb that describes each underlined word.

1. The alarm clock <u>rang</u> (noisily) in my ear.

2. I (quickly) <u>rose</u> and dressed myself.

3. I (carefully) <u>checked</u> the departure time on my airline ticket.

4. Planes (rarely) <u>wait</u> for tardy passengers.

5. My cat <u>watched</u> (sadly) as I ate breakfast.

6. The taxi driver <u>honked</u> the horn (impatiently).

7. He <u>drove</u> (fast), and I held my breath and closed my eyes.

8. When the driver stopped the taxi, I (cautiously) <u>opened</u> my eyes.

9. I paid him and <u>tipped</u> him (generously).

10. I <u>walked</u> (directly) to the ticket counter and checked my baggage.

Name _____

Lesson 19 Underline the prepositional phrase in each sentence. Circle the preposition and draw a box around the noun or pronoun that is the object of the preposition.

1. Rabbits live (near) my [house].

2. I see them (in) the [morning].

3. Low-flying planes can spot them (from) the [air].

4. I watch them (from) my [kitchen].

5. The vegetable garden (behind) my [house] is their favorite spot.

6. Some rabbits sleep (near) [it].

7. Others lie (on) the soft [leaves].

8. They all nibble (on) my [vegetables].

9. Most (of) the [rabbits] move quickly.

10. A few move slowly (through) my [yard].

Lesson 20 Underline each coordinating conjunction. Circle each subordinating conjunction.

1. Tyler <u>and</u> Zoe decided to make homemade pizza.

2. They usually buy it at Giorgio's <u>or</u> the Hopkins Cafe.

3. They thought it would be easy to make, <u>but</u> they weren't sure how to make the crust.

4. (Although) Tyler is an experienced cook, he wanted to follow a recipe.

5. (If) the pizza turned out badly, they would be very disappointed.

6. One cookbook had recipes for pineapple pizza <u>and</u> pesto pizza.

7. (Because) Zoe loves pineapple, it was an easy choice.

8. They put the pizza in the oven <u>and</u> turned on their favorite TV show.

9. (While) they watched TV, the pizza baked.

10. (Before) they tasted the pizza, they let it cool.

Lesson 21 Underline the word in parentheses that will correctly complete each sentence.

1. "Emi and her brother are going to Colorado for (<u>their</u>/there/they're) vacation," Kris said.

2. "I've never been (their/<u>there</u>/they're)," she added enviously.

3. "How are they getting (their/<u>there</u>/they're)?" asked Luis.

4. "(Their/There/<u>They're</u>) flying and then renting a car at the Denver airport," Kris replied.

5. "Do they need someone to water (<u>their</u>/there/they're) plants?" Luis asked.

6. "I live near (<u>their</u>/there/they're) house, so I could do it," he went on.

7. "I hope (their/there/<u>they're</u>) planning to take a lot of pictures," said Kris.

8. "Have you seen the pictures from (<u>their</u>/there/they're) trip to Georgia?" asked Luis.

9. "(Their/There/<u>They're</u>) lucky to be able to travel so much," sighed Kris.

10. "I don't envy (<u>their</u>/there/they're) travels. I like it here at home," said Luis.

Lesson 22 Write *its* or *it's* on the line to complete each sentence correctly. Remember to capitalize a word that begins a sentence.

1. "___It's___ called a tarantula," said Mr. Muñoz, holding up the large, hairy spider for the

   class to see.

2. "It makes ___its___ home in warm areas around the world," he continued.

3. "___It's___ as big as my fist!" exclaimed Carlos.

4. "If you think this species is big, you should see the bird spider, which can spread ___its___

   legs about seven inches," said the teacher.

5. "___It's___ scary looking!" said Darrell.

6. "___It's___ really very friendly," said Mr. Muñoz, letting the spider walk up his arm.

7. "___Its___ bite can kill you!" shouted Alicia.

8. "___Its___ bite was once believed to cause a disease called *tarantism*," Mr. Muñoz explained.

9. "In reality, ___it's___ no more dangerous than a bee," he continued.

10. "There's an Australian tarantula that's much more dangerous than this one," he added.

    "___It's___ one of a group of tarantulas called *funnel-webs*."

Name _____

Lesson 23 Write *your* or *you're* to complete each sentence correctly. Remember to capitalize a word that begins a sentence.

1. "Evie, may I borrow _____your_____ bike today?" asked Jason.

2. "Sure," said Evie, "but if _____you're_____ going to the park, be sure to lock it up."

3. "_____You're_____ late," Juan called when Jason arrived.

4. "Do you want me to play on _____your_____ team or on Dean's team?" Jason asked.

5. "_____You're_____ going to play on my team," answered Juan.

6. "_____You're_____ playing well today," Juan said when Jason caught his second fly ball.

7. "_____Your_____ advice about staying on my toes has really helped," Jason responded.

8. After reviewing the lineup, Juan told Jason, "_____You're_____ up third, so get ready."

9. "_____You're_____ up at bat next," Juan said.

10. "Keep _____your_____ eye on the ball!" he yelled.

Lesson 24 Write *C* if the boldfaced word or phrase in a sentence is used correctly. Write *X* if it is used incorrectly.

1. "Would you **like** to come to my house for dinner tonight?" Claudia asked Malcolm. __C__

2. "Do you think it's, **like**, okay with your parents?" Malcolm asked. __X__

3. "Of course it's okay with them," Claudia said. "**You know** how much they like you." __C__

4. "**You know** what happened the last time you had me over for dinner," Malcolm said. __C__

5. "My mother got angry when you came over because I hadn't, **like**, asked her first,"

   Claudia remembered. __X__

6. "That was pretty, **you know**, embarrassing for me," Malcolm said. __X__

7. "I'm sorry," said Claudia. "Do you **like** hamburgers?" __C__

8. "**You know** I do!" said Malcolm with a big smile. __C__

9. "Well, tonight my father is going to make, **like**, the best hamburgers and homemade

   cole slaw you've ever eaten!" __X__

10. "Great!" exclaimed Malcolm. "I **like** your dad's cooking!" __C__

Lesson 25 Underline the word in parentheses that correctly completes each sentence.

1. My sister thinks that birds make the (best/goodest) pets.

2. I like dogs much (better/gooder) than birds.

3. Dogs are (better/gooder) at playing games than birds.

4. My dog Lucy used to be the (worsest/worst) behaved dog in the world.

5. I took her to obedience school, and her behavior became (gooder/better).

6. Now Lucy is the (best/goodest) student in the class!

7. She's getting (better/gooder) at following my commands.

8. My sister used to complain that Lucy's fur made her allergies (worse/worser).

9. Spring is the (worsest/worst) time of year for allergies.

10. Having a dog in the house does make some people's allergies (worse/worser).

Lesson 26 Write *who, which,* or *that* in the blank to complete each sentence correctly.

1. Halloween, _____which_____ takes place on October 31st, is my favorite holiday.

2. It's fun for children, _____who_____ get to dress up in costumes.

3. I like to wear costumes _____that_____ are wild and original.

4. My mother, _____who_____ is an artist, usually makes my costumes for me.

5. Last year I wore a dragon costume _____that_____ had a long tail and glittering scales.

6. My brother, _____who_____ is older than I, takes me trick-or-treating with him.

7. We only eat treats _____that_____ come wrapped in packages.

8. Last year my neighbor transformed her garage into a haunted house, _____which_____ was very scary.

9. It had fake skeletons _____that_____ popped out from dark corners.

10. On Halloween night, my brother and I ate several pieces of candy, _____which_____ made me feel a little bit ill.

Name _____

Lesson 27 Circle the word in parentheses that correctly completes each sentence.

1. My sister DeShawn is a (**very**/real) good horseback rider.

2. When my parents offered to pay for horseback riding lessons, she was (**very**/real) excited.

3. She showed (very/**real**) talent at the sport, even as a beginner.

4. She could ride horses that were usually (**very**/real) skittish with other riders.

5. She also practiced (**very**/real) hard.

6. DeShawn's riding instructor thought she could be a (very/**real**) champion someday, so she spent extra hours coaching her.

7. We were all (**very**/real) proud of DeShawn the day she won her first blue ribbon at a horse show.

8. Now she lives on a (very/**real**) horse farm and raises horses.

9. She is (**very**/real) lucky to be able to do something she loves.

10. I feel (**very**/real) happy whenever she asks me to visit.

Lesson 28 Write the correct form of *sit* or *set* in each blank.

1. When I got home from school, I _____set_____ my backpack down on the kitchen table.

2. After getting myself a snack, I _____sat_____ down at the table and pulled out my homework assignment.

3. "Jaime, can you please _____sit_____ somewhere else?" Mom asked.

4. I took my belongings up to my room, _____set_____ them on my desk, and tried to start my homework again.

5. A little while later, my mother called, "Jaime, please come help me _____set_____ the table."

6. I carefully _____set_____ eight dinner plates around the table.

7. Then I _____set_____ the napkins, knives, forks, and spoons in their proper places.

8. Just then my father came home and _____set_____ a bag of groceries on the counter.

9. Mom _____set_____ the food on the table while Dad put the groceries away.

10. Finally, we all _____sat_____ down and ate.

Lesson 29 Underline the word in parentheses that correctly completes each sentence.

1. My aunt (<u>knew</u>/known) she wanted to be a policewoman when she was just a little girl.

2. "All my girlfriends wanted to be ballerinas or nurses when they (<u>grew</u>/grown) up," she said to me last week.

3. "I (<u>knew</u>/known) I did not want to dance or work in a hospital," she added.

4. She (<u>grew</u>/grown) up during a time when women didn't have as many job opportunities as they do today.

5. Many people she (<u>knew</u>/known) tried to discourage her from becoming a police officer.

6. "Luckily," she said, "I had (knew/<u>known</u>) several women who had interesting careers."

7. "I also (<u>grew</u>/grown) up in a family that encouraged me to follow my dreams," she added.

8. "I (<u>knew</u>/known) that being a girl wouldn't stop me from doing what I wanted to do," my aunt continued.

9. "You have (grew/<u>grown</u>) up in a time in which it's more acceptable for women to work in a variety of jobs," she told me.

10. I have (knew/<u>known</u>) many helpful people, but my aunt is the one who has encouraged me the most.

Lesson 30 Underline the word in parentheses that correctly completes each sentence.

1. Last summer my father took my sister to the pool to (learn/<u>teach</u>) her how to swim.

2. "First, I'm going to (learn/<u>teach</u>) you how to float on your back," he said to her.

3. My sister soon (<u>learned</u>/taught) that she could float without sinking.

4. After a few days he told her, "Now I'm going to (learn/<u>teach</u>) you some basic strokes."

5. First, he (learned/<u>taught</u>) her how to do the crawl.

6. "You need to (<u>learn</u>/teach) how to move your head correctly when you breathe," he said.

7. "When am I going to (<u>learn</u>/teach) how to dive?" my sister asked him.

8. "I'll (learn/<u>teach</u>) you to dive after you've learned how to swim well," he answered.

9. After that, my sister practiced hard and (<u>learned</u>/taught) her basic strokes very quickly.

10. By the end of the summer, my dad said she was ready to (<u>learn</u>/teach) how to do a swan dive.

Name _____

Extra Practice

Lesson 31 Circle each boldfaced word that is a subject pronoun. Underline each boldfaced word that is an object pronoun.

1. Yesterday (I) helped my grandmother clean out her attic. (It) was full of interesting things.

2. My grandfather died a long time ago. (We) found an old photo of **him**.

3. (He) was wearing a naval uniform in the picture, and he looked handsome to **us**.

4. Grandmother gave the photo to **me**. (She) said she had another copy in her album.

5. (We) dragged a huge trunk out from behind some boxes. Inside **it** (we) found a pile of old-fashioned clothes.

6. (They) had plastic wrapped around **them**. (They) were perfectly preserved.

7. There was a kimono my grandfather had brought back with **him** from Japan. (He) visited Asia in the 1970s.

8. (I) unwrapped a beautiful blue evening gown that had been my grandmother's. I asked **her** if she would try it on.

9. (She) laughed and said that none of the dresses would fit **her** anymore.

10. We wrapped up the dresses and put **them** back in the trunk. Grandmother said that when I was big enough, they would belong to **me**.

Lesson 32 Circle the correct pronoun in each pair.

1. Laney and (me/(I)) made a treasure hunt for my little brother and sister.

2. We drew chalk maps on the sidewalk for him and (she/(her)) to follow.

3. My little sister is a good treasure hunter, so Laney and ((I)/me) had to make her clues hard.

4. My little brother is only four, so I helped (he/(him)) with the clues.

5. ((He)/Him) and I walked all over the yard, following clues.

6. My little sister and Laney worked as a team, competing against my brother and ((me)/I).

7. When my brother and sister got close to the treasure, Laney and (me/(I)) stopped helping.

8. They begged Laney and ((me)/I) to give away the last few clues, but we held firm.

9. Finally, she and (him/(he)) decided to help each other find the treasure.

10. They thanked Laney and ((me)/I) when they found out that the treasure was a big bag of popcorn.

174 **Name** _____

Lesson 33 Circle the correct phrase in parentheses.

1. (Me and Keisha/**Keisha and I**) were teaching Sue and Kim how to jump rope, double-dutch.

2. First, (**Sue and I**/I and Sue) practiced jumping quickly, one foot at a time.

3. Then Sue and Kim turned the ropes for (me and Keisha/**Keisha and me**).

4. (**Keisha and I**/I and Keisha) ran into the twirling ropes together.

5. (I and Keisha/**Keisha and I**) started counting out loud.

6. Sue told (me and Keisha/**Keisha and me**) that we were jumping too fast for her to learn.

7. (I and she/**She and I**) decided to begin again, only more slowly.

8. Sue and Kim tried turning the ropes slowly, but they kept falling on
   (me and Keisha/**Keisha and me**).

9. Then Keisha thought of a way that (I and she/**she and I**) could teach them.

10. (Keisha and me/**Keisha and I**) described what our feet were doing as we jumped.

Lesson 34 Circle the antecedent or antecedents of each boldfaced pronoun.

1. The campers were ready for the annual canoe (race) Any minute now **it** would begin.

2. Five (canoes) were at the starting line. **They** surged forward at the sound of the whistle.

3. At first, (Lisa) and (André) were in the lead. One by one the other teams passed **them**.

4. The blue (canoe) did not stay in the race long. **It** tipped over, and its paddlers had to pull
   the canoe ashore.

5. The (lake) was calm and smooth. The only waves on **it** were created by the racers.

6. (Germaine) and (Jody) were in the red canoe. **They** had won last year, and many people
   thought they would win again.

7. (Lloyd) and (Veronica) were way ahead of the others. The crowd of campers cheered **them** on.

8. The finish (line) was still many yards away. Who would cross **it** first?

9. Suddenly, (Germaine) and (Jody) began catching up. **They** paddled hard until they had
   passed Lloyd and Veronica.

10. The red canoe crossed the finish line first. (Germaine) and (Jody) clapped and cheered as **they**
    floated toward the shore.

Name _____ 175

Lesson 35 Underline the correct form of each verb in parentheses. Make sure the verb agrees with the subject.

1. In the south of France farmers (<u>grow</u>/grows) flowers for French perfume.

2. The Battle of the Flowers (take/<u>takes</u>) place there every February.

3. This twelve-day festival (include/<u>includes</u>) a parade through the city of Nice.

4. The people of Nice (<u>build</u>/builds) beautiful floats for the parade.

5. They (<u>use</u>/uses) flowers to decorate the floats.

6. Many Battles of the Flowers (<u>occur</u>/occurs) during the festival.

7. Each battle (last/<u>lasts</u>) all afternoon.

8. People (<u>bring</u>/brings) lots of flowers to the battle.

9. At the signal, everyone (throw/<u>throws</u>) flowers at one another.

10. Soon, colored petals (<u>cover</u>/covers) the ground.

Lesson 36 Underline the correct form of *be* in each sentence.

1. Traffic lights (is/<u>are</u>) an important safety device.

2. Before the invention of the traffic signal in the early 1920s, drivers (was/<u>were</u>) free to cross an intersection at any time. This caused accidents.

3. Garrett Morgan (<u>was</u>/were) an African American inventor.

4. His electric traffic signal system (<u>was</u>/were) the first of its kind.

5. One day Morgan saw a traffic accident in which several people (was/<u>were</u>) hurt.

6. Morgan (<u>was</u>/were) certain that he could improve traffic safety.

7. The modern traffic light system (<u>is</u>/are) only slightly different from Morgan's original system.

8. Today, this system (<u>is</u>/are) in operation all over the world.

9. Motorists everywhere (is/<u>are</u>) familiar with the traffic signal.

10. Driving (<u>is</u>/are) safer because of Morgan's invention.

Name

Lesson 37 Underline the form of the verb in each sentence that gives the correct sense of time.

1. The Brooklyn Bridge (<u>opened</u>/has opened) in 1883.

2. At the time it (is/<u>was</u>) the longest suspension bridge in the world.

3. Suspension bridges (will hold/<u>hold</u>) up a roadway with cables suspended from towers.

4. Before the Brooklyn Bridge, older suspension bridges (<u>had used</u>/use) iron cables.

5. John Roebling (<u>designed</u>/has designed) the Brooklyn Bridge with light, strong steel cables.

6. It still (stood/<u>stands</u>) today, connecting Brooklyn and Manhattan in New York City.

7. Every day thousands of people (<u>cross</u>/had crossed) the bridge in cars or on foot.

8. For over a hundred years people (<u>have admired</u>/admire) its towers and weblike cables.

9. The bridge (was/<u>has been</u>) a national historic landmark since 1964.

10. Next summer I (<u>will walk</u>/walked) across the Brooklyn Bridge.

Lesson 38 Write *X* next to each sentence with two negative expressions. Then, on another sheet of paper, rewrite these sentences correctly. **Possible answers appear below. Accept all reasonable responses.**

1. "I haven't seen nothing that looks familiar for hours," David told Geena. __X__
   "I haven't seen anything that looks familiar for hours," David told Geena.

2. "I haven't never been so lost in my life," Geena agreed. __X__
   "I have never been so lost in my life," Geena agreed.

3. "This wouldn't have happened if we had paid more attention to the road signs,"

   David said. ____

4. "There isn't no reason to panic," Geena told David. __X__
   "There isn't any reason to panic," Geena told David.

5. "I've never seen anyone look so confused," a police officer said to David. ____

6. "We didn't bring no map with us," David told the officer. __X__
   "We didn't bring a map with us," David told the officer.

7. The officer told them not to have no worries. __X__
   The officer told them not to have any worries.

8. "It won't take long to drive you back to your campsite," he said. ____

9. Police officers don't usually let no pedestrians ride in their police cars. __X__
   Police officers don't usually let pedestrians ride in their police cars.

10. Geena and David had never ridden in no real police car before, and they accepted

    the offer. __X__
    Geena and David had never ridden in a real police car before, and they accepted the offer.

Name _____

Extra Practice

Lesson 39 Underline the correct form of the adjective in parentheses.

1. Liza's dance troupe performed the (more creative/<u>most creative</u>) dance I have ever seen.

2. They combined ballet and gymnastics into a slow, balancing dance that was (most beautiful/<u>more beautiful</u>) than ballet alone.

3. Liza had designed the costumes, using the (lighter/<u>lightest</u>) fabric she could find.

4. The costumes flowed over the dancers' muscles, making them look (<u>more graceful</u>/gracefuler) than dancers in traditional leotards.

5. The music for their dance was (slowest/<u>slower</u>) than the music for the other dances.

6. Mia, the (<u>smallest</u>/smaller) girl in the whole company, amazed everyone.

7. She proved she was (strongest/<u>stronger</u>) than people thought by holding two dancers on her shoulders.

8. At the end of the piece, the applause was the (louder/<u>loudest</u>) I have ever heard.

9. Liza's dance troupe was definitely (<u>better</u>/best) than the other dance troupe.

10. They may be the (better/<u>best</u>) dance troupe in the city!

Lesson 40 Underline the correct form of the adverb.

1. Of all the swimmers at the starting line, Ellen waited the (<u>most nervously</u>/more nervously).

2. She had trained (hardest/<u>harder</u>) for this race than she had for any other race.

3. Ellen dove (<u>more swiftly</u>/most swiftly) than the swimmer next to her.

4. After falling behind in the first lap, Ellen came out of the turn (<u>more quickly</u>/most quickly) than any other swimmer in the race.

5. Her arms pulled her through the water, and soon she was swimming (<u>more smoothly</u>/most smoothly) than she had in the first lap.

6. Ellen's arms got tired (most easily/<u>more easily</u>) than her legs.

7. Still, she kept stroking (most persistently/<u>more persistently</u>) than she had in any other race.

8. Of all the people at the finish line, Ellen's dad cheered the (<u>loudest</u>/louder).

9. Ellen went home (most wearily/<u>more wearily</u>) than she ever had before.

10. Ellen ate the (<u>most hungrily</u>/more hungrily) at the dinner table that night.

Lesson 41 Correct each capitalization and punctuation error. Then label each sentence *declarative, interrogative, imperative,* or *exclamatory.*

1. please pass me the flour?. _____imperative_____
2. What are you making? _____interrogative_____
3. I'm rolling out tortillas for dinner,. _____declarative_____
4. I love your homemade tortillas. _____declarative_____
5. we are also having tamales for dinner and flan for dessert. _____declarative_____
6. is this a special occasion)? _____interrogative_____
7. Yes, uncle Leo got a new job today?. _____declarative_____
8. what great news that is! _____exclamatory_____
9. don't tell anyone yet. _____imperative_____
10. Is it a secret)? _____interrogative_____

Lesson 42 Draw three lines (≡) under each lowercase letter that should be capitalized. Draw a line through each capital letter that should not be capitalized.

1. The washington Monument was built in honor of george washington.
2. It stands between the united states Capitol building and the lincoln memorial.
3. The potomac river is Nearby.
4. Funds for the Washington Monument were raised by the Washington national monument society.
5. The Tower was designed by robert mills.
6. The Walls of the tower are covered in White marble from maryland.
7. Many of the stones for the Washington monument were Donated.
8. Pope pius IX sent a Stone from the Temple of concord in rome, italy.
9. This stone was stolen one night by members of a Group called the Know-Nothings.
10. Today the Washington Monument is a National memorial and is maintained by the National park Service.

Name _____ 179

Lesson 43 Rewrite the items below on the lines. Use abbreviations where you can.

1. Doctor Alison Reid Calloway _____ Dr. A.R. Calloway

2. Tuesday, August 21 _____ Tues., Aug. 21

3. Mister Mark Henry Novak _____ Mr. M.H. Novak

4. 333 Stone Avenue _____ 333 Stone Ave.

5. The Hungry Dog Company _____ The Hungry Dog Co.

6. Doctor Martin Luther King Junior _____ Dr. M.L. King Jr.

7. Peachtree Boulevard _____ Peachtree Blvd.

8. Piranhas Incorporated _____ Piranhas Inc.

9. Mister Joseph David Siegel _____ Mr. J.D. Siegel

10. Friday, February 8 _____ Fri., Feb. 8

Lesson 44 Circle the letters that should be capitalized in each title. Underline or add quotation marks to each title.

1. Sarita wrote a summary of a story titled "legend of the okefenokee lizard."

2. Ami and Malvin went to the movie theater to see norton the alligator goes to france.

3. Jonas lent his book the poems of preston pig to his young cousin Emile.

4. Emile's favorite poem is called "mud is magnificent."

5. What is the best story in the book titled trailside adventures?

6. "Beware of the scorpion" is my favorite story.

7. Neuri watched the movie tornado avengers with Alvin and Rami.

8. They loved the movie's theme song, "the avengers are coming."

9. The librarian suggested Mari read the short story "a girl of the south" before traveling to Louisiana.

10. A magazine has decided to publish my poem "frog music."

Lesson 45 Underline the correct word in each pair. If the word is a possessive, write *possessive*. If the word is a contraction, write the two words it was made from.

1. (Let's/Lets') go to the dog show. _____ **Let us**

2. The (rottweiler's/rottweilers') bodies are massive. _____ **possessive**

3. That (pug's/pugs') face is cute. _____ **possessive**

4. All (pug's/pugs') noses are stubby. _____ **possessive**

5. That (chow's/chows') tongue is black! _____ **possessive**

6. Look, (he's/hes') wagging his tail. _____ **he is**

7. That is the biggest dog (Ive/I've) ever seen! _____ **I have**

8. (It's/Its') an Irish wolfhound. _____ **It is**

9. (Their/They're) the tallest of all breeds. _____ **They are**

10. I think that one is the four (judge's/judges') favorite. _____ **possessive**

Lesson 46 Add commas where they belong. Circle commas that don't belong.

1. This backpack has a large inside pouch, a small outside pouch, and a hidden pocket.

2. Its special lining can keep food hot, warm, or cold.

3. I can use it for hiking, picnicking, or school.

4. When I bring it to school, I keep my lunch in the small pouch, my books in the big pouch, and my keys in the hidden pocket.

5. This backpack has belonged to my uncle, my cousin, my brother, and me.

6. It has traveled to Africa, Asia, and Europe.

7. The places I've visited are New Mexico, Canada, and Oregon.

8. Right now I have pajamas, a sleeping bag, and my toothbrush in the backpack.

9. I'm going on a sleepover with Evan, Michael, Lucas, and Josh.

10. We'll stay up late, eat pizza, and tell scary stories.

Name _____

Lesson 47 Add the missing comma to each sentence. Then decide why the comma is needed. Write *I* for introductory word, *C* for compound sentence, and *D* for direct address.

1. Dave, do you know what that bridge is called? __D__

2. No, I have no idea. __I__

3. I'll give you some hints, and you guess its name. __C__

4. Well, I'll try to guess. __I__

5. It was named after the channel it spans, and the channel was named during the California Gold Rush. __C__

6. Well, does that mean the word *gold* is in the title? __I__

7. Yes, you're getting warm. __I__

8. The second part of the name rhymes with *great*, but there's no *r* in the word. __C__

9. Mom, don't give such easy clues! __D__

10. You only gave me two clues, but I already know that it's the Golden Gate Bridge. __C__

Lesson 48 Add a semicolon where it is needed in each sentence.

1. Soybeans come in many different colors; they can be red, green, yellow, or speckled.

2. Soybeans are easy to grow; they are a popular crop among farmers.

3. Soybean plants are good for the soil; they provide nitrogen, an important nutrient.

4. Many foods are made from soybeans; soy sauce, vegetable oil, soy flour, and tofu all have soy in them.

5. Soybeans can also be used for surprising things; some fire extinguishers contain foam made from soy.

6. Tofu is made by boiling, crushing, and pressing soybeans; this method was invented in China in 164 B.C.

7. The traditional Japanese diet includes tofu; Japan imports large amounts of soybeans.

8. In Japan tofu is served in beautiful ways; sometimes it is carved in the shape of leaves.

9. Tofu can be made to imitate many other foods; it can even be made to taste like ice cream.

10. Tofu is a healthy food; it provides more protein than lean beef.

Lesson 49 Write *I* after each indirect quotation and *D* after each direct quotation. Then add quotation marks and other punctuation to the direct quotations.

1. "I'd like to have a garden, but I live in the city," said Arno. __D__

2. Dinah said that plants will grow well in a sunny window. __I__

3. Arno opened the cupboard and asked, "Can I grow peas, beans, and peppers?" __D__

4. "You can grow all of those things in containers," Charlie said. __D__

5. "A bottle garden is another way to grow plants inside," said Martha. __D__

6. Martha explained that a bottle garden is called a *terrarium*. __I__

7. "First we need a big jar," said Charlie. __D__

8. Charlie said that Arno could put soil and plants in the jar. __I__

9. "What kind of small plants will you put in your terrarium?" asked Martha. __D__

10. "I think I'll put geraniums, moss, and ferns in it," said Arno. __D__

Lesson 50 Rewrite this friendly letter correctly on the blanks below.

Turkey Feather Ranch Peru, IN 46970 March 18, 2012 Dear Anya, My grandmother's ranch is so much fun! This morning, Grandma showed us where the baby turkeys grow. See you soon, Kristen

Turkey Feather Ranch

Peru, IN 46970

March 18, 2012

Dear Anya,

My grandmother's ranch is so much fun! This morning, Grandma showed us where the baby turkeys grow.

See you soon,

Kristen

Extra Practice

Read each sentence and decide which phrase correctly describes it. Fill in the circle next to your answer.

1. All living things contain water, many scientists think that life began in water.
   - (a) fragment
   - **(b) comma splice**
   - (c) compound sentence

2. Water evaporates from lakes and oceans, and it falls back to Earth as rain.
   - (a) fragment
   - (b) run-on
   - **(c) compound sentence**

3. Important to all living things.
   - **(a) fragment**
   - (b) run-on
   - (c) compound sentence

4. Water covers over 70 percent of Earth, but most of it is salt water.
   - (a) fragment
   - (b) run-on
   - **(c) compound sentence**

5. Different forms of water.
   - **(a) fragment**
   - (b) run-on
   - (c) comma splice

Choose the answer that describes the underlined part of each sentence. Fill in the circle next to your answer.

6. <u>Three percent of the world's surface water</u> is fresh water.
   - (a) simple subject
   - **(b) complete subject**

7. Water <u>is essential to all living things</u>.
   - (a) simple predicate
   - **(b) complete predicate**

8. Most of our planet's freshwater supply <u>exists</u> in glaciers.
   - (a) simple subject
   - **(b) simple predicate**

9. Some <u>glaciers</u> extend into the ocean.
   - **(a) simple subject**
   - (b) complete subject

10. Icebergs <u>are broken chunks of glaciers</u>.
    - (a) complete subject
    - **(b) complete predicate**

11. Icebergs <u>pose</u> great danger for ships.
    - **(a) simple predicate**
    - (b) complete predicate

12. A waterspout <u>is</u> a kind of tornado.
    - (a) complete predicate
    - **(b) simple predicate**

13. A waterspout is a tall column <u>of</u> water.
    - **(a) preposition**
    - (b) prepositional phrase

14. It forms <u>over water</u>.
    - (a) complete predicate
    - **(b) prepositional phrase**

15. The column rises <u>into the clouds</u>.
    - (a) preposition
    - **(b) prepositional phrase**

Name _____

16. <u>As the column twists</u>, moist air flows up the column.
    (a) dependent clause   (b) independent clause

17. Although waterspouts can cause damage, <u>tornadoes are more dangerous</u>.
    (a) dependent clause   (b) independent clause

18. Strong <u>winds</u> and heavy <u>rains</u> usually accompany a tornado.
    (a) compound subject   (b) compound predicate

19. Tornadoes can <u>pick</u> up large objects and <u>throw</u> them long distances.
    (a) compound subject   (b) compound predicate

20. <u>Thunder</u> and <u>lightning</u> often accompany a tornado.
    (a) compound subject   (b) compound predicate

21. <u>Cellars</u> and <u>basements</u> offer the best protection.
    (a) compound subject   (b) compound predicate

22. They give <u>people</u> a hiding place from high winds.
    (a) predicate noun   (b) indirect object

23. Tornadoes are very <u>dangerous</u>.
    (a) predicate noun   (b) predicate adjective

24. Tornadoes often destroy <u>buildings</u>.
    (a) predicate adjective   (b) direct object

25. Another name for a tornado is a <u>twister</u>.
    (a) predicate noun   (b) predicate adjective

26. Many scientists study <u>tornadoes</u>.
    (a) predicate noun   (b) direct object

27. The National Weather Service uses <u>radar</u> for tornado detection.
    (a) predicate noun   (b) direct object

28. Radar information can be quite <u>accurate</u>.
    (a) predicate adjective   (b) direct object

29. The information gives <u>scientists</u> a way of predicting tornadoes.
    (a) direct object   (b) indirect object

30. They cannot prevent these <u>storms</u>, however.
    (a) direct object   (b) indirect object

Decide whether each boldfaced word is a preposition, a coordinating conjunction, or a subordinating conjunction. Fill in the circle next to your answer.

1. Garrett Morgan's mother had once been enslaved, **but** he became a successful inventor.
   - (a) preposition   **(b)** coordinating conjunction   (c) subordinating conjunction

2. Morgan invented the traffic light, **and** he also invented the gas mask.
   - (a) preposition   **(b)** coordinating conjunction   (c) subordinating conjunction

3. Morgan's gas mask allowed people to breathe **in** smoky, poisonous environments.
   - **(a)** preposition   (b) coordinating conjunction   (c) subordinating conjunction

4. **When** some gas exploded in a tunnel near Morgan's home, he and his brother put on masks and helped the people trapped inside.
   - (a) preposition   (b) coordinating conjunction   **(c)** subordinating conjunction

5. Morgan's gas masks were very important to soldiers **in** World War I.
   - **(a)** preposition   (b) coordinating conjunction   (c) subordinating conjunction

Which pronoun can replace each boldfaced word or phrase? Fill in the circle next to your answer.

6. Before the 1870s there were few roads across America, and it was difficult to transport mail and goods over **these roads**.
   - (a) it   (b) his   **(c)** them

7. **The stagecoach** was a carriage designed especially for traveling swiftly across rough country.
   - **(a)** It   (b) They   (c) Them

8. Ben Holladay ran a stagecoach company. **Holladay's** coaches were always on time.
   - (a) Him   **(b)** His   (c) Their

9. Once Ben Holladay's coach was held up by bandits, but **Holladay** tricked the bandits into letting him go without stealing much of his money.
   - **(a)** he   (b) they   (c) him

Is each boldfaced word an adjective or an adverb? Fill in the circle next to your answer.

10. In 1804 **two** United States Army officers named Lewis and Clark set out on an expedition.
    - **(a)** adjective   (b) adverb

11. People in the East knew **almost** nothing about the West.
    - (a) adjective   **(b)** adverb

12. President Jefferson **actually** hoped Lewis and Clark would find woolly mammoths there.
    - (a) adjective   **(b)** adverb

13. Sacagawea, a Shoshone woman, guided Lewis and Clark through **unfamiliar** territory.
    - **(a)** adjective   (b) adverb

14. Sacagawea helped them establish friendly relationships with **some** Native American groups.
    - **(a)** adjective   (b) adverb

Name _____

Decide what kind of noun each boldfaced word is. Fill in the circle next to your answer.

15. Franklin Delano **Roosevelt's** legs were paralyzed by polio when he was 39 years old.
    (a) possessive   (b) plural

16. This condition did not prevent Roosevelt from following his **dream** of political success.
    (a) common   (b) proper

17. Roosevelt was president of the United States during the **Depression** and World War II.
    (a) common   (b) proper

18. Roosevelt had a plan to solve **America's** economic problems, and he called it the New Deal.
    (a) singular possessive   (b) plural possessive

19. The New Deal created jobs for thousands of American **men** and women.
    (a) possessive   (b) plural

20. Roosevelt had a special place in **voters'** hearts. He was elected president four times.
    (a) singular possessive   (b) plural possessive

Decide which tense the boldfaced verb is in. Fill in the circle next to your answer.

21. Parts of the United States **were** once Spanish territory.
    (a) present   (b) past   (c) future   (d) present perfect

22. From the 1560s to the 1820s, the Spanish **operated** settlements in America called missions.
    (a) present   (b) past   (c) future   (d) present perfect

23. Native Americans **built** many of the mission buildings out of adobe.
    (a) present   (b) past   (c) future   (d) present perfect

24. Some old adobes **have stood** for hundreds of years.
    (a) present   (b) past   (c) future   (d) present perfect

25. Today the remains of missions **stand** in Florida, Texas, New Mexico, Arizona, and California.
    (a) present   (b) past   (c) future   (d) present perfect

26. Many architects **have imitated** the mission style in modern buildings.
    (a) present   (b) past   (c) future   (d) present perfect

27. As long as they stand, the missions **will remind** us of America's Spanish heritage.
    (a) present   (b) past   (c) future   (d) present perfect

28. Perhaps you **will visit** one of these old missions some day.
    (a) present   (b) past   (c) future   (d) present perfect

Find the correct word to complete each sentence. Fill in the circle next to your answer.

1. Is baseball _____ favorite sport?
   (a) your
   (b) you're

2. _____ going to be a first-rate pitcher someday.
   (a) Your
   (b) You're

3. _____ already an excellent hitter.
   (a) Your
   (b) You're

4. Have you brought _____ glove to practice?
   (a) your
   (b) you're

5. Pablo and Roger do well out _____ in the outfield.
   (a) their
   (b) there
   (c) they're

6. _____ team has an excellent catcher, too.
   (a) Their
   (b) There
   (c) They're

7. _____ not going to beat us, though!
   (a) Their
   (b) There
   (c) They're

8. It's not _____ fault that we're better players.
   (a) their
   (b) there
   (c) they're

9. The tall boy over _____ is our best player.
   (a) their
   (b) there
   (c) they're

10. _____ too bad that my old glove is falling apart.
    (a) Its
    (b) It's

11. _____ stitching is coming undone.
    (a) Its
    (b) It's

12. _____ an old glove.
    (a) Its
    (b) It's

13. Victoria is pitching _____ today than she did in our last game.
    (a) best
    (b) gooder
    (c) better

14. Last week's game was her _____ game of the season.
    (a) baddest
    (b) worst
    (c) worse

15. I think Victoria is a _____ pitcher than Shelly.
    (a) better
    (b) more good
    (c) best

16. Victoria is the one _____ gave me my first baseball card.
    (a) which
    (b) who
    (c) that

Name _____

17. She gave me a card _____ she didn't want anymore.

    (a) which   (b) who   **(c) that**

18. The home runs _____ Willie Aikens hit were in games one and four of the 1980 World Series.

    (a) which   (b) who   **(c) that**

19. Aikens hit more than one home run in two different games in that series, _____ made him a record setter.

    (a) which   (b) who   (c) that

20. It must be _____ exciting to play major league baseball.

    (a) very   (b) real

21. Yes, but professional baseball is a _____ challenging job, too.

    (a) very   (b) real

22. Roberto Clemente of the Pittsburgh Pirates was a _____ hero.

    (a) very   **(b) real**

23. I want to _____ you about some of Clemente's accomplishments.

    (a) teach   (b) learn

24. When Clemente _____ that there had been an earthquake in Nicaragua, he collected supplies to take to the victims.

    (a) taught   **(b) learned**

25. He did not just _____ around and wait for others to help.

    (a) set   **(b) sit**

26. Please _____ that book about Clemente's life on the table.

    (a) sit   **(b) set**

27. I _____ that Clemente had died in a plane crash, but I didn't know he was on his way to help the Nicaraguans.

    (a) knowed   **(b) knew**

28. Lately I've _____ interested in reading about Clemente's life.

    (a) growed   **(b) grown**

Decide whether the boldfaced word or phrase is used correctly in each sentence. Fill in the circle next to your answer.

29. Did **you know** that Clemente finished his career with exactly 3,000 hits?

    (a) correct   (b) incorrect

30. Clemente was, **like**, the eleventh player in history to reach the 3,000 hit mark.

    (a) correct   **(b) incorrect**

Choose the word or phrase that completes the sentence correctly. Fill in the circle next to your answer.

1. ___ wrote a report about cars.
    (a) Mike and me   (b) Mike and I

2. ___ learned about the history of the automobile.
    (a) Me and Mike   (b) Mike and I

3. Our teacher told ___ that early steam-powered cars were built in France in the 1770s.
    (a) Mike and I   (b) Mike and me

4. In 1885 two Germans ___ the first working gasoline engines.
    (a) built   (b) will build

5. Today the United States and Japan ___ the world's leading car manufacturers.
    (a) are   (b) is

6. Henry Ford ___ his first gas-powered car in 1896.
    (a) developed   (b) has developed

7. Those early Ford cars ___ very rare today.
    (a) are   (b) is

8. Most people in our family ___ old cars.
    (a) admire   (b) admires

9. The cars of the 1950s ___ my favorites.
    (a) are   (b) is

10. One of my neighbors ___ old cars.
    (a) collect   (b) collects

11. The cars of the 1940s were ___ than the earlier models.
    (a) longer   (b) longest

12. People drive ___ today than they did long ago.
    (a) faster   (b) fastest

13. Are cars ___ today than they were twenty years ago?
    (a) expensiver   (b) more expensive

14. Yes, but today's cars are the ___ cars that have ever been built, according to some automobile experts.
    (a) most dependable   (b) more dependable

15. Many of today's cars run ___ than cars did fifty years ago.
    (a) more efficiently   (b) most efficiently

Name _____

Which pronoun can replace each boldfaced word or phrase? Fill in the circle next to your answer.

16. My **aunt** loves cars.

    (a) It   (b) She   (c) We   (d) Her

17. My **uncle** took her to a car show on her birthday.

    (a) Him   (b) She   (c) He   (d) Them

18. Ryan lent **Jeanine** some magazines about cars.

    (a) her   (b) it   (c) them   (d) she

19. Jeanine read the **magazines** in two days.

    (a) they   (b) him   (c) them   (d) it

20. Then Jeanine gave the magazines to **Roz**.

    (a) her   (b) she   (c) them   (d) they

21. Bill and **Jeanine** need a new car.

    (a) her   (b) them   (c) she   (d) they

22. My mom told Bill and **Jeanine** to wait for the holiday sale.

    (a) her   (b) them   (c) she   (d) it

23. I asked **Bill** and Jeanine if I could go with them.

    (a) he   (b) them   (c) him   (d) they

Decide which word or phrase the boldfaced word replaces in each sentence. Fill in the circle next to your answer.

24. Bill and Jeanine want a new car right away because **they** need to drive to work every day.

    (a) Bill   (b) Jeanine   (c) Bill and Jeanine   (d) Mom and Jeanine

25. Mom knows a lot about cars, so we go to **her** when we have questions.

    (a) Jeanine   (b) Mom   (c) Mom and Jeanine   (d) Bill and Jeanine

26. Jeanine is usually thrifty, so I hope **she** waits for the best deal.

    (a) Mom   (b) me   (c) Jeanine   (d) Bill

27. Bill values my opinion, so **he** invited me to go car shopping with them.

    (a) Dad   (b) I   (c) Jeanine   (d) Bill

Decide which sentence in each pair uses negative words correctly. Fill in the circle next to the sentence that is written correctly.

28. (a) Most people couldn't afford a car in the early 1900s.

    (b) Most people couldn't afford no car in the early 1900s.

29. (a) Henry Ford didn't want to charge no high price for the Model T Ford.

    (b) Henry Ford didn't want to charge a high price for the Model T Ford.

30. (a) Before Ford used the moving assembly line in 1913, no cars couldn't be built cheaply.

    (b) Before Ford used the moving assembly line in 1913, cars couldn't be built cheaply.

Read each sentence and decide whether it is declarative, interrogative, imperative, or exclamatory. Fill in the circle next to your answer.

1. Do you see the green turtle on the beach?
   - ⓐ declarative   **ⓑ interrogative**   ⓒ imperative   ⓓ exclamatory

2. What a beautiful creature!
   - ⓐ declarative   ⓑ interrogative   ⓒ imperative   **ⓓ exclamatory**

3. It has come out of the sea to lay its eggs in the sand.
   - **ⓐ declarative**   ⓑ interrogative   ⓒ imperative   ⓓ exclamatory

4. Please don't bother the turtle.
   - ⓐ declarative   ⓑ interrogative   **ⓒ imperative**   ⓓ exclamatory

Which boldfaced word needs to be capitalized? Fill in the circle with the letter that matches it.

5. The **american** alligator was once an endangered **species**.   **ⓐ**   ⓑ
   - ⓐ   ⓑ

6. This large **reptile** lives in the swamps of **florida**, Georgia, and Alabama.   ⓐ   **ⓑ**
   - ⓐ   ⓑ

7. The **alligator** got its name from the **spanish** words *el lagarto*.   ⓐ   **ⓑ**
   - ⓐ   ⓑ

Choose the correct way to rewrite the boldfaced part of each sentence. Fill in the circle next to your answer.

8. My neighbor, **Mister Alfred Blake Simmons**, told me that people once made shoes and suitcases out of alligator hides.
   - **ⓐ Mr. A.B. Simmons**   ⓑ Mr' A.B. Simmons   ⓒ mr AB Simmons

9. He lives on **West Elm Avenue**, around the corner from my house.
   - ⓐ W Elm Ave   ⓑ w. Elm ave.   **ⓒ W. Elm Ave.**

10. I read all about alligators in a book called **the life of the american alligator**.
    - **ⓐ The Life of the American Alligator**   ⓑ "The Life of The American Alligator"

11. In my poem, **alligators are all right**, I wrote about how they were saved from extinction.
    - ⓐ Alligators Are all Right   **ⓑ "Alligators Are All Right"**

12. My friend Beth's favorite movie is called **how the alligator got its smile**.
    - **ⓐ How the Alligator Got Its Smile**   ⓑ "How The Alligator Got Its Smile"

13. **The heads of American alligators** are broad and flat.
    - ⓐ American alligator's heads   **ⓑ American alligators' heads**

14. **The head of an American crocodile** is narrow, and the crocodile has two big teeth that stick up on either side of its snout.
    - **ⓐ An American crocodile's head**   ⓑ An American crocodiles' head

15. **That is** how you can tell crocodiles and alligators apart.
    - ⓐ Thats   **ⓑ That's**   ⓒ Thats'

Name _____

Decide where the comma belongs in each sentence. Fill in the circle with the matching letter.

16. Amphibians' markings help them hide, defend themselves and find a mate. (a)●b
                a   b

17. Yellow red, or blue markings on poison-dart frogs warn that they are poisonous. (a)(b)
       a   b

18. "Do you see that toad Jill?" asked Dave. (a)(b)
                  a   b

19. Jill stared at the toad's cage but its camouflage markings disguised its appearance. (a)(b)
                  a   b

20. "No I can't see it yet," she replied. (a)(b)
      a   b

Is a comma or a semicolon needed after the boldfaced word? Fill in the circle next to your answer.

21. The elephant trunk snake is well **named** it looks a lot like an elephant trunk.
    ●a needs a comma   (b) needs a semicolon

22. The scales of the elephant trunk snake are light **gray** and its skin drapes in loose folds.
    ●a needs a comma   (b) needs a semicolon

Decide whether each sentence is missing quotation marks or is correct as written. Fill in the circle next to your answer.

23. Cicely said that the alligator snapping turtle has an unusual way of hunting for food.
    (a) missing quotation marks   ●b correct as written

24. It wiggles its tongue like a worm and tricks fish into swimming into its mouth, she said.
    ●a missing quotation marks   (b) correct as written

Use the friendly letter below to answer each question. Fill in the circle next to your answer.

a   Camp Cayman
     August 4, 2012

b Dear Toby,

c   Today we hiked through the woods. I looked under a log and found a salamander. How are you?

d Your friend,
e Ashley

25. Which part of the letter is the greeting? (a)●b(c)(d)(e)
26. Which part of the letter is the closing? (a)(b)(c)●d(e)
27. Which part of the letter is the body? (a)(b)●c(d)(e)
28. Which part of the letter is the heading? ●a(b)(c)(d)(e)
29. Which part of the letter is the signature? (a)(b)(c)(d)●e
30. To which would you add Ashley's camp's city, state, and zip code? ●a(b)(c)(d)(e)

Grammar, Usage, and Mechanics Handbook
Table of Contents

Mechanics

Section 1 Capitalization 196
Section 2 Abbreviations and Initials 197
Section 3 Titles 197
Section 4 Quotation Marks 198
Section 5 Spelling 198
Section 6 End Marks 198
Section 7 Apostrophes 199
Section 8 Commas and Semicolons 199

Sentence Structure and Parts of Speech

Section 9 The Sentence 200
Section 10 Subjects 200
Section 11 Predicates 201
Section 12 Simple, Compound, and Complex Sentences 201
Section 13 Fragments, Run-ons, and Comma Splices 202
Section 14 Nouns 202
Section 15 Adjectives 202
Section 16 Pronouns 203
Section 17 Verbs 204
Section 18 Adverbs 205
Section 19 Prepositions 205
Section 20 Direct Objects and Indirect Objects 205
Section 21 Conjunctions 205

Usage

Section 22 Negatives 206
Section 23 Comparisons 206
Section 24 Contractions 207
Section 25 Plural Nouns 207
Section 26 Possessive Nouns 207
Section 27 Problem Words 208
Section 28 Homophones 210

Letters and E-mails

Section 29 Letters 211
Section 30 E-mails 212

Research

Section 31 Library Research 212
Section 32 Internet Research 213

Guidelines for Listening and Speaking

Section 33 Listening 214
Section 34 Speaking 214

Name _____

Mechanics

Section 1 Capitalization

- Capitalize the first word in a sentence.
  The kangaroo rat is an amazing animal.

- Capitalize all *proper nouns,* including people's names and the names of particular places.
  Gregory Gordon   Washington Monument

- Capitalize titles of respect.
  Mr. Alvarez   Dr. Chin   Ms. Murphy

- Capitalize family titles used just before people's names and titles of respect that are part of names.
  Uncle Frank   Aunt Mary   Governor Adamson

- Capitalize initials of names.
  Thomas Paul Gerard (T.P. Gerard)

- Capitalize place names.
  France   Utah   China   Baltimore

- Capitalize *proper adjectives,* adjectives that are made from proper nouns.
  Chinese   Icelandic   French   Latin American

- Capitalize the months of the year and the days of the week.
  February   April   Monday   Tuesday

- Capitalize important words in the names of organizations.
  American Lung Association   Veterans of Foreign Wars

- Capitalize important words in the names of holidays.
  Veterans Day   Fourth of July

- Capitalize the first word in the greeting or closing of a letter.
  Dear Edmundo,   Yours truly,

- Capitalize the word *I.*
  Frances and I watched the movie together.

- Capitalize the first, last, and most important words in a title. Be sure to capitalize all verbs including *is* and *was.*
  Island of the Blue Dolphins
  Away Is a Strange Place to Be

- Capitalize the first word in a direct quotation.
  Aunt Rose said, "Please pass the clam dip."

Abbreviations are shortened forms of words. Many abbreviations begin with a capital letter and end with a period.

- **You can abbreviate titles of address and titles of respect when you write.**
  Mister (Mr. Brian Davis)   Mistress (Mrs. Maria Rosario)
  Doctor (Dr. Emily Chu)   Junior (Everett Castle, Jr.)
  Note: *Ms.* is a title of address used for women. It is not an abbreviation, but it requires a period (Ms. Anita Brown).

- **You can abbreviate words used in addresses when you write.**
  Street (St.)   Avenue (Ave.)   Route (Rte.)   Boulevard (Blvd.)   Road (Rd.)

- **You can abbreviate certain words in the names of businesses when you write.**
  Pet Helpers Incorporated (Pet Helpers Inc.)   Zykar Corporation (Zykar Corp.)

- **You can abbreviate days of the week when you take notes.**
  Sunday (Sun.)   Wednesday (Wed.)   Friday (Fri.)
  Monday (Mon.)   Thursday (Thurs.)   Saturday (Sat.)
  Tuesday (Tues.)

- **You can abbreviate months of the year when you take notes.**
  January (Jan.)   April (Apr.)   October (Oct.)
  February (Feb.)   August (Aug.)   November (Nov.)
  March (Mar.)   September (Sept.)   December (Dec.)
  (May, June, and July do not have abbreviated forms.)

- **You can abbreviate directions when you take notes.**
  North (N)   East (E)   South (S)   West (W)

An *initial* is the first letter of a name. An initial is written as a capital letter and a period. Sometimes initials are used for the names of countries or cities.

Michael Paul Sanders (M.P. Sanders)   United States of America (U.S.A.)
Washington, District of Columbia (Washington, D.C.)

Section 3 Titles

- **Underline titles of books, newspapers, TV series, movies, and magazines.**
  <u>Island of the Blue Dolphins</u>   <u>Miami Herald</u>   <u>I Love Lucy</u>
  Note: These titles are put in italics when using a word processor.

- **Use quotation marks around articles in magazines, short stories, chapters in books, songs, and poems.**
  "This Land Is Your Land"   "The Gift"   "Eletelephony"

- **Capitalize the first, last, and most important words. Articles, prepositions, and conjunctions are usually not capitalized. Be sure to capitalize all verbs, including forms of the verb *be* (*am, is, are, was, were, been*).**
  A Knight in the Attic   *My Brother Sam Is Dead*

Section 4 Quotation Marks

- Put quotation marks (" ") around the titles of articles, magazines, short stories, book chapters, songs, and poems.
  My favorite short story is "Revenge of the Reptiles."

- Put quotation marks around a *direct quotation,* or a speaker's exact words.
  "Did you see that alligator?" Max asked.

- Do not put quotation marks around an *indirect quotation,* a person's words retold by another speaker. An indirect quotation is often signalled by *whether* or *that.*
  Max asked Rory whether he had seen an alligator. Rory said that he hadn't.

Writing a Conversation

- Put quotation marks around the speaker's words. Begin a direct quotation with a capital letter. Use a comma to separate the quotation from the speaker's name.
  Rory said, "There are no alligators in this area."

- When a direct quotation comes at the end of a sentence, put the end mark inside the last quotation mark.
  Max cried, "Look out!"

- When writing a conversation, begin a new paragraph with each change of speaker.
  Max panted, "I swear I saw a huge, scaly tail and a flat snout in the water!"
  "Relax," Rory said. "I told you there are no alligators around here."

Section 5 Spelling

Use these tips if you are not sure how to spell a word you want to write:

- Say the word aloud and break it into syllables. Try spelling each syllable. Put the syllables together to spell the whole word.

- Write the word. Make sure there is a vowel in every syllable. If the word looks wrong to you, try spelling it other ways.

- Think of a related word. Parts of related words are often spelled the same.
  Decide is related to *decision.*

When you use the word processing function of a computer to write something, you can use the spell check feature. It will identify possible spelling errors in your writing. A spell checker will not catch errors with homophones, though. For example, if you type *break* instead of *brake,* the spell checker will not catch the mistake, because the word is spelled correctly.

Section 6 End Marks

Every sentence must end with a period, an exclamation point, or a question mark.

- Use a *period* at the end of a statement (declarative sentence) or a command (imperative sentence).
  Dad and I look alike. (*declarative*)   Step back very slowly. (*imperative*)

- Use an *exclamation point* at the end of a firm command (imperative sentence) or at the end of a sentence that shows great feeling or excitement (exclamatory sentence).
  Get away from the cliff! (*imperative*)   What an incredible sight! (*exclamatory*)

- Use a *question mark* at the end of an asking sentence (interrogative sentence).
  How many miles is it to Tucson? (*interrogative*)

An apostrophe (') is used to form the possessive of a noun or to join words in a contraction.

- **Possessives show ownership. To make a singular noun possessive, add 's.**
  The bike belongs to Carmen. It is Carmen's bike.
  The truck belongs to Mr. Ross. It is Mr. Ross's truck.

- **To form a possessive from a plural noun that ends in s, add only an apostrophe.**
  Those books belong to my sisters. They are my sisters' books.

- **Some plural nouns do not end in s. To form possessives with these nouns, add 's.**
  The children left their boots here. The children's boots are wet.

- **Use an apostrophe to replace the dropped letters in a contraction.**
  couldn't (could n<u>o</u>t)   it's (it <u>is</u>)   hasn't (has n<u>o</u>t)
  didn't (did n<u>o</u>t)   I'm (I <u>am</u>)   they'll (they w<u>ill</u>)

Section 8 Commas and Semicolons

Commas in Sentences

- **Use a comma after an introductory word in a sentence.**
  Yes, I'd love to go to the movies.   Actually, we had a great time.

- **Use a comma to separate items in a series. Put the last comma before *and* or *or*.**
  The puppy whined, scratched at the door, and then barked loudly.
  Shall we eat cheese, bread, or fruit?

- **Use a comma when speaking directly to a person.**
  Akila, will you please stand up?   We would like you to sing, Akila.

- **Use a comma to separate a direct quotation from the speaker's name.**
  Harold asked, "How long do I have to sit here?"
  "You must sit there until Anton returns," Vic said.

- **Use a comma with the conjunctions *and, or,* and *but* when combining independent clauses in a compound sentence.**
  Lisa liked the reptiles best, but Lyle preferred the amphibians.

Semicolons in Sentences

- **You may use a semicolon in place of a comma and a conjunction when combining independent clauses.**
  Lisa likes reptiles best; Lyle prefers amphibians.

Commas in Letters

- **Use a comma after the greeting and closing of a friendly letter.**
  Dear Reginald,   Your friend, Deke

Commas with Dates and Place Names

- **Use a comma to separate the day from the date and the date from the year.**
  We clinched the division championship on Saturday, September 19, 2012.

- **Use a comma to separate the name of a city or town from the name of a state.**
  I visited Memphis, Tennessee.

Sentence Structure and Parts of Speech

Section 9 The Sentence

A *sentence* is a group of words that tells a complete thought. A sentence has two parts: a *subject* and a *predicate*.

- The subject tells *whom* or *what* the sentence is about.
  <u>The swimmers</u> race.

- The predicate tells what the subject *is* or *does*.
  The judges <u>watch carefully</u>.

There are four kinds of sentences: *statement, question, command,* and *exclamation*.

- A sentence that tells something is a *statement*. It is also called a *declarative sentence*. A statement ends with a period.
  Jake swam faster than anyone.

- A sentence that asks something is a *question*. It is also called an *interrogative sentence*. A question ends with a question mark.
  Did Sammy qualify for the finals?

- A sentence that tells someone to do something is a *command*. It is also called an *imperative sentence*. A command usually ends with a period, but a firm command can end with an exclamation point.
  Keep your eyes on the finish line.
  Watch out for that bee!

- A sentence that shows excitement or surprise is called an *exclamation* or *exclamatory sentence*. An exclamation ends with an exclamation point.
  Jake has won the race!

Section 10 Subjects

The *subject* of a sentence tells whom or what the sentence is about.

- A sentence can have one subject.
  <u>Mary</u> wrote a book.

- A sentence can have a *compound subject,* two or more subjects that share the same predicate.
  <u>Alex and Mark</u> have already read the book.

The *complete subject* includes all the words that name and tell about the subject.

<u>Many different students</u> have borrowed the book.

The *simple subject* is the most important noun or pronoun in the complete subject.

Many different <u>students</u> have borrowed the book.
<u>They</u> discussed the book yesterday.

Note: Sometimes the simple subject and the complete subject are the same.

<u>Ricardo</u> is writing a book about robots.

Section 11 Predicates

The *predicate* of a sentence tells what happened.

The *complete predicate* includes a verb and all the words that tell what happened.

- A complete predicate can tell what the subject of the sentence did. This kind of predicate includes an action verb.

  Mary <u>won an award</u>.

- A complete predicate can also tell more about the subject. This kind of predicate includes a linking verb.

  Mary <u>is a talented writer</u>.

- A *predicate noun* follows a linking verb and renames the subject.

  Our dog is a <u>retriever</u>.

- A *predicate adjective* follows a linking verb and describes the subject.

  Our dog is <u>friendly</u>.

The *simple predicate* is the verb that goes with the subject. It generally tells what the subject did, does, or will do.

Celia <u>won</u> an award for her performance.

She <u>will receive</u> a trophy next week.

A *compound predicate* is two or more predicates that share the same subject. Compound predicates are often joined by the conjunction *and* or *or*.

Ramon <u>sang</u> and <u>danced</u> in the play.

Mary <u>wrote</u> the play and <u>directed</u> it.

Section 12 Simple, Compound, and Complex Sentences

A *simple sentence* tells one complete thought.

Arthur has a rock collection.

A *compound sentence* is made up of two simple sentences joined by a comma and a conjunction (*and, or, but*). The two simple sentences in a compound sentence can also be joined by a semicolon. Two simple sentences can go together to make one compound sentence if the ideas in the simple sentences are related.

Arthur has a rock collection, <u>and</u> Mary collects shells.

Arthur collects rocks; Mary collects shells.

A *complex sentence* is made up of one *independent clause* (or simple sentence) and at least one dependent clause. A *dependent clause* is a group of words that has a subject and a predicate but cannot stand on its own.

Dependent Clause: when Arthur visited southern Arizona

Independent Clause: He learned a lot about desert plants and animals.

Complex Sentence: When Arthur visited southern Arizona, he learned a lot about desert plants and animals.

Section 13 Fragments, Run-ons, and Comma Splices

A *fragment* is not a sentence, because it is missing a subject or a predicate. A fragment can also be called an incomplete sentence because it does not tell a complete thought.

Sumi and Ali. (*missing a predicate that tells what happened*)
Went hiking in the woods. (*missing a subject that tells who went hiking*)

A *run-on sentence* is two complete sentences that are run together.

Sumi went hiking Ali went swimming.

- To fix a run-on sentence, use a comma and a conjunction (*and, or, but*) to join the two sentences. (You may also join the sentences with a semicolon.)
  Sumi went hiking, **but** Ali went swimming.

A *comma splice* is two complete sentences that have a comma between them but are missing a joining word such as *and, or,* or *but*.

Sumi went hiking yesterday, Ali went swimming.

- To fix a comma splice, add *and, or,* or *but* after the comma.
  Sumi went hiking yesterday, **and** Ali went swimming.

Try not to string too many short sentences together when you write. Instead, combine sentences and take out unnecessary information.

Incorrect: I stared at him and he stared at me and I told him to go away and he wouldn't so then I called my big sister.
Correct: We stared at each other. I told him to go away, but he wouldn't.
Then I called my big sister.

Section 14 Nouns

A *common noun* names any person, place, thing, or idea.

Ira visited an auto **museum** with his **friends**. Ira has always had an **interest** in **cars**.

A *proper noun* names a certain person, place, thing, or idea. Proper nouns begin with a capital letter.

Ira wants to visit the **Sonoran Desert** in **Mexico**.

Section 15 Adjectives

An *adjective* is a word that tells more about a noun.

- Some adjectives tell what kind.
  Jim observed the **huge** elephant. The **enormous** beast towered above him.
- Some adjectives tell how many.
  The elephant was **twelve** feet tall. It weighed **several** tons.
- Sometimes an adjective follows the noun it describes.
  Jim was **careful** not to anger the elephant. He was **happy** when the trainer led it away.
- *A, an,* and *the* are special kinds of adjectives called *articles*. Use *a* and *an* to refer to any person, place, or thing. Use *the* to refer to a specific person, place, or thing. Use *a* before a singular noun that begins with a consonant sound. Use *an* before a singular noun that begins with a vowel sound.
  An elephant is heavier than **a** rhino. **The** elephant in this picture is six weeks old.

- *Demonstrative* adjectives tell which one. The words *this, that, these,* and *those* can be used as demonstrative adjectives. Use *this* and *these* to talk about things that are nearby. Use *that* and *those* to talk about things that are far away.

  <u>This</u> book is about rhinos.   <u>These</u> rhinos just came to the zoo.

  <u>That</u> rhino is enormous!   <u>Those</u> funny-looking creatures are wildebeests.

  Note: Never use *here* or *there* after the adjectives *this, that, these,* and *those.*

- A *proper adjective* is made from a proper noun. Capitalize proper adjectives.

  <u>Italian</u> cooking   <u>Democratic</u> convention   <u>Apache</u> legend

Section 16 Pronouns

A *pronoun* can replace a noun naming a person, place, thing, or idea. Personal pronouns include *I, me, you, we, us, he, she, him, her, it, they,* and *them.*

- A *subject pronoun* takes the place of the subject of a sentence. A subject pronoun is in the *nominative* case. The subject pronouns are *I, you, he, she, it, we,* and *they.*
  Rita is an excellent soccer player. <u>She</u> is an excellent soccer player.

- Do not use both the pronoun and the noun it replaces together.
  Incorrect: <u>Rita she</u> made the team.

  Correct: <u>Rita</u> made the team. OR <u>She</u> made the team.

- An *object pronoun* replaces a noun that is the object of a verb or preposition. Object pronouns are in the *objective case.* The object pronouns are *me, you, him, her, it, us,* and *them.*
  Rita's team played the Bobcats. Rita's team beat <u>them</u>.

- Use a subject pronoun as part of a compound subject. Use an object pronoun as part of a compound object. To test whether a pronoun is correct, say the sentence <u>without</u> the other part of a compound subject or object.
  Incorrect: Rita told Ellen and <u>I</u> it was a close game. (Rita told <u>I</u> it was a close game.)
  Correct: Rita told Ellen and <u>me</u> it was a close game. (Rita told <u>me</u> it was a close game.)

- An *antecedent* is the word or phrase a pronoun refers to. The antecedent always includes a noun.
  <u>The Bobcats</u> are excellent player. (They) won every game last season.

- A pronoun must match its antecedent. An antecedent and pronoun agree when they have the same *number* (singular or plural) and *gender* (male or female).
  <u>Nick</u> saved the game. <u>He</u> kicked a goal at the last minute.
  <u>Nick's mother</u> cheered. <u>She</u> was very excited.
  <u>The Bobcats</u> were upset. <u>They</u> had not lost a game all season.

- Possessive pronouns show ownership. The words *my, your, his, her, its, their,* and *our* are possessive pronouns.
  Those skates belong to my brother. Those are <u>his</u> kneepads, too.

- The interrogative pronouns *who, what,* and *which* are used to ask questions.
  <u>Who</u> has brought the volleyball?   <u>What</u> is a wicket used for?
  <u>Which</u> is the net for volleyball?

- *This, that, these,* and *those* can be used as demonstrative pronouns.
  <u>This</u> is a soft rug.   <u>These</u> are sweeter than those over there.
  <u>That</u> is where I sat yesterday.   <u>Those</u> are new chairs.

An *action verb* shows action in a sentence.

> Scientists <u>study</u> the natural world.   They <u>learn</u> how the laws of nature work.

- Sometimes a *helping verb* is needed to help the main verb show action. A helping verb comes before a main verb.

  Scientists <u>are</u> studying glaciers.   The studies <u>will</u> help us learn about Earth's history.

- Verbs can tell about the present, the past, or the future.

  Few people <u>travel</u> in Antarctica. (*present tense*)

  Explorers first <u>traveled</u> to the South Pole over 100 years ago. (*past tense*)

  Other explorers <u>will travel</u> to the South Pole in the future. (*future tense*)

  Scientists <u>have studied</u> Antarctica for many years. (*present perfect tense*)

- The *present tense* is used to show that something happens regularly, or is true now.

  Squirrels <u>bury</u> nuts each fall.

  Add *s* to most verbs to show present tense when the subject is *he, she, it,* or a singular noun. Add *es* to verbs ending in *s, ch, sh, x,* or *z.* Do not add *s* or *es* if the subject is a plural noun or if the subject is *I, you, we,* or *they.*

add *s*	add *es*	change *y* to *i* and add *es*
speak/speaks	reach/reaches	carry/carries
look/looks	mix/mixes	bury/buries

- The *past tense* shows past action. Add *-ed* to most verbs to form the past tense. Verbs that do not add *-ed* are called *irregular verbs*. Here are some common irregular verbs.

Present	Past	With *have, has,* or *had*
bring	brought	brought
go	went	gone
grow	grew	grown
know	knew	known
take	took	taken

- The *future tense* indicates future action. Use the helping verb *will* to form the future tense.

  Mom <u>will visit</u> Antarctica next year.   She <u>will photograph</u> penguins.

- The *present perfect tense* shows action that began in the past and may still be happening. To form the present perfect tense, add the helping verb *has* or *have* to the past participle of a verb.

  Mom <u>has studied</u> Antarctica for years.   Her articles <u>have appeared</u> in science journals.

- The subject and its verb must agree in number.

  An Antarctic explorer needs special equipment.

  (*singular subject:* **An Antarctic explorer;** *verb + s or es:* **needs**)

  Explorers carry climbing tools and survival gear.

  (*plural subject:* **Explorers;** *verb without s or es:* **carry**)

A *linking verb* does not show action. It connects the subject of a sentence to a word or words in the predicate that tell about the subject. Linking verbs include forms of the verb *be,* such as *am, is, are, was,* and *were. Seem* and *become* are linking verbs, too.

> Explorers <u>are</u> brave. That route <u>seems</u> very long and dangerous.

Note: *Feel, taste, smell, sound,* and *look* can be action or linking verbs.

Section 18 Adverbs

An *adverb* is usually used to describe a verb or an adjective. Most adverbs tell how, when, where, or how much.

- Many adverbs end in *-ly*.
  Andrew approached the snake cage <u>slowly</u>. He <u>cautiously</u> peered inside.

- Some adverbs do not end in *-ly*.
  Andrew knew that snakes can move <u>fast</u>.

- *Very* is an adverb. It means "extremely." Never use *real* in place of *very*.

Incorrect	Correct
The snake's fangs were <u>real</u> sharp.	The snake's fangs were <u>very</u> sharp.

Section 19 Prepositions

A *preposition* shows a relationship between a word in a sentence and a noun or pronoun that follows the preposition. Prepositions help tell when, where, what kind, how, or how much.

- Prepositions include the words *in, at, under, over, on, through, to, across, around, beside, during, off,* and *before.*
  Jeff left the milk <u>on</u> the table.   He knew it belonged <u>in</u> the refrigerator.

- A *prepositional phrase* is a group of words that begins with a preposition and ends with its object. The object of a preposition is a noun or a pronoun. A prepositional phrase can be at the beginning, middle, or end of a sentence.
  Jeff knew his mother would be home <u>in five minutes</u>.
  <u>Within three minutes</u> Jeff had put the milk away.

Section 20 Direct Objects and Indirect Objects

A *direct object* is the word or words that receive the action of the verb. Direct objects follow action verbs. (A linking verb never has a direct object.) To find the direct object, say the verb followed by "Whom?" or "What?" A direct object is always a noun or pronoun.

Jacques painted a <u>picture.</u> (Painted whom or what? Picture. *Picture* is the direct object.)

A sentence with a direct object may also have an *indirect object*. An indirect object is a noun or pronoun and usually tells to whom something is given.

Jacques gave his <u>mom</u> the painting.

Section 21 Conjunctions

The words *and, or,* and *but* are *coordinating conjunctions*. They connect words or groups of words that have the same function.

- Coordinating conjunctions may be used to join words within a sentence.
  My favorite reptiles are snakes <u>and</u> lizards.   Najim doesn't like snakes <u>or</u> lizards.

- A comma and a coordinating conjunction can be used to join two or more simple sentences. (The conjunction *and* does not need a comma if both sentences are short.)
  I like snakes, <u>but</u> he says they're creepy.   We can get a snake, <u>or</u> we can get a lizard.

A *subordinating conjunction* shows how one clause (a group of words with a subject and predicate) relates to another clause. Many dependent clauses begin with a subordinating conjunction. Subordinating conjunctions include *although, because, if,* and *before.*

<u>Before</u> his mom left, Bo cleaned his room. <u>Because</u> he had a favor to ask, he vacuumed, too.

Usage

Section 22 Negatives

A *negative word* says "no" or "not."

- Often negatives are in the form of contractions.
  Do **not** enter that room.   **Don't** even go near the door.

- In most sentences it is not correct to use two negatives.

  Incorrect   Correct
  We **can't** see **nothing**.   We **can't** see anything.
  We **haven't** got **no** solution.   We **haven't** got a solution.

- Do not use the word *ain't*.

Section 23 Comparisons

- The *comparative form* of an adjective or adverb compares two people, places, or things. The comparative form is often followed by "than." To compare two people, places, or things, add *-er* to short adjectives and adverbs.
  An elephant is **tall**. A giraffe is **taller** than an elephant. (*Giraffe* is compared with *elephant*.)
  A lion runs **fast**. A cheetah runs **faster** than any other land animal. (*Cheetah* is compared with *any other land animal*.)

- The *superlative form* of an adjective or adverb compares three or more people, places, or things. The article "the" usually comes before the superlative form. To compare three or more items, add *-est* to short adjectives and adverbs.
  The giraffe is the **tallest** land animal.
  The cheetah runs the **fastest** of any animal now alive.

- When comparing two or more things using the ending *-er* or *-est*, never use the word *more*.

  Incorrect   Correct
  She is **more faster** than he is.   She is **faster** than he is.

- The word *more* is used with longer adjectives to compare two persons, places, or things. Use the word *most* to compare three or more persons, places, or things.
  Mario is **excited** about the field trip.
  Duane is **more excited** than Mario.
  Kiki is the **most excited** student of all.

- Sometimes the words *good* and *bad* are used to compare. These words change forms in comparisons.
  Mario is a **good** athlete.   The basketball court is in **bad** shape.
  Kiki is a **better** athlete.   The tennis court is in **worse** shape than the basketball court.

  Bill is the **best** athlete of all.   The ice rink is in the **worst** shape of all.
  Note: Use *better* or *worse* to compare two things. Use *best* or *worst* to compare three or more things.

Section 24 Contractions

When two or more words are combined to form one word, one or more letters are dropped and replaced by an apostrophe. These words are called *contractions*.

- In the contraction below, an apostrophe takes the place of the letters *wi*.
  he will = he'll

- Here are some other common contractions.

cannot/can't	have not/haven't	she would/she'd
could not/couldn't	I will/I'll	they have/they've
does not/doesn't	it is/it's	we are/we're

Section 25 Plural Nouns

- A *singular noun* names one person, place, thing, or idea.

girl	pond	arrow	freedom

- A *plural noun* names more than one person, place, or thing. To make most singular nouns plural, add *s*.

girl**s**	pond**s**	arrow**s**	freedom**s**

- For nouns ending in *sh, ch, x,* or *z,* add *es* to make the word plural.

bush/bush**es**	box/box**es**
lunch/lunch**es**	quiz/quiz**zes**

- For nouns ending in a consonant and *y,* change the *y* to *i* and add *es*.

penny/penn**ies**	army/arm**ies**

- For nouns that end in *f* or *fe,* replace *f* or *fe* with *ves* to make the noun plural.

shelf/shel**ves**	wife/wi**ves**

- Some words change spelling when the plural is formed.

man/men	woman/women	mouse/mice	goose/geese

- Some words have the same singular and plural form.

deer	sheep

Section 26 Possessive Nouns

A *possessive noun* shows ownership.

- To make a singular noun possessive, add an apostrophe and *s* to make it possessive.

John**'s** bat	the girl**'s** bike

- When a singular noun ends in *s,* add an apostrophe and *s*.

Ross**'s** project	James**'s** glasses

- To make a plural noun that ends in *s* possessive, add an apostrophe.

the soldiers**'** songs	the girls**'** bikes

- When a plural noun does not end in *s,* add an apostrophe and *s* to show possession.

the men**'s** ideas	the children**'s** shoes

Section 27 Problem Words

These words are often misused in writing.

sit	*Sit* means "rest or stay in one place." Sit down and relax for a while.
sat	*Sat* is the past tense of *sit*. I sat in that chair yesterday.
set	*Set* is a verb meaning "put." Set the chair here.
may	*May* is used to ask permission or to express a possibility. May I have another hot dog? I may borrow that book someday.
can	*Can* shows that someone is able to do something. I can easily eat three hot dogs.
learn	*Learn* means "to get knowledge." Who will help you learn Spanish?
teach	*Teach* means "to give knowledge." Never use *learn* in place of *teach*. **Incorrect:** My sister will learn me to speak Spanish. **Correct:** My sister will teach me to speak Spanish.
is	Use *is* to tell about one person, place, or thing. Alabama is warm during the summer.
are	Use *are* to tell about more than one person, place, or thing. Also use *are* with the word *you*. Seattle and San Francisco are cool during the summer. You are welcome to visit me anytime.
doesn't	The contraction *doesn't* is used with the singular pronouns *he, she,* and *it*. He doesn't like sauerkraut. It doesn't agree with him.
don't	The contraction *don't* is used with the plural pronouns *we* and *they*. *Don't* is also used with *I* and *you*. They don't like swiss cheese. I don't care for it, either.
I	Use the pronoun *I* as the subject of a sentence. When using *I* or *me* with another noun or pronoun, always name yourself last. I am going to basketball camp. Renée and I will ride together.
me	Use the pronoun *me* after action verbs. Renée will call me this evening. Also use *me* after a preposition, such as *to, at,* and *with*. Pass the ball to me. Come to the game with Renée and me.
good	*Good* is an adjective.
well	*Well* is an adverb. These words are often used incorrectly. **Incorrect:** Renée plays good. **Correct:** Renée is a good basketball player. She plays well.

like	*Like* means "similar to" or "have a fondness for." Do not use *like* in places where it does not belong. **Incorrect:** I enjoy, like, all kinds of water sports. **Correct:** I like swimming and water polo.
you know	Only use the phrase *you know* when it helps a sentence make sense. Try not to use it in places where it does not belong. **Incorrect:** We can, you know, go canoeing. **Correct:** Did you know that my family has a canoe?
let	*Let* is a verb that means "allow." Please let me go to the mall with you.
leave	*Leave* is a verb that means "go away from" or "let stay." We will leave at noon. Leave your sweater here.
was	*Was* is a past tense form of *be*. Use *was* to tell about one person or thing. Hana was sad yesterday.
were	*Were* is also a past tense form of *be*. Use *were* to tell about more than one person or thing. Also use the word *were* with *you*. Hana and her friend were both unhappy. Were you home yesterday?
has	Use *has* to tell about one person or thing. Rory has a stamp collection.
have	Use *have* to tell about more than one. Also use *have* with the pronoun *I*. David and Lin have a rock collection. I have a bottle cap collection.
who	Use *who* to refer to people. The man who picked me up is my father.
which	Use *which* to refer to things. His rear tire, which was flat, had to be repaired.
that	*That* can refer to people or things. Use *that* instead of *which* to begin a clause that is necessary to the meaning of the sentence. The picture that Stephon drew won first prize.
very	*Very* is an adverb. It means "extremely." I was very tired after the hike.
real	*Real* is an adjective. It means "actual" or "true to life." Never use *real* in place of *very*. **Incorrect:** The hike was real long. **Correct:** I used a real compass to find my way.

Section 28 Homophones

Homophones sound alike but have different spellings and meanings.

are	*Are* is a form of the verb *be*.	We are best friends.
our	*Our* is a possessive pronoun.	Our favorite color is green.
hour	An *hour* is sixty minutes.	Meet me in an hour.

its	*Its* is a possessive pronoun.	The horse shook its shaggy head.
it's	*It's* is a contraction of the words *it is*.	It's a beautiful day for a ride.

there	*There* is an adverb that usually means "in that place." It can also be used in the expressions "there is" and "there are."
	Please put the books there. There are three books on the table.
	There is a library nearby.
their	*Their* is a possessive pronoun. It shows something belongs to more than one person or thing.
	Their tickets are in my pocket.
they're	*They're* is a contraction made from the words *they are*.
	They're waiting for me inside.

two	*Two* is a number.	Apples and pears are two fruits I like.
to	*To* means "toward."	I brought the pot to the stove.
too	*Too* means "also."	I'd like some lunch, too.
	Too can mean "more than enough."	That's too much pepper!

your	*Your* is a possessive pronoun.
	Where are your socks?
you're	*You're* is a contraction made from the words *you are*.
	You're coming with us, aren't you?

whose	*Whose* is a possessive pronoun.	
	Whose raincoat is this?	
who's	*Who's* is a contraction made from the words *who* and *is* or *who* and *has*.	
	Who's at the front door?	Who's taken my book?

ate	*Ate* is a form of the verb *eat*.	We ate lunch together.
eight	*Eight* is a number word.	She had eight marbles.

principal	A *principal* is a person with authority.
	The principal made the rule.
principle	A *principle* is a general rule or code of behavior.
	He lived with a strong principle of honesty.

waist	The *waist* is the middle part of the body.
	She wore a belt around her waist.
waste	To *waste* something is to use it in a careless way.
	She would never waste something she could recycle.

aloud	*Aloud* means out loud, or able to be heard.
	He read the poem aloud.
allowed	*Allowed* is a form of the verb *allow*.
	We were not allowed to swim after dark.

Letters and E-mails

Section 29 Letters

A *friendly letter* is an informal letter written to a friend or family member.

In a friendly letter, you might send a message, invite someone to a party, or thank someone for a gift. A friendly letter has five parts.

- The *heading* gives your address and the date.
- The *greeting* includes the name of the person you are writing to.
- The *body* of the letter gives your message.
- The *closing* is a friendly or polite way to say good-bye.
- The *signature* is your name.

> 35 Rand Street
> Chicago, IL 60606
> July 15, 2012
>
> Dear Kim,
>
>   Hi from the big city. I'm spending the summer learning to skateboard. My brother Raj is teaching me. He's a pro.
>
>   I have one skateboard and hope to buy another one soon. If I can do that, we can practice together when you come to visit.
>
>   Your friend,
>
>   *Art*

A *business letter* is a formal letter.

You would write a business letter to a company, an employer, a newspaper, or any person you do not know well. A business letter looks a lot like a friendly letter, but it also includes the name and address of the business you are writing to, substitutes a colon for a comma after the greeting, omits paragraph indentations, and aligns all of the letter parts along the left-hand margin.

> 35 Rand Street
> Chicago, IL 60606
> July 15, 2012
>
> Swenson Skateboard Company
> 10026 Portage Road
> Lansing, MI 48091
>
> Dear Sir or Madam:
>
> Please send me your latest skateboard catalog. I am particularly interested in your newest models, the K-7 series.
>
> Thank you.
>
> Sincerely yours,
> *Arthur Quinn*
> Arthur Quinn

The envelope below shows how to address a letter. A friendly letter and a business letter are addressed the same way.

> ARTHUR QUINN
> 35 RAND ST
> CHICAGO IL 60606
>
>   KIM LEE
>   1555 MONTAGUE BLVD
>   MEMPHIS TN 38106

An *e-mail* is a note sent from one person to another person, a group, or a company via a computer network. Today, many people use e-mail to stay in touch with friends and family. An e-mail should contain five parts, like a letter does.

- An e-mail contains a *greeting*, a *body*, a *closing*, and your *name*.
- An e-mail *header* contains your e-mail address, the e-mail address of the person you are writing to, the date, and a subject line.

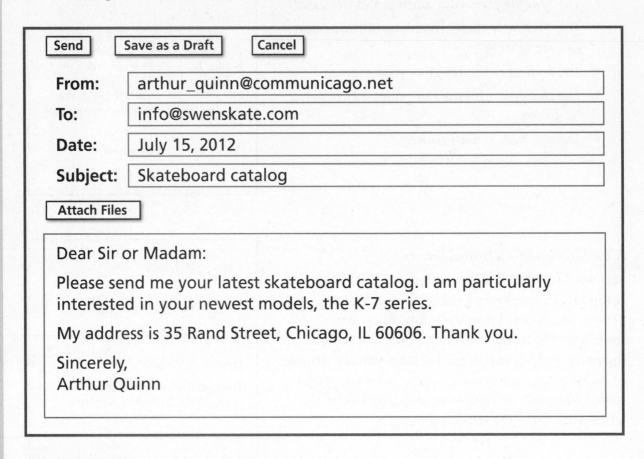

```
Send    Save as a Draft    Cancel

From:     arthur_quinn@communicago.net
To:       info@swenskate.com
Date:     July 15, 2012
Subject:  Skateboard catalog

Attach Files
```

Dear Sir or Madam:

Please send me your latest skateboard catalog. I am particularly interested in your newest models, the K-7 series.

My address is 35 Rand Street, Chicago, IL 60606. Thank you.

Sincerely,
Arthur Quinn

Research

Section 31 Library Research

You can find information for a report or a project in a library.

- Many libraries have an information desk. The person at the desk can help you look for information.
- Libraries have many reference books, including dictionaries, thesauruses, and encyclopedias. You can use these to find information about words, and basic information about topics.
- Libraries have nonfiction books about all kinds of subjects. You can find books on a particular subject by entering that subject into a computer connected to the library's database. This database lists all the publications in the library. The computer will usually list several books on the subject you entered. Each listing will have a code that tells where in the library that book can be found.

You can use online dictionaries, thesauruses, and encyclopedias to find basic information about words and topics. You can also find information for a report or a project by using an Internet *search engine*.

- Think of **key words** that tell what you are looking for. For example, if you need information on animals that live in the rainforest, you might use the key words **rainforest animals**. Type these words into the search engine's text box.

- The search engine will provide you with links to **Web sites**. You can click on a link to visit a Web site.

- When you get to the Web site, you need to judge whether it will be a good source of information.

  — Notice the last three letters of the Web site's Internet address. Sites with a **.gov** and **.edu** are usually more reliable than sites with **.com**.

  — Think about who has written the information. Is the writer an expert on the topic? Is the writer giving facts, or just expressing opinions?

  — Check to see if the information is up-to-date. The site should tell you when it was last updated.

Internet Safety

Be sure to follow safety rules whenever you use the Internet. These rules will help you keep personal information private.

- When you log on to a school computer, you may type your own name as a username. However, when you go on the Internet, you use a screen name. That should never be your real name or nickname. You will also use a password, a secret word or symbol that identifies who you are. Keep your password safe. Do not share it with anyone. Never use your address, birthday, phone number, or pet's name as a password. Those are too easy for someone else to figure out.

- Have you ever received e-mail with an attachment? Usually you must click the attachment to load it into your computer. Never download attachments from strangers. These may harm your computer.

Guidelines for Listening and Speaking

Section 33 Listening

These steps will help you be a good listener:

- **Listen carefully** when others are speaking.
- **Keep in mind your reason for listening.** Are you listening to learn about a topic? To be entertained? To get directions? Decide what you should get out of the listening experience.
- **Look directly at the speaker.** Doing this will help you concentrate on what he or she has to say.
- **Do not interrupt** the speaker or talk to others while the speaker is talking.
- **Ask questions** when the speaker is finished talking if there is anything you did not understand.

Section 34 Speaking

Being a good speaker takes practice. These guidelines can help you become an effective speaker:

Giving Oral Reports

- **Be prepared.** Know exactly what it is that you are going to talk about and how long you will speak. Have your notes in front of you.
- **Speak slowly** and **clearly.** Speak **loudly** enough so everyone can hear you.
- **Look** at your audience.

Taking Part in Discussions

- **Listen** to what others have to say.
- **Disagree politely.** Let others in the group know you respect their point of view.
- **Try not to interrupt** others. Everyone should have a chance to speak.

Topic Index

Unit 1

The World Outside: Water
Erie Canal, 21–22
Glaciers, 17–18
Lakes, 19–20
Oceans, uses of, 13–14
Tides, 11–12
Tsunami, hurricane, monsoon, typhoon, 25–26
Water, bodies of, 15
Water, states of, 9–10
Water, use of, 7–8
Waves, 23–24
Wetlands, 27

Unit 2

Looking Back: United States History
"America the Beautiful," 37–38
Elion, Gertrude, (American medical pioneer), 41–42
Grand Canyon, 49–50
"Little Saigon": Vietnamese community, 43–44
Mississippi River, 39–40
Mount Rushmore, 51–52
National anthem, writing of, 37–38
Outer Banks: Cape Hatteras, North Carolina, 45–46
Route 66, 53
Thanksgiving: colonists; the Wampanoag, 35–36
Uncle Sam: national symbol, 33–34
Whaling, early history of, 47–48

Unit 3

Unforgettable Folks: Athletes
Baseball: Ichiro Suzuki and Jackie Robinson, 67–68
Cycling: Tour de France, 79
Football: Jim Plunkett, 69–70
Gymnastics: Carly Patterson, 73–74
Ice hockey: Mario Lemieux, 71–72
Ice skating: Michelle Kwan, 63–64
Soccer: Briana Scurry, 77–78
Softball: Cat Osterman, 65–66
Swimming: Maritza Correia, 75–76
Table tennis: Jan-Ove Waldner, 61–62
Track: Billy Mills, 59–60

Unit 4

Grab Bag: Cars
24 Hours of Daytona, 97–98
Demolition derby, 89–90
Drag races, 87–88
Formula One cars, 93–94
Indy 500, 85–86
Midget racecars, 103–104
Mille Miglia, 99–100
New York-to-Paris race (1908), 91–92
Soap box racers, 101–102
Stock car races, 95–96
Sutton, Kelly (NASCAR driver), 105

Unit 5

Beasts and Critters: Amphibians and Reptiles
Amphibians, 119–120
Boa constrictors, 115
Chameleons, 125–126
Chinese alligators, 113–114
Frogs, 123–124
Leatherback turtles, 111–112
Lizards: chuckwallas and iguanas, 131
Rattlesnakes, 127–128
Salamanders, 121–122

Language Index

a and *an*, 45–46, 202
abbreviations, 115–116, 197
adjectives, 45–46, 71–72, 101–102, 113–114, 196, 202–203, 206
adverb usage, 47–48, 59–60, 71–72, 103–104, 205, 206
and, 11–12, 21–22, 51–52, 121–122, 201, 202, 205
antecedents, 91–92, 203
apostrophes, 35–36, 119–120, 199, 207
articles, 45–46, 202
be, forms of, 95–96, 204, 208
but, 21–22, 51–52, 201, 202, 205
capitalization, 33–34, 111–112, 113–114, 115–116, 117–118, 127–128, 129–130, 196, 197, 198, 203
clauses, dependent, 23–24, 51–52, 201, 205
clauses, independent, 21–22, 23–24, 51–52, 123–124, 125–126, 199, 201
command, 111–112, 198, 200
commas, 21–22, 121–122, 123–124, 127–128, 129–130, 198, 199, 201, 202, 211
commas after introductory words, 123–124, 199
commas in a series, 121–122, 199
commas in compound sentences, 21–22, 123–124, 199, 201
commas in direct quotations, 127–128, 198, 199
commas in letters, 129–130, 199
comma splice, 25–26, 202
commas to separate nouns of direct address, 123–124, 199
common nouns, 33–34, 202
comparatives, 67–68, 101–102, 103–104, 206
comparing with *good* or *bad*, 67–68, 206
complex sentences, 201
compound sentences, 21–22, 125–126, 201
conjunctions, coordinating, 21–22, 51–52, 121–122, 201, 202, 205
conjunctions, subordinating, 51–52, 205
contractions, 59–60, 61–62, 63–64, 99–100, 119–120, 199, 208
declarative sentences, 111–112, 198, 200
demonstrative adjectives, 45–46, 203
demonstrative pronouns, 203
direct objects, 13–14, 205
e-mail format, 129–130, 212
end marks, 111–112, 127–128, 198, 200
exclamatory sentences, 111–112, 198, 200
fragments, 25–26, 202
future tense verbs, 41–42, 204
helping verbs, 41–42, 43–44, 75–76, 204
imperative sentences, 111–112, 198, 200
indirect objects, 15–16, 205
initials, 115–116, 197
interrogative sentences, 111–112, 198, 200
introductory words, 123–124, 199
I or *me*, 89–90, 203, 208
irregular verbs, 41–42, 43–44, 75–76, 204
its and *it's*, 61–62, 210
know and *grow*, 75–76, 204
learn and *teach*, 77–78, 208
letter format, 129–130, 199, 211
like and *you know*, 65–66, 209
linking verbs, 17–18, 204
naming yourself last, 89–90, 208
negatives, 99–100, 206, 208
nouns, 15–16, 33–34, 35–36, 113–114, 119–120, 200, 202, 203, 207

object of preposition, 19, 49, 205
object pronouns, 85–86, 87–88, 89–90, 203, 208
or, 11–12, 21–22, 51–52, 121–122, 201, 202, 205
past participles, 43–44, 204
past tense verbs, 41–42, 75–76, 204
possessive nouns, 35–36, 119–120, 199, 207
predicate, 7–8, 9–10, 11–12, 201
predicate adjective, 17–18, 201
predicate, complete, 7–8, 201
predicate, compound, 11–12, 201
predicate noun, 17–18, 201
predicate, simple, 9–10, 201
prepositions, 19–20, 49–50, 205
prepositional phrases, 19–20, 49–50, 205
present perfect tense, 43–44, 204
present tense verbs, 39–40, 93–94, 204
pronouns, 37–38, 61–62, 63–64, 69–70, 85–86, 87–88, 89–90, 91–92, 203, 209, 210
pronouns, interrogative, 203
pronouns, personal and possessive, 37–38, 61–62, 63–64, 203, 210
proofreading checklist, 28, 54, 80, 106, 132
proofreading practice, 27, 53, 79, 105, 131
proper adjectives, 113–114, 196, 203
proper nouns, 33–34, 113–114, 196, 202
question, 111–112, 198, 200
question mark, 111–112, 198, 200
quotation marks, 127–128, 198, 199
quotations, direct and indirect, 127–128, 198, 199
real, 71–72, 209
regular verbs, 93–94, 204
run-on sentences, 25–26, 202
semicolons, 125–126, 199
sentences, 21–22, 25–26, 111–112, 200, 201, 202
set, 73–74, 208
simple sentences, 21–22, 201
singular and plural nouns, 35–36, 119–120, 207
sit, 73–74, 208
statement, 111–112, 198, 200
subject, 7–8, 9–10, 11–12, 85–86, 87–88, 89–90, 93–94, 95–96, 200, 203, 208
subject, complete, 7–8, 200
subject, compound, 11–12, 200
subject pronouns, 85–86, 87–88, 89–90, 203
subject, simple, 9–10, 200
subject, singular and plural, 93–94, 95–96
subject-verb agreement, 93–94, 95–96, 204
superlatives, 101–102, 103–104, 206
that, 69–70, 203
the, 45–46, 101, 202, 206
their, there, and *they're*, 59–60, 210
titles (book, movie, poem, song, story), 117–118, 197
titles of respect, 113–114, 115–116, 196, 197
verbs, 9–10, 39–40, 41–42, 43–44, 73–74, 75–76, 77–78, 93–94, 95–96, 97–98, 201, 204, 208, 209
verb tense, proper, 97–98, 204
very, 71–72, 209
which, 69–70, 203
who, 69–70, 203
writing sentences correctly, 111–112, 198, 199, 200
your and *you're*, 63–64, 210